THE COMPLETE IDIOT'S GUIDE TO

The Internet UK and Eire 2003 Edition

by Peter Kent

UK edition adapted by Rob Young

Prentice Hall

An imprint of Pearson Education

PEARSON EDUCATION LIMITED

Head Office:
Edinburgh Gate
Harlow CM20 2JE
Tel: +44 (0)1279 623623
Fax: +44 (0)1279 431059

London Office:
128 Long Acre
London WC2E 9AN
Tel: +44 (0)20 7447 2000
Fax: +44 (0)20 7447 2170

First published in Great Britain in 1998
Second edition published 2000 by Pearson Education Limited
Third edition published 2001 by Pearson Education Limited
Fourth edition published 2002 by Pearson Education Limited
This fifth edition published 2003 by Pearson Education Limited

Authorized adaptation from the English language edition published by Que Corporation
Copyright © 2003
Adaptation published by Pearson Education Limited
© Pearson Education Limited 2003

The rights of Peter Kent and Rob Young to be identified as
Authors of this Work have been asserted by them in accordance
with the Copyright, Designs and Patents Act 1988.

ISBN 0-130-39914-0

British Library Cataloguing in Publication Data
A CIP catalogue record for this book can be obtained from the British Library.

10 9 8 7 6 5 4 3 2

Typeset by Pantek Arts Ltd, Maidstone, Kent.
Printed and bound in Great Britain by Biddles Ltd, Guildford and King's Lynn.

The Publishers' policy is to use paper manufactured from sustainable forests.

Contents At A Glance

Contents

ix

Acknowledgements

We are grateful to the following for permission to reproduce copyright material:

AOL UK Ltd; Bandwidth Communications Ltd, Whatsonstage.com; Bigfoot Communications (Hong Kong) Ltd; Bonus.com; BTLookSmart Europe Ltd; Climate Action Network; Department of Physics and Astronomy, Stephen F. Austin State University; Financial Times; Freeserve.com; Maps.com; MediaRing.com Ltd; MX Financial Solutions; NetDive, Inc; Pearson Education, Inc; QUALCOMM, Inc; Karl Resch. EXTsearch; Stephen P. Ryder, Editor, Casebook: Jack the Ripper; Stephanie and Peter da Silva, http://paml.net; SunSITE; Tesco Stores Ltd; Tjerk Vonck, mIRC; Virgin Atlantic Airways Ltd.

Screenshot on page 61 © 2002, Southern Living, Inc. Reprinted with permission; Screenshot on page 94 from www.virginradio.co.uk reprinted with permission of Virgin Radio Ltd; Screenshot on page 125 Copyright Jupitermedia. All rights reserved. Reprinted with permission from http://www.internet.com; Screenshot on page 171 © Matrox Electronic Systems Ltd. Matrox is a registered trademark of Matrox Electronic Systems Ltd; Screenshot on page 247 © Yell.com 2002, reprinted with permission; Screenshot on page 286 from www.ukonline.net/travel, reprinted with permission of UK Online; Screenshots on pages 301 and 302 from www.amazon.co.uk. Amazon.co.uk is a registered trademark of Amazon.com, Inc. in the US and/or other countries. © 2002 Amazon.com. All rights reserved; Screenshot on page 311 from www.onelook.com, Copyright 2002 Datamuse; Screenshots reprinted by permission from Microsoft Corporation; Netscape website © 2002 Netscape Communications Corporation. Screenshots used with permission; Netscape browser window © 2002 Netscape Communications Corporation. Used with permission. Netscape Communications has not authorized, sponsored, endorsed, or approved this publication and is not responsible for its content.

In some instances we have been unable to trace the owners of copyright material, and we would appreciate any information that would enable us to do so.

Introduction

Welcome to *The Complete Idiot's Guide to the Internet*, 2003 Edition. That's nine editions in just eight-and-a-half years. Sometimes it's hard to imagine that, to most people just eight years ago, the Internet was little more than some strange computer thing they'd heard about on television. Now it's become a necessity for many of us – it's hard to imagine life without it. Not for you, though. If you're reading this book, chances are you're what's known in *Internetspeak* as a 'newbie' – a newcomer. Well, I've got good news for you.

If you're just starting to learn about the Internet, in one important way you're lucky. Eight years ago most Internet users were computer boffins, and that was fine because without a high degree of 'boffinity' you weren't going to get far on the Net anyway. Getting an Internet account was like stepping back in time to the 1970s, when computers were driven by obscure text commands and a mouse was furry and ate cheese.

Today the majority of new users are firmly in the 21st century. Thousands of fancy new Internet programs have been written in the last few years that make the Internet friendlier and easier to use. Today, it's easier to get on the Internet than it ever has been, and it's a lot easier to find your way around once you're there.

So Why Do You Need This Book?

To misquote L.P. Hartley, the Internet is a foreign country; they do things differently there. Different customs, different places to see, different ways to get things done, different rules. Chances are that if you've picked up this book, you're not an experienced international traveller along the highways and byways of this amazing system. You probably need a little help. Well you've come to the right place.

Yes, the Internet is far easier to get around now than it was in the mid-90s. But there's still a lot to learn. The journey will be far more comfortable than it was back then, and you can travel much farther.

Now, I know you're not an idiot. What you do, you do well. But right now, you don't do the Internet and you need a quick way to get up and running. You want to know what the fuss is about, or maybe you already know what the fuss is about and you want to find out how to get in on it. Well, I'm not going to teach you how to become an Internet guru, but I will tell you the things you really *need* to know, such as:

> ➤ How to get up and running on the Internet.

> ➤ How to send and receive email messages.

> ➤ How to move around on the World Wide Web (and what is the Web, anyway?).

> ➤ How to find what you are looking for on the Internet.

> ➤ How to protect life and limb in the fast lane of the information superhighway.

> ➤ How to participate in Internet discussion groups (that could take over your life and threaten your relationships if you're not careful).

> ➤ How to make your fortune in cyberspace.

I am, however, making a few assumptions. I'm assuming that you know how to use your computer, so don't expect me to give basic lessons on using the mouse, switching between windows, working with directories and files, and all that stuff. There's enough to cover in this book without all that. If you want really basic beginner's information, check out *The Complete Idiot's Guide to PCs* (also from Alpha), a great book by Joe Kraynak.

But Why A *UK* and *Eire* Guide To The Internet?

In the UK and Eire we use the Internet differently from our American counterparts: different companies provide the services we need, charge different prices for them, and give us different options to choose from. And once we're connected, we want to find the information that matters to *us*, so we need to look in different places to find it. In addition, because we're not American (or French, or Italian ...), our interests, habits, laws, environment and whole way of life, differ enormously. These affect both the *way* we use the Internet and what we use it *for*.

> ➤ Most American users have access to free local phone calls, which means that they can stay connected to the Internet all day long for no extra charge. In the UK, where many of us still pay by the minute, to follow some of the suggestions given in an American guide could end up costing a small fortune! Throughout this book, it's assumed that you want your time on the Internet to have as little impact as possible on the size of your phone bill.

➤ As a local user, you want to find local information. For example, you want to read local newspapers and magazines; see local weather forecasts; check local TV listings and sports results; find out what's showing at your nearest cinema; use local travel agents, hotels, airlines and trains; plan days out at local theme parks, museums and so on.

➤ Many Internet sites give support, help and advice on any subject you can imagine. Although some American Internet books can point you towards valuable information, they won't tell you where to get the best UK and Eire legal or consumer advice, find a job, or discuss financial matters with other UK and Eire investors.

➤ You can now buy almost anything from 'cyberstores' on the Internet. But do you really want to do your shopping in dollars and wait for the goods to be shipped from America when there are plenty of UK and Eire shopping sites just a couple of mouse clicks away? In fact, if you want to use the Internet to arrange car insurance, manage your bank account, or book theatre tickets, among other things, you'll have to find the right sites in the UK and Eire!

How Do You Use This Book?

I've used a few conventions in this book to make it easier for you to follow. For example, when you need to type something, it will appear in bold like this:

type **this**

If I don't know exactly what you'll have to type (because you have to supply some of the information), I'll put the unknown information in italics. For example, you might see the following instructions. In this case, I don't know the file name, so I made it italic to indicate that you have to supply it.

type **this** *file name*

Also, I've used the term 'Enter' throughout the book, even though your keyboard may have a 'Return' key instead.

In case you want a greater understanding of the subject you are learning, you'll find some background information in boxes. You can quickly skip over this information if you want to avoid all the gory details. On the other hand, you may find something that will help you out of trouble. Here are the special icons and boxes used in this book.

Check This Out

These boxes contain notes, tips, warnings, and asides that provide you with interesting and useful (at least theoretically) titbits of Internet information.

Technical Talk

The 'Techno Talk' icon calls your attention to technical information you might spout off to impress your friends, but that you'll likely never need to know to save your life.

Acknowledgements

Thanks to the huge team at the publishers who helped me put this together. There's a lot more to writing a book than just, well, writing. I'm very grateful to have people willing and able to do all the stuff that comes once the words are on the computer screen.

Part 1
Start At The Beginning

You want to start and you want to start quickly. No problem. In Part 1, you're going to do just that. First, I'll give you a quick overview of the Internet and then I'll have you jump right in and use the two most important Internet services: email and the World Wide Web. (The Web is so important these days that many people think the Internet is the Web. I'll explain the difference in Chapter 1.)

By the time you finish this part of the book, you'll be surfing around the Web like a true cybergeek – and you'll be ready to move on and learn about the other Internet services.

Your Connection To The Online Universe

Your journey into cyberspace begins with figuring out how to get online... which is far easier to do today than back in 1993 when the first edition of this book was written. Today the difficulties lie in choice, not implementation; that is, you may well spend more time figuring out which Internet service to use than getting up and running after you've decided. (You may also spend time figuring out which service you want, and then discovering that you can't *have* it, as you'll hear in a moment.) But before I help you make your choice, here's a little background information.

What Is The Internet?

Let's start with the basics. What's a computer network? It's a system in which computers are connected so they can share 'information'. (I'll explain what I mean by that word in a moment.) There's nothing particularly unusual about this in today's world. There are millions of networks around the world. True, they are mostly in the industrialized world, but there isn't a nation in the world that doesn't have at least a few. (Okay, I don't know that for sure, but I can't think of one.)

The Internet is something special, though, for two reasons. First, it's the world's largest computer network. Second, and what makes it *really* special, is that it's pretty much open to anyone with the entrance fee, and the entrance fee is constantly dropping. In fact, the majority of UK users now have free accounts, but that doesn't mean the entrance fee can't drop any further: some enterprising companies have reduced the cost of phone charges for Internet connections, and many more offer deals that give you free calls during evenings and weekends.

Just how big is the Internet? Well, you should first understand that many of the numbers we've heard in the last few years are complete nonsense. In 1993, people were saying 25 million. Considering that the majority of Internet users at the time were in the US, and that 25 million is 10 per cent of the US population, and that most people in that great nation thought that computer networks were something used to enslave them in the workplace, it's highly unlikely that anywhere near 25 million people were on the Internet. In fact, they weren't.

These days, estimates vary all over the place, ranging from the high tens of millions to the low hundreds of millions. In January of 1998, Nua Internet Surveys estimated more than 100 million and today they're claiming 407 million. The truth is that nobody knows how many people are using the Internet. Remember, though, that many users are only infrequent visitors to cyberspace, visiting perhaps once a week or so.

What Exactly Is 'Information'?

What, then, do I mean by 'information'? I mean anything you can send over lines of electronic communication and that includes quite a lot these days (and seems to include more every day). I mean letters, which are called *email* on the Internet. I mean reports, magazine articles and books, which are called *word processing files* on the Internet. I mean music, which is called *music* on the Internet.

You can even send your voice across the Internet; you'll learn how to do that in Chapter 13. And let me just say that you'll find it much cheaper than talking long-distance on the phone – as long as you can find someone to talk to at the other end. You can grab computer files of many kinds (programs, documents, clip art, sounds, and anything else that can be electronically encoded) from huge libraries that collectively contain literally millions of files.

4

A Word About Numbers

When I first started writing about the Internet, I used to try to be specific; I might have said '2.5 million files'. However, I've given up that practice for two reasons. First, many of the numbers were made up; no, not by me, but by Internet gurus who were trying to be specific and made 'educated' guesses. Second, even if the numbers were correct when I wrote them, they were too low by the time the book got to the editor, *much* too low by the time the book got to the printer, and *ridiculously* low by the time the book got to the readers. But you can be pretty sure that there are at least a few million files available for you to copy.

But 'information' could also be a type of conversation. You want to talk about politics? There's a discussion group waiting for you. Do you want to meet like-minded souls with a passion for daytime soap operas? They're talking right now.

Anything that can be sent electronically is carried on the Internet and much that can't be sent now probably will be sent in a few months. 'Such as?', you ask. How about a three-dimensional image of your face? In the next year or so, special face scanners will appear on the scene. You'll be able to scan your face and send the 3D image to someone, or use the image for your chat *avatar*. You'll learn about avatars in Chapter 12, 'Online Chat Rooms And Instant Messaging'.

The Internet Services

To be specific, take a quick look at the Internet services available to you.

➤ **Email.** This is the most used system. Hundreds of millions of messages wing their way around the world each day, between families, friends and businesses. The electronic world's postal system, email is very much like the real world's postal system, except that you can't send fruit, bombs, or this month's selection from the Cheese of the Month club. (You *can*, however, send letters, spreadsheets, pictures, sounds, programs, and more. See Chapters 2 and 3 for more info.)

➤ **Chat.** Chat's a bit of a misnomer. There's not much chatting going on here, but there is an awful lot of typing. You type a message and it's instantly transmitted to another person, or to many other people, who can type their responses right away. You'll learn more about this in Chapter 12.

➤ **Internet Phones.** Install a sound card and microphone, get the Internet phone software and then talk to people across the Internet. This is not very popular today, and to be quite honest, despite all the hype, it probably won't be popular anytime soon, either. But just think: you can make international phone calls for 60p an hour ... We'll come back to this in Chapter 13.

➤ **FTP.** FTP is the grand old man of the Internet. The whole purpose of the Internet was to transfer files from one place to another and, for years, FTP was how it was done. FTP provides a giant electronic 'library' of computer files; you'll learn how to use it in Chapter 11.

➤ **World Wide Web.** It's the Web that's really driving the growth of the Internet, 'cause it's *cool*! (Are you sick of that word yet?) Containing pictures, sounds and animation, the Web is a giant 'hypertext' system in which documents around the world are linked to one another. Click on a word in a document in, say, Sydney, Australia, and another document (which could be from Salzburg, Austria) appears. You'll learn about this amazing system in Chapters 4–8.

➤ **Newsgroups.** Newsgroups are discussion groups. Want to find out the latest on the Euro? (Or, at least, what the members of the discussion group say?) Want to learn an unusual kite-flying technique? Want to learn about ... well, anything really. There are over 50,000 internationally distributed newsgroups and you'll find out how to work with them in Chapters 9 and 10.

➤ **Mailing lists**. If 50,000 discussion groups are not enough for you, here are thousands more. As you'll also learn in Chapter 10, the mailing lists are another form of discussion group that work in a slightly different manner.

This is not an exhaustive list. Other systems are available; these are simply the most important ones.

But these are all tools, not reasons to be on the Internet. As a wise man once said, 'Nobody wants a $\frac{1}{4}$-inch drill bit, they want a $\frac{1}{4}$-inch hole'. Nobody wants the Web, FTP or mailing lists either; they want ... well, what do they want? As you read this book, you'll get plenty of ideas for how you can use the Internet tools for profit and pleasure.

Getting On The Net

So you think the Net sounds great. How do you get to it, though? You might get Internet access in a number of ways:

➤ Your college provides you with an Internet account.

➤ Your company has an Internet connection from its internal network.

➤ You've signed up with an online service such as America Online (AOL), CompuServe, or the Microsoft Network (MSN).

➤ You've signed up with an Internet service provider.

➤ You book a few hours at one of the Internet pubs and cafés springing up all over the land.

The Internet is not owned by any one company. It's more like the world's telephone system: each portion is owned by someone and the overall system hangs together because of a variety of agreements between those organizations. So there is no *Internet, Ltd.* where you can go to get access to the Internet. No, you have to go to one of the tens of thousands of organizations that already have access to the Internet and get a connection through them.

You'll learn more about finding a connection in Appendix D.

What Do You Need?

What does it take to get onto the information superhighway? Many of you already have Internet accounts; our high-priced research shows that most readers buy this book *after* they have access to the Internet (presumably because they got access and then got lost). However, to make sure we're on the same wavelength before we get going, let's consult the checklist to see what you need and what you've got. Actually, it's a very short list: you need a telephone line, a computer, a modem and an Internet access account. Let's look at each one in a little more detail:

Turn Off Call Waiting

If you have the Call Waiting service on your phone line, make sure you turn it off every time you go online (by dialling # 43 #) and back on again when you've finished (* 43 #). Otherwise, an incoming call at the wrong moment could disconnect you and cancel anything you were doing – particularly irritating if you were waiting for a huge file to download and were just seconds away from completing!

Computer

Yes, you *knew* you needed a computer! But a common misconception is that you've got to have a fast, powerful computer to surf the Net. In fact, almost *any* computer will be up to the task. I do have a few suggestions that will enrich your online time though:

➤ Windows 95, NT 4, and later operating systems all have built-in support for Internet connections that make all the setting-up and connecting happen smoothly and simply.

➤ To hear the Internet's musical offerings and use Internet telephony software (see Chapter 13) you'll need a soundcard.

➤ To enjoy the World Wide Web at its graphical, vibrant best, you'll be happiest with at least a high-colour, 800 × 600 display. On modern computers that's a standard setup, so don't worry if that's all Greek to you!

➤ Finally, a large hard disk. It's not vital – you'll have to install a few new programs, but they won't take up more than a few megabytes – but you'll find it hard to resist downloading some of the free or inexpensive software you'll find on the Net!

Modem

The modem is the device that converts the information on a computer into sound that can be sent down a phone line and converts it back to meaningful information again when it gets to the other end. The most important thing to look for when buying a modem is its *speed* – how much information it can move around per second. The faster your modem (in theory, at least), the quicker you'll get everything done that you planned to do, cutting your phone bill and any online charges as a result.

Is A Fast Modem Really Worth The Extra Money?

Generally speaking, yes it is. But you've heard the term 'superhighway' used to describe the Internet. Like any highway, there's a lot of people all trying to get to the same place and things can get jammed solid, so while the person with the slow modem is gazing at his screen for some sign of information arriving, the person with the fast modem is doing just the same. But, when everything's running smoothly, a 56Kbps modem is streets ahead of a 28.8, and digital access such as Home Highway (explained later in this chapter) is far better than analogue.

At the moment, the fastest modems shift data around at a maximum speed of 56Kbps (56 thousand bits per second). There have been slower models available in the past (28.8Kbps and 33.6Kbps could still be bought until recently) but the price of the 56K modem has fallen to rock bottom, so no-one's building the slower models any more, other than as PC Card devices for notebook computers. Slower modems really are a false economy: if you connect to the Net for more than a few minutes a week at these speeds you'll be miserable. Most new desktop computers come with a built-in modem (some notebook and handheld computers do too), but if you do have to buy one, avoid anything slower than a 56Kbps model.

You'll also get a choice between an internal and an external model. Although the external modem is slightly more expensive I'd go for it every time. It's much easier to install (just plug in the phone cable, serial or USB cable and main plug), and the lights on the front make it easier to tell what's going on.

Internet Access Account

With all the necessary hardware bits and bobs in place, the final thing you need is a way to connect to a computer that is a part of the Internet. There are hundreds of companies in the UK who specialize in selling dial-up links to the Internet via their own computers, so the next step is to choose one of these companies and set up an account with them.

This leads to the final decision you have to make: do you want an account with an **Internet service provider** (often just called an ISP) or with an **online service**?

Online Services And Internet Service Providers – What's The Difference?

The most important thing that Internet service providers and the major online services have in common is that they both let you connect to the Internet. It's the way they do it and what else they have to offer that makes them different, along with their methods of deciding how much you should pay. Let's take a look at the two options and the pros and cons of each.

Online Services

You may have heard of the 'big three' online services, **America Online** (AOL), **CompuServe** (CSi), and the **Microsoft Network** (MSN). In fact, if you buy computer magazines, you're probably snowed under with floppy-disks and CD-ROMs inviting you to sign up to one or other of these. One of the main plus-points about these online services is the speed and ease with which you can sign up: just this one disk and a credit or debit card number is all you need.

But don't confuse online services with the Internet itself. An online service is like an exclusive club: once you subscribe you'll have access to a range of members-only areas such as discussion forums, chat rooms and file libraries. Although you can 'escape' to the Internet from here, non-members can't get in. You won't find much in the members-only areas that you can't find on the Internet itself, but online services do have the combined benefits of ease of use, online help if you get lost, and a friendly all-in-one program that lets you reach everything you need. Although the Internet certainly isn't the chamber of horrors that some newspapers would have you believe, there's little control over what gets published there; online services carefully filter and control their members-only content, making them the preferred choice for getting the whole family online.

How 'Easy' Is It To Connect To An Online Service?

I knew you'd ask, so I've just signed up with a major online service (I won't say which). It took 12 minutes from inserting the CD-ROM to officially 'arriving online'. Yes, I know, I've done it before; the point is that the most difficult thing I had to do was read those shiny numbers on my credit card.

So online services give you the Internet, plus a bit more. In the past, what counted against online services was the monthly charge, but with the arrival of free Internet service providers the online services have had to run to keep up. At the time of writing, AOL is offering *unmetered access* (more about that a little later) at a similar price to the ISPs, £15.99 per month, so it really all boils down to the simple question, *Is this the kind of service you'd like to use?*

Internet Service Providers

An Internet Service Provider gives you access to the Internet, plain and simple. When you dial in to your access provider's computer, you'll see some sort of message on the screen that tells you you're connected, but you won't feel the earth move. Instead, you'll start your email program or your Web *browser* and start doing whatever you wanted to do.

The Internet service provider (ISP) account has several valuable points in its favour. The first is pricing: the competition among companies to gain subscribers means that you can now access the Internet without paying a penny (apart from your telephone bill, although that's starting to change too). If you prefer to pay – and there may be reasons why you would, as we'll see in a moment – a single low monthly charge will give you unrestricted Internet access with no extra charges for the time you spend online. The second benefit is that you'll have far greater flexibility in your choice of software. Most service providers will give you a bundle of programs when you sign up, but you don't have to use them – you can try out all the programs you want to until you find the ones you're happy with. In most cases, signing up with an ISP is as straightforward as signing up with an online service these days, particularly for Windows users: follow the instructions that come with the CD-ROM and you'll usually be online in minutes.

Phone Calls And Connections

Whether you choose to hook up with an ISP or an online service, you'll have to dial in to that company's computer every time you want to use the Internet. This means that if you connect for 20 minutes you're making a 20-minute phone call (although it's your modem using the line, not your phone). The call may cost you money, and you might also have to pay a monthly or annual fee to your service provider.

Although that sounds like bad news for your bank account, it probably isn't. The first piece of good news is that you should always be able to connect through a local phone number. At the time of writing, British Telecom's local rate (per minute) is 4p peak, 1.7p cheap, and 1p at weekends. Add your dial-up number to your 'Friends & Family' list and you'll save at least 10 per cent. And if your phone bill is high enough to qualify for the PremierLine scheme you'll be able to knock off another 15 per cent. (Different phone companies' charges vary, of course, so make sure you check these details before relying on them!)

Another piece of good news is that you may not have to pay your ISP. Many ISPs offer free access (which we'll look at in a moment), leaving you with nothing but the calls to pay for.

It May Be Free!

Here's one more piece of good news: many ISPs are now offering premium-rate services (some using a British Telecom package called **SurfTime**). For a fixed monthly fee of £6 to £9 you receive access to the Internet for as long as you like during evenings and the weekend, with no call changes. (At other times, of course, call charges do apply.)

Free Access Pros And Cons

Although it's a recent innovation in the UK, the free-access bandwagon has gained immense speed with all manner of companies jumping on board. Well-known names like Dixons, Tesco and Virgin now offer free Internet access; telecommunications companies are trying to steal us away from BT by providing free access combined with lower call charges; and established ISPs like BT Internet have introduced free accounts to cling on to their existing users.

Free Internet Access? What's The Catch?

The main catch is that you'll be paying upwards of 50p per minute for calls to the company's help line if you get stuck. It's a pretty small catch though: you're not going to get stuck very often, and you may never need to phone the help line at all.

The obvious benefit of using a free ISP is that you don't pay, thereby saving yourself £6 to £15 per month. That leads to a couple more benefits:

➤ If you find the service poor or unreliable you can stop using it and pick another without the aggravation of cancelling your subscription and stopping payments.

➤ You can sign up with several ISPs – still at no cost – as an increasing number of Internet users choose to do.

The negative side of free access providers is that they're heavily geared towards the home user – if you want to get your company online or set up a business Web site, a free ISP probably won't be flexible enough for you. The result is that the folk who subscribe to free ISPs are home users who all pile onto the Net at the same time: evenings and weekends. If your chosen ISP hasn't invested enough in its service to cope with these sudden rushes, you may find things a bit slow or unreliable.

Don't let the paragraph above put you off, though! I have accounts with several ISPs – some free, some not – and I don't find much to choose between them in terms of reliability and speed. Unless you have a good reason not to, free access is still the route to take.

Service Provider

A company that sells access to the Internet. You dial into its computer, which connects you to the Internet. The online service providers are an anomaly. Strictly speaking, they are Internet service providers because they provide Internet access. However, they aren't called 'service providers'; instead, they're called 'online services'. The companies called service providers generally provide access to the Internet and little, if anything, more. The online services, on the other hand, have all sorts of file libraries, chat services, news services, and so on, within the services themselves.

Unmetered Access (At Last!)

Only a few short years ago, Internet users paid their ISP upwards of £10 a month *and* paid all call charges. The arrival of the free ISP accounts made a huge difference to the cost of going online, but it was still the call charges that got you. What the UK has been waiting for is **unmetered access**, and at last it's here.

With unmetered access, you pay one monthly fee to your ISP or online service and you can stay online continuously, day and night, without paying a penny in call charges. Well, okay, not actually *continuously* because most companies limit you to 'reasonable use' in their small print (anything over about 12 hours being considered unreasonable) but you get the idea. Many ISPs and online services offer unmetered access, and they all charge a similar price of around £14 to £16 per month – you can find a few to choose from in Appendix D.

Broadband And Other Options

Up to this point I've assumed that you have a modem and you want to use it for your Internet access – modem connections are cheap, easy and convenient. But there are other options you might want to consider later on, such as the latest **broadband** connections, which offer faster ways to connect to the Net. These tend to be the domain of companies and individuals who use the Internet extensively, and they replace the humble modem. Not surprisingly, they're also more expensive than a modem connection, which is why they're best ignored for the time being, but here's a brief description of each.

Techno Talk

Broadband

The word 'broadband' is a catch-all term for the latest high-speed digital connections. Broadband connections currently come in two delicious flavours, ADSL and cable, but other broadband options are beginning to appear such as SDSL (available in parts of Scotland) and some unusual modem/satellite hybrid systems.

➤ **Home Highway.** This service from British Telecom replaces your modem with a new device called an ISDN card or Terminal Adaptor and puts a larger phone-socket junction box on your wall. This gives you two phone lines with speeds of 64Kbps each (a little faster than the fastest modem), allowing you to surf the Net while sending faxes or making phone calls. In theory, you can link the two lines together to give yourself a 128Kbps connection, but there are currently few access providers who allow you to connect this way (and you'll be paying double the price for your phone calls). Apart from the cost of the ISDN card (around £60), installation costs around £75 and the quarterly rental is roughly £75. If you already have Internet access, you can find out more about Home Highway and its sister service, Business Highway, on BT's Web site at **http://www.bt.com/homehighway**. If you're tempted by this, here's one extra bonus: making connections to your service provider takes only a couple of seconds and is completely silent – a big difference from the 30-odd seconds of whistling and screeching you have to endure with a modem.

13

➤ **ISDN line.** The details and benefits of an ISDN line are similar to those of Home Highway, but this option requires the installation of a digital phone line which, together with a few other subtle differences, results in higher costs. ISDN may be the best connection method for some businesses, but home users will usually ignore this one.

Dig Deeper

If you're seriously considering an ISDN line, make sure you check access providers' charges too – some require a higher monthly subscription for an ISDN connection than for a modem connection.

➤ **Leased line.** This is a mind-bogglingly fast direct connection to the Internet. Leased lines (also known as *permanent* connections) are often used by large organizations such as universities, groups of schools, and corporations. The organization has to set up special equipment to connect its network to the Internet and it has to lease a special telephone line that can transfer data very quickly. Because that organization has a leased line, it is always connected to the Internet, which means there's no need to make a telephone call and use a modem to reach the service provider's computer. A leased line will set you back anything from £2000 upwards annually, so don't buy one until you're sure you need it!

➤ **ADSL.** This digital system from BT offers one of the new breed of broadband connections, giving you a permanent link to the Internet and a download speed of between 50Kpbs and 2Mbps (10 to 40 times the maximum speed of a modem). As with Home Highway, you can use your line to make and receive phone calls while online. ADSL connections are desirable things, and getting your hands on an ADSL account is easy, with big names such as BTOpenWorld, Demon Internet, Virgin Net and America Online all offering them. Prices vary, but the current average is around £25 per month, plus the cost of installation and equipment. Installation could be over £200, but the simple self-install package reduces this to about £80. So ADSL accounts are easy to come by, and pretty affordable, so why don't we all have them? The main catch is that you need to be located within 3½ miles of an ADSL-enabled telephone exchange, but according to BT that now covers 90% of the population. If you have Internet access already, visit BTOpenWorld online at **http://www.btopenworld.com** to find out whether that 90% includes you.

➤ **Cable connection.** If you can get one, you probably want one! Cable modems and their broadband connections are very fast, and may be permanent, similar to a leased line. Like ADSL, however, the drawback is that they're more expensive than an ordinary modem connection at between £15 and £40 per month depending upon the speed you need. If your home is cable-connected, visit the Web site of one of the companies providing cable connections to find out more: blueyonder at **http://www.blueyonder.co.uk** and NTL at **http://www.ntl.com**.

Do You Need Speed?

Stuck with a slow connection? Don't get too jealous of people using faster connections. The Internet can be very slow at times, and even if you have a very fast connection from your service provider to your computer, you might still find yourself twiddling your thumbs. For instance, when you're using the Web, the server you've connected to might be slow. Or the lines from that server across the world to your service provider might be slow. Or your service provider's system may be clogged up with more users than it can handle.

Oh, all right, I'll tell you the truth. A fast connection is fantastic – the Internet is a completely different experience. Sure, you'll run across slow servers now and then, although there seem to be fewer and fewer of them. But all of a sudden you'll find that the things you'd always avoided like the plague over a slow modem (video in particular) really work well. I've also run across sites that seem to be designed for broadband users, sites I wouldn't have the patience to visit with a standard modem. A fact of Internet life over the years is that as connection speeds have increased, Web site designers haven't been slow to take up the slack and add heavyweight features to their sites. Right now broadband connections are great luxuries; in a few years, though, they could be a necessity.

You Want Help Setting Up?

Unfortunately, I can't help you with the initial setup of your software. There are too many different systems to cover. So here's my (very general) advice: if your service provider or online service can't help you set up, *find another one!*

Don't let me frighten you. In many cases, the initial setup is actually quite easy. You simply run some kind of setup program and follow any instructions and in a few minutes, you'll be up and running.

Some providers – in particular many of the small service providers – are not terribly helpful. However, things are certainly better than they were three or four years ago, when many service providers had the attitude 'we give you the account to connect to, it's up to you to figure out how to do it!' These days, most are making more of an effort. But if you run into a service provider that isn't willing to explain, absolutely clearly, what you need to do to connect, you should move on. This is a very competitive business and there are many good companies that are willing to help you.

15

That's All, Folks!

We don't need to talk any more about getting an Internet account. Most of you already have an account, so it's time to move on and get down to the meat of the subject: how to work with the account you have. If, on the other hand, you *don't* have an account yet, flip to Appendix D, in which I explain how to find one. In fact, even if you *do* have an account, you should look in the appendix because you might eventually want to swap to a cheaper or more reliable service.

Moving along, we'll assume that you have an Internet account you are completely happy with and that you know how to log on to that account. (Check with your system administrator or look in your service documentation if you need information about logging on to the Internet.)

The Least You Need To Know

➤ The Internet is the world's largest computer network, an enormous public information highway.

➤ You can do many things on the Internet: send email, join discussion groups, grab files from electronic libraries, cruise the World Wide Web, and much more.

➤ There are four types of Internet connection available: a standard dial-up connection using a modem and ordinary phone line (the cheapest, and a perfectly adequate method); an ISDN or Home Highway digital connection (faster and more reliable, but also more expensive); an ADSL or cable permanent connection (very fast and rather expensive); and a leased line permanent connection (extremely fast and frighteningly expensive).

➤ The Internet is a public system. The online services – America Online, CompuServe, the Microsoft Network, et al. – are private services, with 'gateways' to the Internet.

➤ A member of an online service can use the Internet, but an Internet user cannot use an online service unless he joins.

➤ You can get Internet access through your company or school, a small local Internet service provider, a giant Internet service provider (such as Freeserve or BT Internet), or an online service.

The Premier Internet Tool: Email

Some of you might think the title of this chapter is a joke. It's not. Although email may not be exciting, 'cool', or 'compelling', it is the most popular and, in many ways, the most useful Internet service. More people use email on any given day than use any other Internet service. Tens of millions of messages fly across the wires each day.

Despite all the glitz of the Web (you'll learn about that glitz in Chapters 4–8), the potential of Internet Phone systems (Chapter 13), and the excitement – for some – of the many chat systems (Chapter 12), email is probably the most productive tool there is. It's a sort of Internet workhorse, getting the work done without any great fanfare.

After spending huge sums of money polling Internet users, we've come to the conclusion that the very first thing Internet users want to do is send email messages. It's not too threatening and it's an understandable concept: you're sending a letter. The only differences are that you don't take it to the post office and that it's much faster. So that's what I'm going to start with: how to send an email message.

Why Should I Use Email?

Three good reasons. First, it's incredibly cheap – for one fifth the price of a 1st class stamp you can send dozens of messages anywhere in the world. Second, it's amazingly fast: mere seconds or minutes rather than days. And third, it's easy to keep copies of the email you send and receive, and it's also easy to sort and locate individual messages quickly.

What Email System?

Which email system do you use? Well, if you are a member of an online service, you have a built-in mail system. But, if you are not a member of one of the major online services   ... who knows what you are using! Even with an online service, there are different options; CompuServe, for instance, offers a number of different programs you can use.

Basically, it all depends what your service provider set you up with. You might be using Netscape, a World Wide Web browser (discussed in Chapter 4) that has a built-in email program. Likewise, you might be using Microsoft Messaging, Exchange, or Internet Mail, which come with Windows 95, or Outlook Express which is included with Windows 98 onwards and some of the later editions of Windows 95. You could be using Eudora, which is probably the most popular email program on the Internet. Or you might be using something else entirely.

Luckily, the email concepts are all the same, regardless of the type of program you are using – even if the actual buttons you click are different.

To POP Or Not To POP?

POP (Post Office Protocol) is a very common system used for handling Internet email. A POP server receives email that's been sent to you and holds it until you use your mail program to retrieve it. However POPs are not ubiquitous: some online services and many companies don't use POP.

Generally, of course, you don't care what system is used to hold your mail. However, if your email service doesn't use POP and you want to switch to a particular email program, you might find that you can't, and the most advanced email programs are designed to be used with POP servers. For instance, at the time of writing, you couldn't use a POP program with an America Online account. On the other hand, CompuServe now does provide POP mail but you have to sign up for this optional service online. (For some bizarre reason, the more recent CompuServe 2000 release does not have a POP system.)

Another common mail system, IMAP (Internet Message Access Protocol), is generally used by corporate networks, not Internet service providers. If you're using a corporate network, you probably won't have much choice about which mail program you can use.

You Have A New Address!

I recently discovered how you can tell an absolute beginner on the Internet; he often talks about his email 'number', equating email with telephones. Well, they are both electronic, after all. However, you actually have an email *address*. That address has three parts:

➤ Your account name

➤ The 'at' sign (@)

➤ Your domain name

What's your account name? It's almost always the name you use to log on to your Internet account. For instance, when I log on to my CompuServe account, I have to type 71601,1266. That's my account name. When I log on to MSN I use CIGInternet, and on AOL, I use PeKent. (Note that the CompuServe account name is a special case; when using this account in an email address, I have to replace the comma with a dot: 71601.1266@compuserve.com.)

Start With What You Were Given

I suggest you start off using the email program that you were given when you set up your account. But if you'd like to get a copy of Eudora later, go to **http://www.qualcomm.com/**. The current version of Eudora offers several different 'modes' including a free cut-down mode, or a free fully-featured mode supported by advertising as well as the more traditional 'buy it and use it' mode. You won't be able to use Eudora with the online services, though, only with true Internet service providers.

After your account name, you use the @ sign. Why? Well, how else would you know where the account name ends and domain name starts, eh?

Finally, you use the domain name, which is the address of your company, your service provider, or your online service. Think of it as the street address line in your full address. After all, a person can address a real letter to any other person using *your* street address. It's the same with the Internet: one street address (the domain name) can be used for thousands of account names.

Account Names: They're All The Same

Actually, CompuServe calls the account name a *User ID*, MSN calls it a *Member Name*, and AOL calls it a *Screen Name*. In addition, you might hear the account name called a *user name* or *logon ID*. All of these names mean the same thing: the name by which you are identified when you log on to your account. Most online services and Internet service providers will let you choose a unique account name when you sign up, and it can be just about anything you like, as long as it contains no spaces. You might want a variation of your name, such as j.smith or john_smith, or something more sophisticated like zapdoodle or jellyfish.

Where do you get the domain name? If you haven't been told already, ask the system administrator or tech support. (Later in this chapter, you'll learn the domain names of the larger online services.)

Pronouncing Your Email Address

Here's the 'correct' way to say an email address out loud. You say 'dot' for the full stops and 'at' for the @ sign. Thus pkent@topfloor.com is 'p kent at topfloor dot com'.

A Word About Setup

You *might* need to set up your email system before it will work. In many cases, this setup will already be done for you. If you are with one of the online services, you don't need to worry – it's done for you. Some of the Internet service providers also do all this configuring stuff for you. Others, however, expect you to get into your program and enter some information. It doesn't have to be difficult. The following figure shows some of the options you can configure in Netscape Messenger, the email program that comes – along with Navigator – as part of the Netscape Communicator package.

Whatever program you have, you might have to enter the following information:

➤ **Incoming Mail Server.** This is usually a POP account, although if you're on a corporate network it might be an IMAP (Internet Message Access Protocol) account. When you connect to your service provider, your email program needs to check with the post office (a program running on your service provider's system) to see if any mail has arrived. This post office actually holds the messages that arrive for you until your mail program asks for them. Your account name is usually the same as the account name that you use to log on to your service. You might need to enter the full account name and the POP host name (for instance, in Eudora Light, I enter pkent@mail.usa.net). Or you might have to enter the account name (pkent) in one box and the POP host name (mail.usa.net) in another.

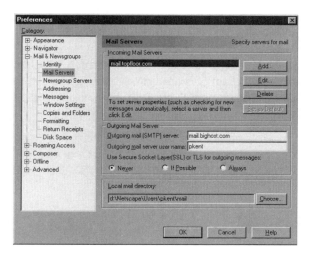

One of several mail-related panels in Netscape Messenger's Preferences dialog box, in which you can configure the mail program before you use it.

➤ **Password.** You'll need to enter your password so the email program can check the POP for mail. This is generally the same password you use to log onto the system.

➤ **Real Name.** This is, yes, your actual name. Most mail programs will send your name along with the email address when you send email.

➤ **SMTP (Simple Mail Transfer Protocol) Host.** This is another mail program. This one's used to send mail. While the POP holds your incoming mail, the SMTP is used to transmit your messages out onto the Internet. This time, you'll enter a hostname (mail.usa.net) or maybe a number (192.156.196.1) that you've been given by your service provider.

➤ **Return or Reply To Address.** If you want, you can make the email program place a different Reply To: address on your messages. For instance, if you send mail from work but want to receive responses to those messages at home, you'd use a different Reply To address. If you do this, make sure you enter the full address (such as pkent@topfloor.com).

➤ **All Sorts of Other Stuff.** There are all sorts of things you can get a good mail program to do. You can tell it how often to check the POP to see if new mail has arrived, choose the font you want the message displayed in, and/or

What Can I Do With My Mail Program?

Check This Out...

You might be able to do lots of things. Check your documentation or Help files, or simply browse through the configuration dialog boxes to see what you can do. Note, however, that the online services' email programs generally have a limited number of choices. Email programs such as Eudora have more choices.

get the program to automatically include the original message when you reply to a message. You can even tell it to leave messages at the POP after you retrieve them. This might be handy if you like to check your mail from work; if you configure the program to leave the messages at the POP, you can retrieve them again when you get home, using the program on your home machine. You can also define how the program will handle 'attachments', but that is a complicated subject that I'll get to later in this chapter.

There are so many email programs around, I can't help you configure them all. If you have trouble configuring your program, check the documentation or call the service's technical support. And as I've said before, if they don't want to help, find another service!

Sending A Message

Now that you understand addresses and have configured the mail program, you can actually send a message. So, who can you mail a message to? Well, you may already have friends and colleagues who you can bother with your flippant 'hey, I've finally made it onto the Internet' message. On the other hand, why not send yourself a message and kill two birds with one stone: you'll learn how to send one, and then you can see what to do when you receive a message!

So start your email program and then open the window in which you are going to write the message. You may have to double-click an icon (such as Eudora, for instance) or choose a menu option that opens the mail's Compose window. In Eudora, once the program is open, you click the **New Message** icon or choose **Message**, **New Message**.

Online Services

If you are working in one of the old CompuServe programs, choose **Mail**, **Create New Mail**. With CompuServe 2000, click the big **Create Mail** button in the toolbar. In AOL, choose **Mail Room**, **Write An Email** or click the **Write** button in the main toolbar.

In all of the email programs, the Compose window has certain common elements. In addition, some have a few extras. Here's what you might find:

➤ **To:** This is the address of the person you are mailing to. If you are using an online service and you are sending a message to another member of that service, all you need to use is the person's account name. For instance, if you are an AOL member and you're mailing to another AOL member with the screen name of PeKent, that's all you need to enter. To mail to that member from a service *other* *than* AOL, however, you enter the full address: pekent@aol.com. (I explain more about mailing to online services in the section 'We Are All One – Sending Email To Online Services', later in this chapter.)

➤ **From:** Not all mail programs show this, but it gives your email address, which is included in the message 'header' (the clutter at the top of an Internet message). It lets the recipient know who to reply to.

➤ **Subject:** This is a sort of message title – a few words summarizing the contents. The recipient can scan through a list of subjects to see what each message is about. (Some mail programs won't let you send a message unless you fill in the subject line; others don't mind if you leave it blank.)

➤ **Cc:** You can enter an address here to send a copy to someone other than the person whose address you placed in the To: line.

➤ **Bc:** This means 'blind copy'. As with the Cc: line, a copy of the message will be sent to the address (or addresses) you place in the Bc: (or Bcc:) line; however, the recipient of the original message won't be able to tell that the Bcc: address received a copy. (If you use Cc:, the recipient of the original message sees a Cc: line in the header.)

➤ **Attachments:** This is for sending computer files along with the message. (Again, I'll get to that later in this chapter, in the section 'Sending Files Is Getting Easier'.)

➤ **A big blank area:** This is where you type your message.

Email programs vary greatly, and not all programs have all of these features. Again, the online service mail programs tend to be a bit limited. The following figures show the Compose window in two very different mail programs.

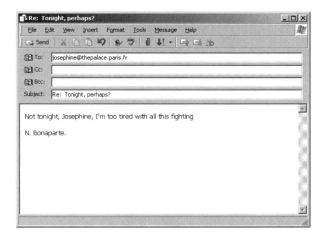

This is Outlook Express's mail composition window.

This is AK-Mail, my current favourite, from http://akmail.com.

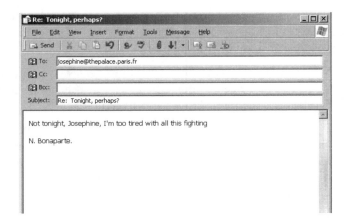

Go ahead and type a To: address. Why not use your own address? If you are in an online service, you might as well use the entire Internet address. The message will probably go out onto the Internet and then turn around and come back to you. I'll explain those online service addresses in the next section.

Don't Cc: To A List!

If you want to mail a message to a large list of people, don't put all the addresses into the Cc: line. Addresses in the Cc: line will be visible to all recipients, and most people don't like the idea of their email address being given away to strangers. Instead put the list into the Bcc: line. Addresses in the Bcc: line will not be displayed anywhere in the email (which also makes each message smaller and therefore quicker to send and receive).

We Are All One – Sending Email To Online Services

One of the especially nice things about the Internet, from an email point of view, is that because all the online services are now connected to the Internet, you can send email between email services. Perhaps you have an America Online account because … well, because they sent you a disk in the mail. And perhaps your brother has a CompuServe account because … well, because he's a geek and that's where the geeks have been hanging out for years. (Before you email me to complain, I've had a CompuServe account for almost 20 years.) You can send email to each other, using the Internet as a sort of bridge. How? Well, you just have to know the other person's account name on that service and that service's domain name.

For instance, CompuServe has this Internet domain name: compuserve.com. Say you want to send an email message to someone at CompuServe who has the account name (well, User ID or Screen Name they call it on CompuServe) of 71601,1266. You add the two together with the @ in the middle. Then you have 71601,1266@compuserve.com. However, you can't have a comma in an Internet address. So you replace it with a dot, and you end up with 71601.1266@compuserve.com. (Some CompuServe users have 'proper' email addresses, names instead of numbers. If you use CompuServe and want one of those real addresses, use GO REGISTER.)

The other major online services are very straightforward. To send email to an AOL member, for example, follow the user's AOL Screen Name with @aol.com. Similarly, to email a Microsoft Network (MSN) user, you'd tag @msn.com onto the member name.

Most online services and Internet service providers have domain names that are just as plain-sailing as these. Of course, there are more complicated Internet addresses, but you'll rarely run into them. If you have trouble mailing someone, though, call and ask *exactly* what you must type as his or her email address. (There's no rule that says you can't use the telephone any more!)

Write The Message

Now that you have the address on-screen, write your message – whatever you want to say. Then send the message. How's that done? There's usually a big Send button, or maybe a menu option that says Send or Mail. What happens when you click the button? That depends on the program and whether or not you are logged on at the moment. Generally, if you are logged on, the mail is sent immediately. Not always, though. Some programs will put the message in a 'queue' and won't send the message until told to do so. Others will send immediately and if you are not logged on, they will try to log on first. Watch closely and you'll usually see what's happening. A message will let you know if the message is being sent. If it hasn't been sent, look for some kind of Send Immediately menu option, or perhaps Send Queued Messages. Whether the message should be sent immediately or put in a queue is often one of the configuration options available to you.

Where'd It Go? Incoming Email

You've sent yourself an email message, but where did it go? It went out into the electronic wilderness to wander around for a few seconds, or maybe a few minutes. Sometimes a few hours. Very occasionally, it even takes a few days. (Generally, the message comes back in a few minutes, unless you mistyped the address, in which case you'll get a special message telling you that it's a bad address.)

Now it's time to check for incoming email. If you are using an online service, as soon as you log on, you'll see a message saying that email has arrived. If you are already online, you may see a message telling you that mail has arrived, or you may need to check; you may find a Get New Mail menu option. If you are working with an Internet service provider, you generally won't be informed of incoming mail; rather, your email program has to go and check. Either you can do that manually (for instance, in Eudora, there's a File, Check Mail command), or you can configure the program to check automatically every so often.

Fancy Fonts

Some of the online services allow you to use fancy text formatting features. For example, AOL lets you use colours, indents, different fonts, bold, italic, and so on. But in general these features only work in messages sent *within* the online services. Internet email is plain text – nothing fancy. Don't bother getting fancy in your Internet email because the online service's email system will strip out all that attractive stuff when the message is sent out onto the Internet. However, there is a system you can use to send formatted email, if both you and the recipient have the right type of mail program – HTML Mail. We'll take a quick look at HTML Mail in Chapter 3, 'Advanced Email: HTML And Encryption'.

What Now?

What can you do with your incoming email? All sorts of things. I think I'm pretty safe in saying that *every* email program allows you to read incoming messages. Most programs also let you print and save messages (if your program doesn't, you need another). You can also delete them, forward them to someone else, and reply directly to the sender.

These commands should be easy to find. Generally, you'll have toolbar buttons for the most important commands and more options available if you dig around a little in the menus, too.

A Word About Quoting

It's a good idea to 'quote' when you respond to a message. This means that you include part or all of the original message. Some programs automatically quote the original message. And different programs mark quoted messages in different ways; usually, you'll see a 'greater than' symbol (>) at the beginning of each line. The following figure shows a reply message that contains a quote from the original message.

You aren't required to quote. But if you don't, the recipient might not know what you are talking about. I receive dozens of messages a day and I know people who get

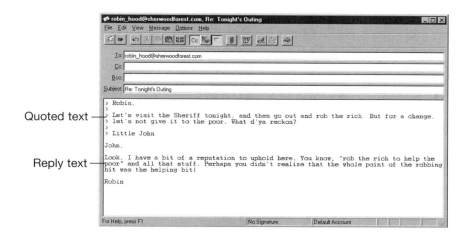

Quoted text ──

Reply text ──

You should quote the original message when responding, to remind the sender what he said.

literally hundreds. (Of course, the radiation emitted from their computer screens is probably frying their brains.) If you respond to a message without reminding the recipient exactly which of the 200 messages he sent out last week (or which of the five he sent to you) you are responding to, he might be slightly confused.

Quoting is especially important when sending messages to mailing lists and newsgroups (discussed in Chapters 9 and 10), where your message might be read by people who didn't read the message to which you are responding.

Sending Files Is Getting Easier

I used to hate sending files. Not because it's so difficult to send files across the Internet (although it is – or at least used to be until very recently), but because it was sort of embarrassing to admit how difficult it was. Now before you misunderstand, let me say that I *did* know how to send files across the Internet. However, very few other people seemed to understand, and even when they did understand, they didn't seem to have software that worked properly. Unless both parties involved (the sender and the recipient) understood the process and had the correct software, things sometimes didn't work.

I recall, for instance, the incredible problems I had transferring computer files to a magazine early in 1995. It didn't matter what transmission format I used (I'll discuss that in a moment), nor what program I was working with; the staff at the magazine couldn't seem to open those files – never mind that this magazine just happened to be a major *Internet* magazine. Today the situation is much improved, and the problems inherent in file transfers are, for many users, a thing of the past.

I'll assume you're working with decent software. Most programs these days can transmit and receive files. You can email files from Outlook to Eudora, from Eudora to CompuServe, from CompuServe to AOL, and from AOL to Pegasus Mail, and so on.

Your program will have some kind of command that enables you to attach a file. For instance, in Eudora choose **Message**, **Attach File**. In Outlook Express choose **Insert**, **File Attachment**. In AOL click the **Attach** button.

In The Old Days

There used to be four ways to send files. Using **MIME** (Multipurpose Internet Mail Extensions); **uuencode** (the file was converted to plain ASCII text); **BinHex** (a system similar to uuencode, used by Macintosh computers); and various methods used by online services. These days the situation is much improved and you can let your email program figure out how to transmit files.

Sending a file with your email is usually as simple as clicking a button and selecting the file.

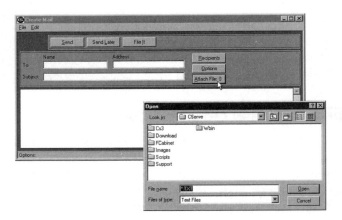

Fatal Attachment

Despite the occasional scare-stories about so-called 'email viruses', email messages are just plain text and therefore can't harbour computer viruses. But files included as attachments may be executable programs or documents that can contain executable macros such as Microsoft Word files, and these certainly can carry viruses. You should always check these attachments with a virus-checker utility before running them.

Cool Things You Can Do With Email

Once you understand your email system and realize that it won't bite, you might actually begin to enjoy using it. The following list contains suggestions of some things you might want to do with your email program.

➤ **Create a mailing list.** You can create a special mailing list that contains the email addresses of many people. For instance, if you want to send a message to everyone in your department (or family, or club) at the same time, you can create a mailing list. Put all the addresses in the list and then send the message to the list. Everyone on the list receives the message and you save time and hassle. Some programs will have a mailing list dialogue box of some sort; others let you create a 'nickname' or 'alias' for the mailing list and then associate the addresses with it.

➤ **Create an address book.** Virtually all email systems have address books and they're usually quite easy to use. You can store a person's complicated email address and then retrieve it quickly using the person's real name.

➤ **Use aliases.** An alias, sometimes known as a nickname, is a simple identifier you give to someone in your address book. Instead of typing **peter kent** or **pkent@topfloor.com**, for instance, you could just type a simple alias like **pk** to address a message to that person.

➤ **Work with mail while you're off-line.** Most programs these days let you read and write email off-line. This is of particular importance with the online services, which are often expensive. Figure out how to use these systems – it's worth the effort.

➤ **Forward your mail.** After being on the Internet for a while, there's a risk of attaining real geekhood, and getting multiple Internet accounts, such as one with your favourite online service, one at work, one with a cheap service provider, and so on. (Right now, I have about eight, I think.) That's a lot of trouble logging on to check for email. However, some services let you forward your email to another account so that if a message arrives at, say, the account you use at home, you can have it automatically sent on to you at work. Very handy. Ask your service provider how to do this. While most Internet service providers let you do this, the online services generally *don't*.

➤ **Create a 'holiday' message.** When you go on holiday, your email doesn't stop. In fact, that's why so many cybergeeks never go on holiday or take a laptop if they do: they can't bear the thought of missing all those messages. Still, if you manage to break away, you may be able to set a special 'holiday' message, an automatic response to any incoming mail, that says basically, 'I'm away, be back soon'. (You get to write the response message.) Again, ask your service provider. And again, the online services generally *don't* have this service.

29

➤ **Filter your files.** Sophisticated email programs have file-filtering capabilities sometimes known as 'message rules'. You can tell the program to look at incoming mail and carry out certain actions according to what it finds. You can place email from your newsgroups into special inboxes, grab only the message subject if the message is very long, automatically delete messages from a particular sender, and so on.

Caution: Email Can Be Dangerous!

The more I use email, the more I believe that it can be a dangerous tool. There are three main problems: 1) people often don't realize the implications of what they are saying, 2) people often misinterpret what others are saying, and 3) people are comfortable typing things into a computer that they would never say to a person face-to-face. Consequently, online fights are common both in private (between email correspondents) and in public (in the newsgroups and mailing lists).

The real problem is that when you send an email message, the recipient can't see your face or hear your tone of voice. Of course, when you write a letter, you have the same problem. But email is actually replacing conversations as well as letters. The Post Office is as busy as ever, so I figure email is *mainly* replacing conversations. That contributes to the problem because people are writing messages in a chatty conversational style, forgetting that email lacks all the visual and auditory 'cues' that go along with a conversation.

In the interests of world peace, I give you these email guidelines to follow:

➤ **Don't write something you will regret later.** Lawsuits have been based on the contents of electronic messages, so consider what you are writing and whether you would want it to be read by someone other than the recipient. A message can always be forwarded, read over the recipient's shoulder, printed out and passed around, backed up onto the company's archives and so on. You don't *have* to use email – there's always the telephone.

➤ **Consider the tone of your message.** It's easy to try to be flippant and come out as arrogant, or to try to be funny and come out as sarcastic. When you write, think about how your words will appear to the recipient.

➤ **Give the sender the benefit of the doubt.** If a person's message sounds arrogant or sarcastic, consider that he or she might be trying to be flippant or funny! If you are not sure what the person is saying, ask him or her to explain.

➤ **Read before you send.** It will give you a chance to fix embarrassing spelling and grammatical errors – and to reconsider what you've just said.

➤ **Wait a day – or three.** If you typed something in anger, wait a few days and read the message again. Give yourself a chance to reconsider.

➤ **Be nice.** Hey, there's no need for vulgarity or rudeness (except in certain newsgroups, where it seems to be a requirement for entrance).

➤ **Attack the argument, not the person.** I've seen fights start when someone disagrees with another person's views and sends a message making a personal attack upon that person. (This point is more related to mailing lists and newsgroups than email proper, but we are on the subject of avoiding fights …) Instead of saying, 'anyone who thinks *EastEnders* is not worth the electrons it's transmitted on must be a halfwitted moron with all the common sense of the average pineapple', consider saying 'you may think it's not very good, but clearly many other people find great enjoyment in this show'.

You're Being Baited

Some people send rude or vicious messages because they actually *enjoy* getting into a fight like this – where they can fight from the safety of their computer terminals.

➤ **Use smileys.** One way to add some of those missing cues is to add smileys – keep reading.

Smile And Be Understood!

Over the last few years, email users have developed a number of ways to clarify the meaning of messages. You might see **<g>** at the end of the line, for example. This means 'grin' and is shorthand for saying, 'you know, of course, that what I just said was a joke, right?' You may also see **:–)** in the message. Turn this book sideways, so that the left hand side of this page is up and the right hand side is down and you'll see that this is a small smiley face. It means the same as **<g>**, 'of course, that was a joke, okay?'

Emoticons Galore

Little pictures are commonly known as 'smileys'. But the smiley face, though by far the most common, is just one of many available symbols. You might see some of the Emoticons in the following table and you may want to use them. Perhaps you can create a few of your own.

Share The Smiles

Many people simply call these character faces 'smiley faces'. But if you'd like to impress your friends with a bit of technobabble, you can call them *Emoticons*. And if you really want to impress your colleagues, use your web browser to visit http://www.emoticon.com, where you'll find more smileys than you can shake a stick at.

Commonly Used Emoticons

Emoticon	Meaning
:-(	Sadness, disappointment
8-)	Kinda goofy-looking smile, or wearing glasses
:-)	A smile
;-)	A wink
*<|:-)	Santa Claus
:-&	Tongue-tied
:-o	A look of shock
:-p	Tongue stuck out

Personally, I don't like smileys much. They strike me as being just a tiny bit too cutesy. However, I do use them now and again to make absolutely sure that I'm not misunderstood!

Message Shorthand

There are a couple of other ways people try to liven up their messages. One is to use obscure acronyms like the ones in this table.

The real benefit of using these is that they confuse the average neophyte. I suggest that you learn them quickly, so you can pass for a long-term cybergeek.

You'll also see different ways of stressing particular words. (You can't use bold and italic in Internet email, remember?) You might see words marked with an underscore on either side (_now!_) or with an asterisk (*now!*).

Online Shorthand

Acronym	Meaning
BTW	By the way
FWIW	For what it's worth
FYI	For your information
IMHO	In my humble opinion
IMO	In my opinion
LOL	Laughing out loud (used as an aside to show your disbelief)
OTF	On the floor, laughing (used as an aside)
PMFBI	Pardon me for butting in
PMFJI	Pardon me for jumping in
RTFM	Read the &*^%# manual
ROTFL or ROFL	Rolling on the floor laughing (used as an aside)
ROTFLMAO	Same as above, except with 'laughing my a** off' added on the end. (You didn't expect me to say it, did you? This is a family book and, anyway, the editors won't let me.)
TIA	Thanks in advance
YMMV	Your mileage may vary

The Least You Need To Know

➤ There are many different email systems, but the basic procedures all work similarly.

➤ Even if your online service lets you use fancy text (colours, different fonts, different styles) within the service, that text won't work in Internet messages.

➤ Sending files across the Internet is much easier now than it was a year or two ago. Sending files within the online services is always easy.

➤ Get to know all the neat little things your email program can do for you, such as create mailing lists and carry out file-filtering.

➤ Be careful with email; misunderstandings (and fights) are common.

Advanced Email: HTML And Encryption

Email has changed quite a bit over the past couple of years and will continue to change dramatically, thanks to two important systems: HTML Mail and encryption.

The first of these, HTML Mail, livens up email a little – in some cases, quite a lot. HTML Mail enables you to use different colours for the text in your messages, to work with different font sizes and styles, to create bulleted lists and centred text, and even to insert pictures and sounds.

Although encryption has been available for a few years, it was too complicated to catch on. Now email encryption – the ability to encrypt, or scramble, email messages to make them unreadable to all but the recipient – is being built into email programs, which makes it easier to use. I used to predict that everyone would be using encryption pretty soon, but I've given up on that prediction. Most people just don't seem to care. Still, the systems are available if you need them, so I'll explain what encryption can do for you and how to use it.

Banish Dull Email With HTML Mail

HTML Mail is a system in which HTML tags can be used within email messages. HTML means Hypertext Markup Language, and as you'll learn in the World Wide Web chapters of this book, HTML is used to create World Wide Web pages. HTML tags are the codes inserted into a Web page that tell a Web browser how to display the page. These tags can be used to modify the manner in which text appears on the page – its colour, size, style, and so on – and where the text appears on the page. They can be used to create tables, insert pictures and Java applications, and plenty more. Now that HTML is coming to email, email messages can be far more than just plain text.

To use HTML Mail, you need two things. First, you need an HTML Mail program. Second (but just as important), you need to ensure that the recipient has an HTML Mail program. If you send an HTML Mail message to someone who doesn't have an HTML Mail program, that person won't see all the formatting you've added to the message. Worse, depending on the program you've used, the message the person receives may be very difficult to read because it will be full of HTML tags. (Some HTML Mail programs insert a plain-text version of the message at the beginning of the message, so a recipient who isn't using an HTML Mail program can still read the message.)

Finding An HTML Mail Program

Most recent mail programs can work with HTML Mail in some form or another. If you're working with Netscape Messenger or Microsoft Outlook Express, the two most commonly-used programs on the Net, you have an HTML Mail-capable program. Most other major programs also work with HTML Mail – Eudora and Pegasus, for instance. You can see a couple of the HTML programs at work in the following figures.

Unfortunately, some of the online services' email systems use a different method. Some allow you to format your messages with colours, bolding, and so on, and even to insert images. But they're not using HTML Mail, so people receiving the messages in an HTML Mail program won't be able to view them properly. Similarly, if people with HTML Mail programs send formatted mail to those services, it won't be received in the correct format, either.

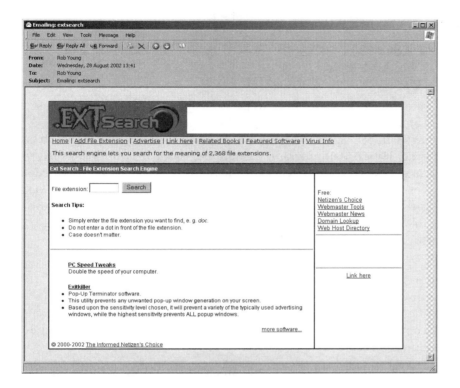

This is a Web page transmitted to Outlook Express. Because Outlook Express works well with HTML Mail, it can display the page inside the message.

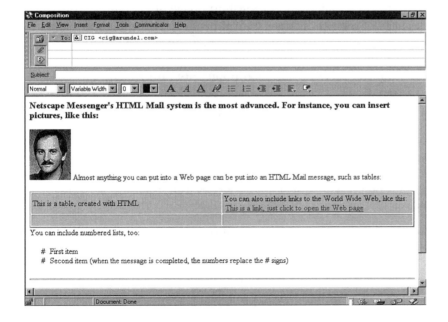

Netscape Messenger, the program that introduced HTML Mail to the world.

Different Programs, Different Abilities

Just because an email program supports HTML Mail doesn't mean that it supports it well or in the best way. Some programs can handle a few simple things, but not the more complicated processes involved with HTML Mail.

Suppose you insert an image into a message using Netscape Messenger. That image will be transferred along with the email message. If the recipient has Netscape Messenger, the image will be displayed within the message exactly where it should be. If the user has another HTML Mail program, though, the image may not be displayed in the message; it may be saved on the recipient's hard disk instead. Some HTML Mail programs won't even send the inserted image with the message. The early HTML Mail versions of Netscape's mail program (the program included with Netscape Navigator 3) inserted a link to the image instead of transferring the image itself. That caused problems, of course, because the image might be on the user's hard disk and unavailable to the recipient.

Some HTML Mail programs may be unable to display some forms of HTML Mail message, too. For instance, the program may be able to display simple HTML Mail messages from Outlook Express or Netscape Messenger, but not the more complicated messages sent by companies who specialize in delivering email versions of magazines and news publications by HTML Mail.

It's worth remembering, too, that taking full advantage of the HTML Mail possibilities isn't always a good thing, even if you and all your friends and colleagues use software that can cope with it. Just by adding a background image, for example, your email message becomes at least ten times larger than it needs to be, taking ten times as long to send and receive. While a sprinkling of text formatting can be effective for emphasis or style, bombarding your friends with messages containing pictures, animations and backgrounds could zero your popularity rating in no time!

Keep Away Prying Eyes With Encryption

The other major change coming to email is the capability to encrypt messages. In other words, messages can be scrambled so that they can't be read if intercepted. Before a scrambled message can be read it must be decrypted, that is, converted back to its original form. Then it will be legible. If all goes well, the only person who can decrypt the message is the intended recipient.

There was a great deal of interest in data encryption late in 1994 and early in 1995. Most of this interest centred around a program called PGP (Pretty Good Privacy). This program is able to encrypt a message so solidly that it's essentially unbreakable. It's almost certainly impossible to break a PGP-encrypted message using current computer technology, and even when technology improves a little, breaking such a message may remain prohibitively expensive. (As I'll explain, there are different levels of encryption; although it's possible to break messages encrypted using the lower levels, the most secure messages cannot be broken.) For instance, breaking into a message to your Aunt Edna explaining when you're going to arrive for Christmas dinner would probably cost the CIA more than engineering a coup in a mid-size Central American republic. Thus your mail will likely remain completely safe. (This, of course, upsets the US government, along with many other governments around the world.)

I know exactly when this intense interest in PGP occurred because I made a shameless attempt to cash in on the interest by writing a book about PGP. I also know exactly when this interest subsided – about three days before my book was published. Why the sudden decline in interest in a technology that could be so useful? Because it's so hard to use.

I wrote my book based on an application called WinPGP, a Windows program that insulates the user from many of the intricacies of using PGP. Still, even using a front end like WinPGP, PGP remained a little complicated, and I told anyone who would listen to me that 'encryption won't be popular until it's built into email programs and is as easy to use as clicking a button'. I'd like to say that everyone took my advice and immediately began work on email programs with built-in encryption, but actually few people listen to me (except my family, and I suspect they're just pretending). Nonetheless, such email programs have begun appearing on the scene, most notably Netscape Messenger, the email portion of Netscape Communicator, and Microsoft's Outlook Express. Encrypting email messages is still a little more complicated than clicking a button, but it's certainly much simpler than it all used to be.

Why Encrypt Your Email?

Email can get you in a lot of trouble. It got Oliver North in hot water, and people have lost their jobs or been sued over things they've said in email. Several things can go wrong when you use email:

➤ The recipient might pass the email on to someone else.

➤ The message can be backed up to a backup system and later read by someone other than the recipient.

➤ Someone could spy on you and read your email looking for incriminating comments.

➤ Your boss may decide to read your email, based on the idea that if it's written on company time and company equipment, it's company property (and the courts will almost certainly back him up).

The most likely scenario is that the recipient intentionally or thoughtlessly passes your message to someone who you didn't count on seeing it. Unfortunately, encryption can't help you with that problem. The second problem – that the message could be copied to a backup system – has got many, many people into trouble. Even if you delete a message and the recipient deletes the message, it may still exist somewhere on the network if the system administrator happened to do a backup before it was deleted. So if you are ever the subject of some kind of investigation, that message could be revived. This is more of a problem on the Internet because a message goes from your computer, to your service provider's computer, to the recipient's service provider's computer, to the recipient's computer – at least four places from which it could be copied. Finally, someone might be out to get you. Internet Email is basic text, and a knowledgeable hacker with access to your service provider's system (or the recipient's service provider's system) can grab your messages and read them.

What do you do, then? The simplest solution is to avoid putting things in email that you would be embarrassed to have others read. The more complicated solution is to encrypt your email.

Public-Key Encryption: It's Magic

Email encryption systems depend on something known as *public-key encryption*. I'd like to give you a full and detailed description of exactly how it works, but I don't know exactly how it works (I'm no mathematician, and encryption is done using the sort of maths that only a geek could love), so I'll give you the simple answer: it's magic. Perhaps that's insufficient; I'll endeavour to explain a little more without getting more complicated than necessary.

First, let me describe *private-key encryption*, which you may have already used. A computer file can be encrypted – turned into a jumble of garbage characters that makes it useless – using a program that works with a private key (also known as a secret key or even simply called a *password*). The *private key* is a sort of code word. Tell the program the name of the file you want to encrypt and the private key, and the program uses a mathematical algorithm to encrypt the file. How can you decrypt the file? You do the same thing: give the program the name of the encrypted file and the private key, and it uses the algorithm to reverse the process and decrypt the file. You may have used private-key encryption already, because many computer programs use it. For instance, if you use the Protect Document command in Word for Windows, you are using private-key encryption. The password that the program asks you for is, in effect, the private key.

Public-key encryption is where the process starts to get a little weird. Public-key encryption uses two keys: a private key and a public key. Through the wonders of mathematics, these keys work together. When you encrypt a file with one key (the public key, for example), the file can only be decrypted with the other key! You can't decrypt the file with the key you used to encrypt it; you must use the other key. Sounds a little odd, but that's how it works. (Okay, this is where my knowledge breaks down. Don't ask me how the mathematics work; as far as I'm concerned, it's magic!)

Public-Key Encryption And Your Email

How, then, does public-key encryption apply to email encryption? An email program with built-in encryption uses public-key encryption to encrypt your email message before it sends it. When you want to send an encrypted message to someone, you have to get hold of that person's public key. These keys are often posted – yes, publicly – on the Internet. There's no need to worry about who gets hold of the public key because it can't be used to decrypt an encrypted message. Using the recipient's public key, you encrypt a message and send it off. The recipient then uses his private key to decode the message.

Where do you find someone's public key? It used to be complicated; you might have to go to a key server, a Web or FTP site that stored thousands of public keys. Or you could ask the person to send you the key. A new system is greatly simplifying the task, though. Some email programs, such as Netscape Messenger, enable a user to include a digital 'certificate', containing his public key, in what's known as a *Vcard*, a special block of information that can be tacked onto the end of an email message. The user can set up Messenger so that every time it sends a message it includes the Vcard, which includes the public key. The email program receiving the message can then extract the public key and place it into a directory of public keys (assuming, of course, that the email program can work with Vcards, and currently most can't). Netscape Communicator's Messenger email program will automatically extract certificates from incoming email. With another program, you may have to choose to save the certificate.

Outlook Express, the new program in Windows 98/Me/2000/XP and some versions of Windows 95 and NT, handles certificates a little differently. It doesn't use a Vcard, but it does attach the certificate containing the public key to a message. If you receive an email message containing a digital certificate, you can add the certificate to your address book by selecting **File**, **Properties**, clicking the **Security** tab, and clicking the **Add Digital ID to Address Book** button.

So, here's how it works:

1. Someone sends you an email message. She's using a Vcard-enabled program and has a public key in the Vcard.

2. When your email program receives the message, it extracts the sender's public key and saves it.

3. Later, you decide that you want to send a private message back, one that's so sensitive it must be encrypted. So you write the message, and then click the **Encrypted** check box. (Netscape Messenger has an Encrypted check box; other programs may have a button or menu command.)

4. You click the **Send** button, and the mail program sees that you want to encrypt the file. The program looks through its list of public keys, searching for one that is related to the recipient's email address. When it finds the public key, it uses the key to scramble the message, then it sends the message across the Internet.

5. The recipient's email program receives the message and sees that it has been encrypted. It takes a closer look and sees that it has been encrypted with the recipient's own public key, so it uses her private key to decrypt the message. The recipient can now read the message.

What happens if someone other than the intended recipient receives the message? The recipient won't be able to decrypt the message because he won't have the correct private key. Well, you assume he won't, but that's a weakness of the system. If the private key is stolen, the security is compromised. Where the system breaks down completely is that just because the message is encrypted doesn't mean the recipient won't decrypt it and then share it with someone else.

Digital Signatures

You can encrypt messages with either the public or private key. Encrypt with one key, and only the matching key can decrypt it. Of course, it wouldn't be a good idea to secure a message by encrypting it with your private key. Remember, a message encrypted with your private key can be decrypted with your public key, and the public key is, well, public. However, if the message can be decrypted with your public key, it means that it must have been encrypted with the corresponding private key, your private key. If you assume that only you have access to the private key, you've just signed the message. In other words, you can sign messages by encrypting them with your private key. As long as your private key remains secure, then the recipient can be sure that the message came from you.

Just to clarify all this, remember these key points:

➤ To send an encrypted message to someone, use that person's public key.

➤ To send a signed message to someone, use your private key.

➤ To send an encrypted message to someone and sign it, use your private key and the recipient's public key.

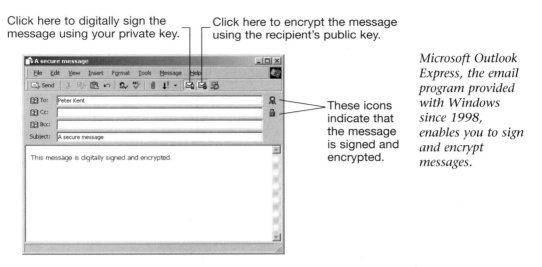

Click here to digitally sign the message using your private key.

Click here to encrypt the message using the recipient's public key.

These icons indicate that the message is signed and encrypted.

Microsoft Outlook Express, the email program provided with Windows since 1998, enables you to sign and encrypt messages.

You don't have to remember all this – an email program will handle it for you. In Netscape Messenger, for instance, if you want to sign a message, click the **Signed** check box. The program will automatically encrypt your message using your private key.

I'm Sold; Where Do I Get My Keys?

Keep in mind that there are two types of email encryption in use. Some email programs use PGP encryption. To work with this type of encryption, you have to download PGP and create your public and private key pairs. Working with PGP can be complicated, though; if you want more information, search for PGP at one of the Web search sites (see Chapter 16, 'Finding Stuff On The Internet'), or go to **http://www.nai.com**.

Probably the most common system, the system that will win the encryption war, is the one being used by Netscape Communicator in the Netscape Navigator and Netscape Messenger programs and, recently, by Microsoft in Outlook Express. This system doesn't use PGP. Rather, you must get hold of a *personal certificate*, a special digital certificate that contains your private and public keys.

Where do you get your certificate? From a *key server,* a site with the necessary software to issue certificates. There are both public- and private-key servers. You can get a certificate from a variety of places, the two most commonly used being VeriSign (**http://www.verisign.com**) and Thawte (**http://www.thawte.com**). (I'd recommend Thawte; they give certificates away, while VeriSign charges an annual fee.) Install the email program you've chosen, and then go to one of these sites and follow the instructions for creating and installing the personal certificate (called a Digital ID by VeriSign) in the program.

Of course, to use this system you'll need a mail program that supports it. Here are a few:

➤ Netscape Messenger (**http://www.netscape.com**)

➤ Microsoft Outlook and Outlook Express (**http://www.microsoft.com**)

➤ Email Connection (**http://email-connection.com**)

➤ Tumbleweed Secure Messenger (**http://www.tumbleweed.com**)

➤ TrustedMIME (**http://www.guardeonic.com**)

Different Size Keys

The size of the keys determines the security of the encryption system. For instance, the Netscape Messenger security software used to come in two versions: a 40-bit version and a 128-bit version. The same applied to Microsoft's security software. These numbers refer to the length of the key (the code) that is used to encrypt the data. The longer the key, the more secure the transmission.

How Much Stronger Is 128-Bit Encryption?

Much, much stronger. For instance, Pretty Good Privacy, Inc. says that the 128-bit PGP software creates messages that are 309,485,009,821,341,068,724,781,056 times more difficult to break than 40-bit messages. They also quote a US government study that found it would take '12 million times the age of the universe, on average, to break a single 128-bit message encrypted with PGP'.

The 128-bit software is built into the Netscape and Microsoft programs available to customers in the United States; until recently, customers outside the US got the 40-bit versions. So why were there two different versions at all? The reason is ITAR, the US government's International Traffic in Arms Regulations. Encryption software using keys more than 40 bits long was, as far as ITAR was concerned, on a par with armaments and could not be exported. Ridiculous, but true. So ridiculous, in fact, that people found all kinds of ingenious ways to make strong encryption software available in other countries without actually 'exporting' it, and the rules had to be relaxed. Nowadays, although 40-bit software is strong enough for all but the most critical uses, 128-bit encryption is far more commonplace.

Sending Voice Messages

It's possible – although perhaps not desirable – to send voice messages in your email messages. Quite frankly, this is a technology that is barely used right now. I've never received a voice message inside an email message. And there are problems – if you're communicating with people who are using slow modem connections, they may not want to receive voice messages because of the size.

Still, if you want to play with voice, try a program such as Eudora (**http://www.eudora.com**) which has a built-in voice attachment system, or Voice E-Mail from Bonzi (**http://www.bonzi.com**).

Another, perhaps minor, problem with voice-annotated email; the recipient must have some kind of player. In the case of Bonzi's Voice E-mail, for instance, you can send the recipient a player, so that even if he doesn't have the same program he can still hear your message. But such players are sometimes a nuisance. In the case of Eudora, for example, the Windows version of the player is 1.32 MB.

Finally... are you sure the recipient's computer is properly configured to play sounds? Thanks to the vagaries of Windows a large number of machines that, in theory, should be able to play sounds, in fact, can't. And many older machines simply aren't properly equipped with a sound card and speakers.

The Least You Need To Know

➤ HTML Mail enables you to create email messages with colours, special fonts, pictures, tables, and more.

➤ Both the sender and recipient must have HTML Mail-compatible programs, or the system won't work. For the moment at least, the online services don't work with HTML Mail.

➤ Email encryption uses a system called public-key encryption; you'll need to get a personal certificate and install it in a compatible email program.

➤ Email programs that allow encryption also allow you to digitally sign messages, proving that they've come from you.

➤ Encryption is not legal everywhere. Some versions of the email software can only be sold in the United States.

➤ The longer the key, the safer the encryption, but even 40-bit keys are safe enough for day-to-day use.

Working On The World Wide Web

The World Wide Web is also known as *The Web, WWW*, and sometimes (among really geeky company) *W3*. And, in really confused company, it's called *the Internet*. I'd better clear up that little confusion about the Web and the Internet right away.

The World Wide Web is not the Internet. It's simply one software system running on the Internet. Still, it's one of the most interesting and exciting systems, so it has received a lot of press, to the extent that many people believe that the terms Web and Internet are synonymous. However, the Web seems to be taking over roles previously carried out by other Internet services and at the same time, Web programs – *browsers* – are including utilities to help people work with non-Web services. For instance, you can send and receive email with some Web browsers, and you can read Internet newsgroups with some.

What's The Web?

Imagine that you are reading this page in electronic form, on your computer screen. Then imagine that some of the words are underlined and coloured. Use your mouse to point at one of these underlined words on your screen and press the mouse button. What happens? Another document opens, a document that's related in some way to the word you clicked.

That's a simple explanation of *hypertext*. If you've ever used Apple's Hypercard or a Windows Help file, you've used hypertext. Documents are linked to each other in some way, generally by clickable words and pictures. Hypertext has been around for years, but until recently most hypertext systems were limited in both size and geographic space. Click a link and you might see another document held by the same electronic file. Or maybe you'll see a document in another file, but that's on the same computer's hard disk, probably the same directory.

The World Wide Web is like a hypertext system without boundaries. Click a link and you might be shown a document in the next city, on the other side of the country, or even on another continent. Links from one document to another can be created without the permission of the owner of that second document. And nobody has complete control over those links. When you put a link in your document that connects to someone else's, you are sending your readers on a journey that you really can't predict. They will land at that other document, from which they can take another link somewhere else – another country, another subject, or another culture – from which they can follow yet another link … and on and on.

The Web has no capacity limit, either. Web pages are being added every minute of the day, all over the world. In fact, the Web is really pushing the growth of the Internet. It's so easy to create and post a Web page that thousands of people are doing it and more are joining them each day.

If you haven't seen the Web, this may all sound a little mundane. Okay, so one document leads to another that leads to another … I try to avoid the Internet hype we've been inundated with over the last couple of years, but the Web really is a publishing revolution. It has made publishing to an international audience quick and simple. I don't mean to imply (as some Internet proponents seem to) that every Web page is a jewel that is widely read and appreciated (much of it is closer to a sow's ear than to silk). But it's a medium with which people can make their words available so that they *can* be widely read if they have some value.

Let's Start

If you want to listen to a CD, you need a CD player. If you want to watch a video, you need a video player. And if you want to view a Web page, you need a Web player: a *Web browser*.

There are actually two parts to the Web equation. First, there's a Web server, a special program running on a host computer (that is, a computer connected directly to the Internet). This server administers a Web site, which is a collection of World Wide Web documents. The second part is the *browser*, a program on your PC that asks the server for the documents and then displays the documents so that you can read them.

There are two major contenders in the Web browser war (yes, there's a war going on, or at least there has been until recently). One is Netscape Navigator. Right now, somewhere around 12% of all Web users are working with Netscape, although in the past Netscape owned 80% or more of the market. Netscape Navigator is now part of the Netscape Communicator suite of programs, available in versions for all Windows editions, the Macintosh and various flavours of UNIX.

Servers And Clients

Techno Talk

If you hang around on the Internet long enough, you'll hear the terms 'server' and 'client' used over and over. A *server* is a program that provides information that a *client* program can use in some way.

Netscape Navigator, part of the Netscape Communicator suite of programs.

In an attempt to revive their flagging market share, Netscape released a new browser in late 2000, simply named Netscape 6. Like Communicator, Netscape 6 includes extra tools such as an email client, this time wrapped up into a more compact package.

Netscape Navigator

This browser is manufactured by Netscape Communications. You might think it would be known as Navigator for short, but for 'historical' reasons it's always been called Netscape. When Netscape Navigator version 4 was released, a suite of programs named Communicator arrived with it: to this day, you can choose either the browser by itself or the entire suite. Netscape 6 arrived as an all-new browser intended to challenge Microsoft's dominant position with Internet Explorer, but its many bugs and lukewarm reception suggest that it's 'too little, too late'.

The other popular browser is Internet Explorer from Microsoft (shown in the following figure), claiming close to 90% of the browser market. Versions of Internet Explorer are available for all editions of Windows, along with Mac, UNIX and other operating systems. From Windows 98 onwards, a copy of Internet Explorer was built into the operating system, so the majority of Windows users already have a copy of Internet Explorer installed.

Microsoft Internet Explorer, the winner of the 'browser war'.

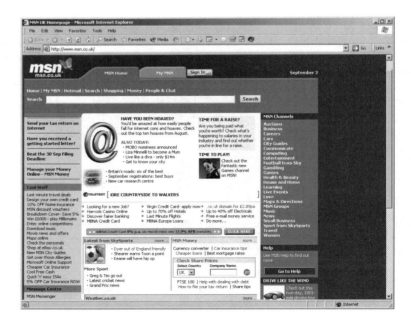

Getting A Browser

Which browser should you use? If your service provider has given you one, I suggest you start with that. You'll probably be given either Netscape or Explorer – most likely Internet Explorer these days because CompuServe, AOL, and (of course!) Microsoft Network provide that browser to their members. If you use Windows 98 or later, you already have Internet Explorer, so don't try to install it again. But if you want to give Netscape a go, you can still do so.

If you have to pick a browser, try Internet Explorer first then try Netscape later and see if you like it. Although there's not a lot of difference between them, Internet Explorer is faster and less likely to crash than Netscape. It seems to be a fact of life that Internet browsers have to have some irritating bugs (sloppy programming that results in odd behaviour when you use the program in certain ways): each new Internet Explorer version fixes old bugs but always adds new ones; Netscape updates seem to routinely ignore old bugs but won't necessarily make anything worse than it was. You might also try Opera, a small, smart (and above all, *reliable*) browser from a small Norwegian company. Turn to Appendix C to find out where to download these browsers and see what others are available.

For now, I'm going to assume that you have a Web browser installed, and that you have opened it and are ready to start. One nice thing about Web browsers is that they all work similarly – and they look very similar, too. So whatever browser you use, you should be able to follow along with this chapter.

Browsing Begins At Home

When you open your browser, whatever page you see is, by definition, your *home page*. (I like that kind of definition; it's easy to understand.) Ideally, the home page is a page that has lots of useful links, which take you to places on the Web that you will want to go to frequently. You can create your own home page by using something called HTML, the Web document language (see Chapter 8, 'Setting Up Your Own Web Site') or even using one of the fancy new customizing systems you'll find on the Web. Both Netscape and Microsoft have systems that automatically create customized pages for you, if you have their browsers. Go to **http://www.netscape.com/ custom/index.html** for the Netscape system or **http://www.msn.co.uk/ personalizing/content/** for the Microsoft system (Internet Explorer 4 and 5 have an Internet Start button you can click to get to this page). I'll explain how to use these 'addresses' later in this chapter, in the section 'A Direct Link: Using The URLs'.

Home Page, Start Page

Microsoft's programmers can't seem to decide whether to use the term *home page* or *start page*. The term home page originally meant the page that appeared when you opened your browser or when you used the Home button. Then all of a sudden, everybody was using the term to mean a person or company's main Web page (the page you see when you go to that Web site) such as NEC's home page, Netscape's home page, and so on. So Microsoft's programmers evidently thought it made more sense to rename the home page to 'start page'. Unfortunately, they're using *both* terms, so Internet Explorer 3, 4 and 5 have a Home button on the toolbar; Explorer 3 has a Go, Start Page menu option; some versions of Explorer 4 have a Go, Home Page menu option and a Home button, but mention start page in the options dialog box. More recent versions of Explorer have completely replaced the term start page with home page.

Moving Around On The Web

Whatever browser you are using, you'll almost certainly find links on the home page. Links are the coloured and underlined words. You may also find pictures that contain links, perhaps several different links on a picture (a different link on each part of the picture). Use your mouse to point at a piece of text or a picture; if the mouse pointer changes shape – probably into a pointing hand – you are pointing at a link. (Just to confuse the issue, some pictures contain links even though the pointer doesn't change shape.)

Click whatever link looks interesting. If you are online (I'm assuming you are!), your browser sends a message to a Web server somewhere, asking for a page. If the Web server is running (it may not be) and if it's not too busy (it may be), it transmits the document back to your browser, and your browser displays it on your screen.

You've just learned the primary form of Web 'navigation'. When you see a link you want to follow, you click it. Simple, eh? But what about going somewhere useful, somewhere interesting? Most browsers these days either have toolbar buttons that take you to a useful Web page or come with a default home page with useful links. For example, in Netscape Navigator 4, you can click the Guide button to open the Guide page, or click the Guide button and hold it down to display a number of options that lead you to pages that help you find your way around the Internet. In Navigator 4.5, though, they removed the Guide button. Instead, at the NetCenter page (the page that appears each time you open the browser or click the Home button) they provide a page full of options that can help you find maps, businesses, people, and Web pages.

How Does The Browser Know Where To Go?

How does your browser know which server to request the document from? What you see on your computer screen is not quite the same document that your browser sees. Open the source document (which you can probably do using the **View**, **Page Source** menu option), and you'll see what the Web document *really* looks like. (You'll learn more about these source documents in Chapter 8.) The source document is just basic ASCII text that contains all sorts of instructions. One of the instructions says, in effect, 'if this guy clicks this link, here's which document I want you to get'. You don't normally see all these funky commands because the browser *renders* the page, removing the instructions and displaying only the relevant text.

Internet Explorer 3 has a special QuickLinks toolbar (click **QuickLinks** in the Address toolbar to open the QuickLinks toolbar). In Explorer 4, 5 and 6, this toolbar is simply named the Links bar and can be opened or closed by selecting **View, Toolbars, Links**. On this toolbar, you'll find a variety of buttons designed to take you to useful starting points. (The button names vary between versions.)

Whatever browser you are using, take a little time to explore. Go as far as you want. Then come back here, and I'll explain how to find your way back to where you came from.

Link Colours

Some links change colour after you click them. You won't see it right away, but if you return to the same page later, you'll find that the link is a different colour. The colour change indicates that the particular link points to a document that you've already seen. The 'used-link' colour does expire after a while, and the link changes back to its original colour. How long it takes for this to happen is something that you can generally control with an option in your browser's Preferences or Options area.

The Hansel And Gretel Dilemma: Where Are You?

Hypertext is a fantastic tool, but it has one huge drawback: it's easy to get lost. If you are reading a book and you flip forward a few pages, you know how to get back. You flip back, right? But with hypertext, after a few moves through the electronic library, you can become horribly lost. How do you get back to where you came from? And where did you come from, anyway?

Over the years, a number of systems have been developed to help people find their way around this rather strange freeform medium. This table explains some tools you can use in most Web browsers to move through the pages and sites you've seen.

Web Page Navigation Tools

Button	Description
Back	Click the **Back** button or choose **Back** from a menu (probably the **Go** menu) to return to the previous Web page.
Forward	Click the **Forward** button or choose the **Forward** menu option to return to a page you've just come back from.
Home	Click the **Home** button (or the **Start** button on some versions of Internet Explorer) to go all the way back to your home page or start page.
Bookmarks or Favorites	You can set bookmarks on pages you think you'll want to come back to (they're known as Favorites in Internet Explorer); bookmarks can be very helpful because you don't have to struggle to find your way back to the page the next time.
History	This is a list of pages you've seen previously. The **Back** and **Forward** commands take you back and forward through this list. You can also go directly to a page in the history list by selecting it from the **Go** menu. (In Explorer 2, you select from the **File** menu. In Explorer 4, 5 and 6, click the small triangle on the **Back** button.)

Bookmarks

The bookmark system (known as Favorites in Internet Explorer) is an essential tool for finding your way around. Get to know it right away.

In most browsers, you can just click a button or select a menu option to place a bookmark. Each system works a little differently, of course. In Netscape, choose **Bookmarks**, **Add Bookmark** (Navigator 3), or click the **Bookmarks** button and choose **Add Bookmark** (Navigator 4) or **Add Current Page** (Netscape 6). The bookmark is added to the bottom of the Bookmark menu (you can move it to a folder or submenu later). In Navigator 4, you can even select which folder you want to put the bookmark in by clicking the **Bookmarks** button and then choosing **File Bookmark**.

In Internet Explorer, choose **Favorites**, **Add to Favorites**, and then click the **Create In** button and select the folder into which you want to place the bookmark.

Both systems have Bookmarks windows and an associated Bookmarks menu. (In Explorer, they're called the Favorites window and menu.) Creating a folder in the window automatically creates a submenu in the menu.

To open Netscape's Bookmarks window choose **Bookmarks**, **Go to Bookmarks** (Navigator 3) or **Bookmarks**, **Edit Bookmarks** (Navigator 4) or **Bookmarks**, **Manage Bookmarks** (Netscape 6). In the latest version of Explorer, you can click the **Favorites** button in the toolbar to open a Favorites panel in the browser window.

You can even search Bookmarks or Favorites. For instance, you can search Internet Explorer's Favorites using the Windows 95 or 98 **Find** tool on the **Start** menu. In Explorer 4, 5 and 6, right-click a folder in the Favorites list and choose **Find** to search the folder.

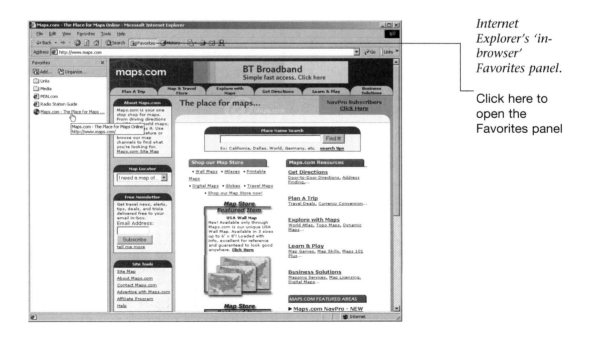

Internet Explorer's 'in-browser' Favorites panel.

Click here to open the Favorites panel

A Little History

The history list varies tremendously. Netscape 3's history list is not very helpful. It lists some, but not all, of the pages you've visited in the current session. Other browsers, including Netscape Navigator 4, show much more, often listing pages from previous sessions. Explorer, for instance, keeps a record of up to 3000 pages (including all the pages from the current session and earlier sessions). You can view the list in a window (see the following figure) sorted by date or by name. Double-click an entry in the history list to open that Web page.

In Or Out?

In Internet Explorer 2, the History window is separate from the browser window; in version 3 and later, the history list is shown within the browser window. Click on Internet Explorer 4, 5 or 6's **Favorites** button, and a panel opens on the left side of the browser window to display the Favorites list. But select **Favorites**, **Organize Favorites** to open a separate Favorites window.

Whatever system you have, though, using the history list is simple. In Netscape Navigator, you can select an entry from the **Go** menu. To keep us on our toes, Microsoft's programmers keep moving the history list. In Internet Explorer 2, you'll find the history entries on the **File** menu; in Explorer 3 and some versions of 4, the history list is on the **Go** menu. Versions 5, 6, and some later editions of version 4, don't have a Go menu; instead, click the little black triangle on the right side of the Back button and a menu drops down showing the pages you've seen most recently.

You can also open the history window to see more history entries, perhaps thousands. In versions 4, 5 and 6 of Internet Explorer, click the **History** button on the toolbar; in version 3 choose **Go**, **Open History Folder**. In Netscape, choose **Window**, **History** (or **Communicator**, **Tools**, **History** if you have the Communicator suite). In Netscape 6, it's **Tasks**, **Tools**, **History**.

A Direct Link: Using The URLs

Earlier in this chapter I mentioned a couple of *URLs*. URLs are Web addresses, such as **http://www.msn.com/** or **http://www.netscape.com/**. These addresses provide a direct link to a particular Web page. Instead of clicking links to try to find your way to a page, you can tell your browser the URL and say 'go get this page'.

Most browsers have a bar near the top in which you can type the URL of the page you want to go to. The bar's almost certainly already displayed; it's a long text box. If it's not there, someone must have removed it; in Netscape, use the **View**, **Show**, **Location Toolbar** (in Navigator 4) or **View**, **Toolbars**, **Navigation Toolbar** (in Netscape 6) menu command to display the bar; in Internet Explorer, choose **View**, **Toolbar**, or **View**, **Toolbars**, **Address Bar**.

Title	Location	First Visited	Last Visited	Expiration	Visit C...	
	http://www.netscape.co...	1 hours ago	1 hours ago	6/14/1997 1...	2	
PowerStart Setup Instructions	http://www.netscape.co...	1 hours ago	1 hours ago	6/14/1997 1...	1	
Netscape PowerStart Setup	http://www.netscape.co...	1 hours ago	1 hours ago	6/14/1997 1...	1	
Macmillan Publishing USA	http://www.mcp.com/	1 hours ago	1 hours ago	6/14/1997 1...	2	
Featured Book	http://www.mcp.com/ge...	1 hours ago	1 hours ago	6/14/1997 1...	1	
Welcome to Netscape	http://home.netscape.co...	20 hours ago	1 hours ago	6/14/1997 1...	3	
About SCISM	http://www.scism.sbu.ac...	4 hours ago	3 hours ago	6/14/1997 8...	2	
Courses at SCISM	http://www.scism.sbu.ac...	4 hours ago	3 hours ago	6/14/1997 8...	3	
Short Courses Programme	http://www.scism.sbu.ac...	4 hours ago	3 hours ago	6/14/1997 8...	1	
BIT Home Page	http://www.scism.sbu.ac...	4 hours ago	4 hours ago	6/14/1997 8...	1	
Name search request sent!	http://www.idot.aol.com...	14 hours ago	14 hours ago	6/13/1997 1...	1	
Namesearch Form	http://www.idot.aol.com...	14 hours ago	14 hours ago	6/13/1997 1...	2	
More information needed!	http://www.idot.aol.com...	14 hours ago	14 hours ago	6/13/1997 1...	1	
NameSearch Menu	http://www.idot.aol.com...	14 hours ago	14 hours ago	6/13/1997 1...	1	
	http://www.rage.com/	16 hours ago	16 hours ago	6/13/1997 8...	1	
POP3 Mail Beta	http://mail.csi.com/mail/...	20 hours ago	20 hours ago	6/13/1997 4...	1	
License Agreement for POP3	http://mail.csi.com/mail/	20 hours ago	20 hours ago	6/13/1997 4...	2	
Directory of /deskapps	ftp://ftp.microsoft.com/d...	22 hours ago	22 hours ago	6/13/1997 1...	1	
Company Information	http://world.compuserve...	23 hours ago	22 hours ago	6/13/1997 1...	22	
Company Information	http://world.compuserve...	22 hours ago	22 hours ago	6/13/1997 1...	1	
Welcome to CompuServe	http://world.compuserve...	23 hours ago	23 hours ago	6/13/1997 1...	1	

With Netscape Navigator 4's history list, you can go back days or even weeks in your Web travels. The list even indicates how long it's been since you visited the page and how often you've been there.

If you don't want the bar there all the time (after all, it takes up room that is sometimes better given to the Web pages), you can leave it turned off. If you keep it turned off, you can generally use a shortcut key to display a dialog box in which you can type a URL. In Netscape, press **Ctrl+O** to open the box (or try **Ctrl+L** if that doesn't work; the shortcut key varies between versions); in Internet Explorer, choose **File**, **Open** or press **Ctrl+O**. In either case, you type the URL in the box that appears. If you prefer to use the Address or Location box at the top of the browser window, click in the box, type the address, and press **Enter**.

> *Check This Out...*
>
> ## New History List Trick
>
> Starting with version 4, the Internet Explorer and Netscape Navigator browsers have a handy new feature that enables you to see the history list from the **Back** and **Forward** buttons. In Navigator, click the button and hold down the mouse button; in Explorer, right-click the button, or click the little downward pointing arrow on the button. In both cases, you'll see a list of pages that you've visited.

Techno Talk

URL

This acronym stands for Uniform Resource Locator, which is a fancy name for Web address.

Maximizing The Web Page

Browsers have so many controls and tools that sometimes there's not enough room for the Web page. Internet Explorer 4 and later have a 'new' feature. Click the **Fullscreen** button (or press F11) to remove almost all the controls (except a small toolbar at the top of the window), giving the Web page the maximum room. You can even remove the small toolbar using an Autohide feature similar to that used by the Windows taskbar (right-click the toolbar and select **Autohide**). Actually this feature isn't new; it's from the ancient history of the graphical Web browser (way back in 1994). It used to be called a Kiosk feature, but it disappeared for a while.

The URL Explained

A URL consists of certain distinct parts. For example, here's a long URL:

http://www.poorrichard.com/newsltr/instruct/subsplain.htm

Each part of this URL has a specific meaning:

http://	This part tells the browser that the address is for a Web page. The http:// stands for *Hypertext Transfer Protocol*, the system used on the Internet to transfer Web pages. In addition to http://, you might see similar prefixes for an FTP site or a Gopher menu (see the following table).
www.poorrichard.com	This part is the hostname, the name of the computer holding the Web server that is administering the Web site you want to visit.
/newsltr/instruct/	This part is the directory in which the Web server has to look to find the file you want. In many cases, multiple directories will be listed, so the Web server looks down the directory tree in subdirectories. In this example, the Web server has to look in the instruct directory, which is a subdirectory of the newsltr directory.
subsplain.htm	This part is the name of the file you want, the Web page. These files are generally .HTM or .HTML files (that extension stands for Hypertext Markup Language, the 'coding' used to create Web pages). Sometimes the URL has no filename at the end; in that case, the Web server generally sends a default document for the specified directory.

The URL is not complicated; it's just an address so your browser knows where to look for a file. The different types of URLs are identified by a different *protocol* portion of the address. The Web page URLs all begin with http://. This table lists some other protocols you'll see on the Internet.

Other Internet Protocols

Protocol Prefix	Description
ftp://	The address of an FTP file library; you'll learn more about FTP in Chapter 11, 'Downloading files with FTP'.
gopher://	The address of a Gopher site, the forerunner to the World Wide Web.
news:	The address of a newsgroup, discussed in Chapter 9, 'Newsgroups: The Source Of 'All Wisdom'. Note that this prefix doesn't have the // after the name; neither does mailto: (below).
mailto:	When you use this prefix, the browser's email program opens so you can send mail. Web authors often create links using the mailto: URL so that when someone clicks the link, he can quickly send a message to the author.
telnet://	The address of a Telnet site.
tn3270://	The address of a tn3270 site. This protocol is similar to Telnet.
wais://	The address of a WAIS site; WAIS is a little-used database-search tool, and you probably won't run into many WAIS links. In any case, most browsers don't recognize the wais:// protocol.

Forget http://

In most browsers these days (including Netscape and Internet Explorer), you don't need to type the full URL. You can omit the http:// piece, and the browser will assume that the http:// piece should be added. If you type something beginning with gopher (as in gopher.usa.net, for instance) or ftp (as in ftp.microsoft.com), you can omit the gopher:// or ftp:// part, too. Also, in some browsers, you can even drop the www. and .com bits. For instance, in Internet Explorer, you can type **mcp** and press **Ctrl+Enter** to get to the http://www.mcp.com/ Web site (this only works if the domain ends with .com). The newest browsers, Explorer 5 and 6, and Netscape 6, have an auto-fill-in feature, something you may have seen in personal finance programs. Start typing a URL, and if the browser recognizes that you've entered it before, it will fill in the rest for you.

What Will You Find On Your Web Journey?

When you travel around the Web, you'll find a lot of text documents and much, much more. As a system administrator at a Free-Net once said to me, 'The Web is for people who can't read!'. It was a slight exaggeration, perhaps, but his point was that, on the Web, the nontext stuff is often more important than the words.

While travelling around the Web, you'll find these sorts of things:

➤ **Pictures.** You'll find pictures both inside the text documents and on their own. Sometimes when you click a link (at a museum site, for example), a picture – not a document – is transferred to your browser.

➤ **Forms.** These days, most browsers are forms-compatible (Navigator and Explorer have always been forms-compatible). In other words, you can use forms to interact with the Web site to send information about yourself (to subscribe to a service, for instance), to search for information, or to play a game, for example.

➤ **Sounds.** Most browsers can play sounds, such as voices and music. Many Web sites contain sounds. For instance, IUMA (the Internet Underground Music Archive at **http://www.iuma.com**/) has song clips from many new bands.

➤ **Files.** Many Web sites have files you can download, such as shareware, demos of new programs, and documents of many kinds. When you click a link, your browser begins the file transfer (see Chapter 5, 'More Web Basics – Searching Saving And More').

➤ **Multimedia of other kinds.** All sorts of strange things are on the Web: 3D images, animations, Adobe Acrobat .PDF hypertext files, videos, slide shows, 2D and 3D chemical images, and plenty more. Click a link, and the file starts transferring. If you have the right software installed, it automatically displays or plays the file. For instance, in the following figure, you can see an iPix image. (See **http://www.ipix.com/** for information about iPix, and Chapter 6, 'Forms, Applets, And Other Web Weirdness' and Chapter 7, 'Web Multimedia' to learn more about multimedia.)

Where Do I Find What I Want On The Web?

You can follow any interesting links you find, as discussed earlier in this chapter. You can also search for particular subjects and Web pages by using a Web search site, as discussed in Chapter 16, 'Finding Stuff On The Internet'.

An iPix image in Internet Explorer. You can move around the room, viewing up, down, and all around.

© 2002, Southern Living, Inc. Reprinted with permission.

Speeding Up Your Journey By Limiting Graphics

The Web used to be a very fast place to move around. The first Web browsers could display nothing but text, and text transfers across the Internet very quickly. These days, though, thanks to something commonly known as 'progress', things move more slowly. The things I just mentioned – pictures, video, sounds, and so on – slow down the process. Although video is the slowest thing on the Web (moving at an almost glacial pace in most cases), pictures are more of a nuisance; very few sites use video, but most use static pictures.

Most browsers provide a way for you to turn off the display of pictures. In Netscape Navigator 4, choose **Edit**, **Preferences**, and then click the **Advanced** category and clear **Automatically Load Images**. In Netscape 6, go to **Edit**, **Preferences**, choose the **Advanced** category and check **Do not load any images**. In Internet Explorer you can turn off images in the Options dialog, and you can turn off sounds and video, too. Choose **Tools, Internet Options** and click the **Advanced** tab, and then clear the **Show Pictures** check box in the list below **Multimedia**. Because the images are no longer transmitted to your browser, you see the pages much more quickly.

Of course, you often need or want to see those images. Many images have links built into them, and although some Web pages have both graphic links and corresponding text links (for people using a browser that can't display pictures), other Web pages are unusable unless you can see the pictures. However, you can usually grab the picture you need quickly. Where there *should* be a picture, you'll see a little icon that functions as a placeholder.

In Netscape, you can right-click the placeholder and choose **Load Image** (**Show Image** in some versions) from the shortcut menu that appears. Or you can click the **Images** button in the toolbar to see all of them. To view an image when you have images turned off in Internet Explorer, right-click the placeholder and choose **Show Picture** from the shortcut menu. In Netscape 6, unfortunately, you have to revisit the **Edit**, **Preferences** dialog to turn image display back on. A promising-looking **View**, **Show Images** menu item does nothing, while right-clicking the placeholder and choosing **View Image** tries and fails to display the image in a separate window.

There's Plenty More!

There's a lot more to say about the Web than I've said in this chapter. In fact, one could write a book about it (I already have: *Using Netscape Communicator 4*). In the next few chapters, you'll learn a few advanced Web travel tips and all about Web multimedia.

The Least You Need To Know

➤ The World Wide Web is a giant hypertext system running on the Internet.

➤ The two best browsers available are Netscape Navigator and MS Internet Explorer.

➤ The home page (sometimes called the start page in Internet Explorer) is the page that appears when you open your browser.

➤ Click a link in a document to see another document. To find your way back, use the **Back** or **Home** button.

➤ The history list shows where you've been. In Netscape Navigator 3, it includes just some of the pages you've seen in the current session; in some other browsers, including Netscape Navigator 4 and Internet Explorer, the history list includes all the pages from the current session and many pages from previous sessions.

➤ A URL is a Web address. You can use the URL to go directly to a particular Web page.

Chapter 5

More Web Basics – Searching, Saving And More

In This Chapter

➤ Running multiple Web sessions

➤ Opening files from your hard disk

➤ All about the cache and reloading

➤ Searching documents and using the pop-up menu

➤ Copying things you find to the Clipboard

➤ Saving images, documents, and files

You've seen the basic moves, now you are ready to learn more techniques to help you find your way around the Web. In the last chapter, you learned how to move around on the Web using a Web browser such as Netscape or Internet Explorer. In this chapter, you'll find out how to run multiple Web sessions at the same time, how to deal with the cache, how to save what you find and so on. You need to know these advanced moves to work efficiently on the Web.

Multiple Windows – Ambidextrous Browsing

These days, most browsers allow you to run more than one Web session at the same time. Why would you want to do that? Well, there could be many reasons. Everyone's in such a hurry these days … . While you wait for an image to load in one window, you can read something in another window. Or maybe you need to find information at another Web site but don't want to 'lose your place' at the current one. (Yes, you have bookmarks and the history list, but sometimes it's just easier to open another window.) You can open one or more new browser windows, as shown in the following figure, so that you can run multiple Web sessions. In this example you can see two Internet Explorer windows. To make the one at the back take up the entire screen, I pressed **F11** to use the **Fullscreen** feature (earlier versions had a **Fullscreen** button), then right-clicked the bar and selected the **Autohide** feature (see Chapter 4, 'The World Of The World Wide Web').

Opening multiple windows is a good way to do more than one thing at a time. In this illustration, one Internet Explorer sits over another that has been maximized using the Fullscreen command (press F11).

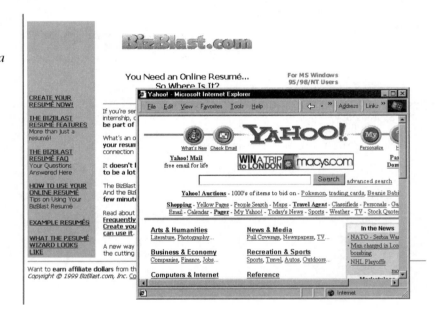

Exactly how you open a new window varies between browsers; however, you'll probably find that most are similar. Here's how the two most popular browsers, Netscape and Internet Explorer, let you open windows.

Netscape gives you two ways to do this:

➤ Right-click the link that you want to 'follow' in a new window, and then choose **Open in New Window**. A new Netscape window opens and the referenced document opens in that window.

➤ Choose **File**, **New Web Browser** (or **File, New, Navigator Window**), or press **Ctrl+N** to open a new window displaying the home page.

Internet Explorer gives you four options:

➤ Right-click the link you want to follow, and then choose **Open in New Window.** A new window opens, displaying the referenced document.

➤ Press **Tab** until the link becomes highlighted and then press **Shift+Enter**.

➤ Choose **File, New Window** (or, in some versions, **File, New, Window**), or press **Ctrl+N** to open a new window that displays the same document as the one you've just viewed.

➤ Type a URL into the Address text box and then press **Shift+Enter** to display that document in a new window.

As you might guess, you could encounter some problems when running multiple sessions. First, there's the memory problem. Web browsers are turning into real memory hogs, so you may find that you simply don't have enough memory to run multiple sessions or to run more than one additional session. And remember that there's only so much work your modem can do. If you have several Web windows open and each is transferring things at the same time, every transfer will be slower than if it were the only thing the modem had to do.

Automatic Multiple Sessions

Now and then, windows will open automatically. If you suddenly notice that the browser's Back button is disabled, it may be that when you clicked a link, a secondary window opened and you didn't notice. Web authors can create codes in their Web pages that force browsers to open secondary or targeted windows.

Your Hard Disk As Web Server?

If you enjoy working on the Web you'll eventually end up with .HTM or .HTML files on your hard disk. You'll have them in your cache (discussed next), or you may save documents using the **File**, **Save As** command. Your browser provides a way to open these HTML files – generally a **File**, **Open** command or something similar. In the current versions of Internet Explorer and Netscape Navigator, click the **Browse** or **Choose File** button and you'll see a typical Open box from which you can select the file you want to open.

HTM Or HTML?

Depending to some degree on the operating system you use, the file extension of the HTML Web files might be .HTM or .HTML. Originally, the Web was developed using UNIX computers and Web files had the extension .HTML. Later, when Windows 3.1 machines started appearing on the Web, the .HTM extension came into use because Windows 3.1 could work only with three-character file extensions. Today, you commonly see both extensions; even though Windows 95 and 98 accept four-letter extensions, not all Windows HTML-editing programs can. And many Windows 3.1 machines are still being used to create Web pages.

Here's a geek trick for you. If you know the exact path to the file you want to open and if you can type quickly, click in the **Address** or **Location** text box. Then type the entire path and file name, such as **C:/Program Files/Netscape/Navigator/ownweb. htm**. This should work in both Netscape and Internet Explorer. In some browsers, however, you may need to use the more formal (and older) method by entering the file path in this format: **file:///C|/Program Files/Netscape/Navigator/ownweb.htm**. Notice that in the second format, you precede the path with **file:///** and replace the colon after C with a pipe symbol (|).

Turbo Charging With The Cache

Have you noticed that when you return to a Web document that you've previously viewed, it appears much more quickly? That's because your browser isn't taking it from the Internet; instead, it's getting it from the *cache*, an area on your hard disk or in your computer's RAM (memory) in which it saves pages. This capability is really handy because it greatly speeds up the process of working on the Web. After all, why bother to reload a file from the Internet when it's already sitting on your hard drive? (Okay, you may think of some reasons to do so, but we'll come back to those when we talk about the Reload command.)

Forward Slash Or Backslash

UNIX computers use a forward slash (/) between directory names. DOS computers use a backslash(\). As the Web was developed on UNIX computers, URLs use forward slashes. Thus C:/Program Files/Netscape/Navigator/ownweb.htm is correct, even though in normal DOS notation this would appear as C:\Program Files\Netscape\Navigator\ownweb.htm. However, you can type it whichever way you please when you're opening a file on your hard disk or a page on the Web; both Internet Explorer and Netscape will figure it out.

Here's how this all works. When the browser loads a Web page, it places it in the cache. You can generally control the size of the cache. Not all browsers let you do so, but Netscape, Internet Explorer and many others do. When the cache fills up, the oldest files are removed to make room for newer ones.

Each time the browser tries to load a page, it *might* look in the cache first to see if it has the page stored. (Whether or not it does depends on how you set up the cache.) If it finds that the page is available, it can retrieve the page from the cache very quickly.

Putting The Cache To Work

To take full advantage of the cache's benefits, you need to do some configuring. To configure the cache in Netscape Navigator 2 or 3, choose **Options**, **Network Preferences** and then click the **Cache** tab. In Navigator 4 and Netscape 6, select **Edit**, **Preferences** and then open the **Advanced** category and click the **Cache** subcategory. The following figure shows Netscape's cache information.

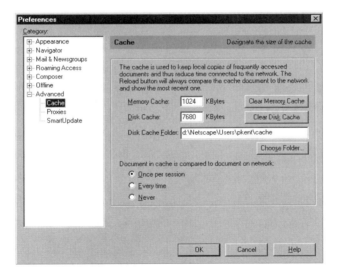

You have several options when setting up Netscape's cache.

Configure any of the available settings to meet your needs:

➤ **Memory Cache.** You can tell Netscape how much of your computer's memory you want to assign to the cache. Netscape stores a few documents in the memory so that it can retrieve them extremely quickly. The button to the right of this option enables you to remove all the pages from the memory cache.

➤ **Disk Cache.** You can also tell Netscape how large the disk cache should be – that is, how much of your disk space you want to give to Netscape. How much should you give? That all depends on how much disk space you have free. (I always say that you can never have too much hard-disk space, money, or beer; I've been proven wrong once or twice, though.) The button to the right of this option enables you to clear out the disk cache, which is handy when you finally run out of disk space.

➤ **Disk Cache Folder.** You can tell Netscape *where* to place the disk cache. If you have several hard disks, put it on the fastest disk or the one with most room.

➤ **Document in cache is compared to document on network.** Now for the complicated one. This tells Netscape when to verify documents. When you request a document (by clicking a link or entering a URL), Netscape can send a message to the Web server saying (basically) 'has this document changed since the last time I grabbed it?'. If it has changed, Netscape downloads a new copy. If it hasn't changed, Netscape grabs the page from the cache. You can configure Netscape to ask the Web server to verify documents **Once per session** (in which case, it checks the first time you try to retrieve a document, but it doesn't bother after that); **Every time** (so that it checks every time you try to get a document, regardless of how many times you view that document in a session); or **Never** (in which case, Netscape doesn't even bother to check to see if it's been updated, unless you use the Reload command).

Check This Out...

The Hard Disk Cache

Note that you are not reserving an area of your hard disk for the cache. For instance, if you have a 30,000K (almost 30Mb) disk cache, your browser doesn't create a 30,000K file that prevents other programs from using that disk space. You're just telling the browser that it can use up to that much disk space for the cache *if it's available* – if other programs don't use up the space first.

➤ **Allow Persistent Caching of Pages Retrieved Through SSL.** This feature is in older versions of Netscape (it's not in the latest version) and it's related to Internet security. SSL stands for Secure Sockets Layer (which probably means no more to you than SSL, so I'm not sure why I told you that). An SSL Web browser can use secure transmission of information; the information is encrypted before being transmitted. This feature tells the browser to cache pages that were sent in a secure manner.

Internet Explorer 5 and 6 use a similar system. Choose **Tools, Internet Options**, and click the **General** tab. (As you may have noticed by now, Microsoft keeps moving things around; in some versions of Explorer you'll need to select **View, Options** – or perhaps **Internet Options** – and then click the **General** tab, or maybe the **Advanced** tab.) Then click the **Settings** button in the **Temporary Internet Files** area.

Although Explorer's programmers (even the innovators) have taken to referring to the cache as Temporary Internet Files, it's the same thing. Near the top of the box, you can tell the browser when to check to see whether there's a newer version of the file. You can tell it to check **Once per session** in Explorer 3; this option is ambiguously labelled **Every time you start Internet Explorer** in Explorer 4 and 5, but it's the same thing. Or you can turn it off altogether (select **Never**). In Explorer 4 and 5, you also have the option to check **Every visit to the page**. And Explorer 5 has yet another option, **Automatically**. This starts off working the same as **Every time you start Internet Explorer**, but, in theory, the browser learns how often a particular page changes, and if it doesn't change often eventually the browser stops checking quite so frequently.

You can also modify the size of the cache by dragging a slider to set the percentage of the drive you want to use (instead of entering a megabyte value). You can select the cache directory using the **Move Folder** button, but notice that Explorer offers something extra: a **View Files** button. Click the **View Files** button to display a list of the files stored in the cache; you can double-click a file to open it in the browser. Explorer 5 and 6 and some versions of Explorer 4 also have a **View Objects** button, which opens a window containing ActiveX controls downloaded to your computer (see Chapter 6, 'Forms, Applets, And Other Web Weirdness'). You can also empty the cache; in more recent versions there's a **Delete Files** button back in the Internet Options dialog box, while earlier versions had an **Empty Folder** button in the cache's Settings dialog box.

Internet Explorer allows you to modify the cache and view its contents directly.

Decisions, Decisions

Which of the cache options should you use? I prefer **Never** because it makes my Web sessions *much* quicker. Whenever I tell a browser to go to a Web page that's already in the cache, it loads the page from the hard disk right away, without sending a verification message to the server first. Even if the browser doesn't have to retrieve the page again – because the page hasn't changed – simply checking with the Web server can slow you down noticeably.

On the other hand, I have to remember to keep using the Reload command to make sure I'm viewing the latest version of the Web pages. Some people may prefer to use the Once per Session option to ensure that they're always looking at the latest page.

What Is Reload?

Sometimes you *do* want to get a file from the Web again. Reload is a 'cure' for the cache. If you get a page from the cache, you are not getting the latest document. Sometimes getting the most recent document doesn't matter, but in a few cases, it *does*.

For instance, say you want to return to a site you visited several weeks ago. If you have a very large cache, that document may still be available. If you have the Never option button selected in the Preferences dialog box, your browser displays the *old* document, without checking to see if the corresponding document stored on the Web has changed. Or perhaps you are viewing a Web document that changes rapidly, such as a stock-quote page. Even if you viewed the page only a few minutes ago, it could already be out of date.

The cure for replacing those old, stale Web pages is to reload them. Click the **Reload** button or choose **View**, **Reload**. Internet Explorer's programmers, in their attempt to rename everything they can, use the term Refresh instead of Reload. (The fact that Reload is a term the Web's been using for several years and that Refresh has a different meaning – Netscape has a Refresh command that simply 'repaints' the display using the contents of the memory cache – doesn't seem to matter.) The Reload command (Refresh in Explorer) tells the browser 'throw away the copy held in the cache and go get the latest version'.

You'll sometimes see a Reload Frame command, which reloads just one frame in a framed document. (Chapter 6 covers frames.) Both Navigator and Explorer have 'super reload' commands too that few people know about. Holding down the Shift key in Navigator, or the Ctrl key in Explorer, and then selecting the Reload or Refresh command tells the browser 'make sure you really do reload everything from scratch, whatever it is!'. Along with getting around a small but persistent bug in Navigator's Reload command, this option ensures that forms, scripts and applets (and some of the other fancy stuff we'll look at in Chapter 6) are reloaded together with the rest of the page.

Long Documents – Finding What You Need

Some Web pages are large. In fact, some are very large – dozens of pages long – with links at the top of the document that take the user to 'sections' lower on the same page. Many Web authors prefer to create one large page than to create lots of small linked ones, the advantage being that once the page has been transferred to your browser, you can use links to move to different parts of the page very quickly.

Virtually all browsers have some kind of
Find command – generally **Edit**, **Find** or
a **Find** button on the toolbar. Internet
Explorer's programmers have a command
called **Edit**, **Find (on this page)**, which
I must admit is a very good idea. This
command tells the browser to search the
current page instead of the Web itself; I'm
sure some new users get confused about
that issue. (On the other hand, Explorer's
Search toolbar button is *not* the same as
the Find command; it's for searching the
Web.) You'll learn how to search the Web in Chapter 16.

**Don't Forget
Find**

Don't forget the
Find command. It
can come in very
handy for searching long FTP file
listings (Chapter 11), as well as
large Web documents.

The Find command works in a way that's very similar to what you've probably used in
other programs (in particular, in word processors). Click the **Find** button, or choose
Edit, Find and the Find dialog box opens. Type the word or words you are looking
for, choose **Match Case** (if necessary) and then click **Find Next**. The browser moves
the document so that the first line containing the word or words you are searching for
is at the top of the window.

Remember To Right-Click

Remember to use the shortcut menus that appear when you right-click on items. Both
Netscape and Internet Explorer use them, as do some other browsers. The shortcut
menu is a new toy in the programmer's toy box – and a very nice one at that. (The
Macintosh mouse has only one button; on Macintosh browsers, you may be able to
access a pop-up menu by pressing the button and holding it down.) Experiment by
right-clicking links, pictures, or the background and you'll find all sorts of useful commands, such as those listed here:

➤ **Copy Shortcut** or **Copy Link Location.** Copies the URL from the link to the
Clipboard.

➤ **Open.** Opens the related document, just as if you clicked the link.

➤ **Open in New Window.** Opens a new window and loads the document
referenced by the link you clicked.

➤ **Save Target As** or **Save Link As.** Transfers the referenced document and saves
it on your hard disk without bothering to display it in the browser first.

➤ **Add Bookmark** or **Add to Favorites.** Places an entry for the document
referenced by the link in the bookmark or Favorites system.

That's not all, of course. Look to see what else is available. You'll find commands for moving back through framed documents, saving image files, saving backgrounds and so on. Oh, which reminds me: maybe you should learn how to save such things from the Web, eh?

Is It Worth Saving?

A lot of it really is. Yes, I know that multimedia consultant and author William Horton has called the Web a 'GITSO' system. You've heard of GIGO, haven't you? Garbage In, Garbage Out. Well, the Web is a Garbage In, Toxic Sludge Out system.

There really is a lot of sludge out there. But obviously, it's not all sludge. Much of it really is worth saving. And now and then, that's just what you'll want to do: save some of it to your hard disk. Let's look at two aspects in particular: how to save and what you can save.

You can save many things from the Web. Most browsers work in much the same way, though one or two have a few nice little extra 'save' features. Here's what you can save:

➤ **Save the document text.** You can copy text from a browser to the Clipboard and then paste the text into another application. Or, you can use the **File, Save As** command, which enables you to choose to save the document as plain text (that is, without all the little codes used to create a Web document; you'll look at those in Chapter 8). In Internet Explorer you can save the entire page, images and all, by choosing **File, Save As**, then picking **Web Archive** from the **Save as type** drop-down list.

➤ **Save the HTML *source* document.** The source document is the HTML (HyperText Markup Language) document used to create the document that you actually see in your browser. The source document has lots of funky little codes, which you'll understand completely after you read Chapter 8. Once you begin creating your own Web pages (you were planning to do that, weren't you?; everyone else and his dog is), you may want to save source documents so you can 'borrow' bits of them. Use **File, Save As** and choose to save as HTML.

It's Not Yours

Remember that much of what you come across on the Web is copyrighted material. Unless you are sure that what you are viewing is not copyrighted, you should assume that it is.

➤ **Save the text or HTML source for documents you haven't even viewed.** You don't have to view a page before you save it (though to be honest, I haven't yet figured out why you would want to save it if you haven't seen it). Simply right-click the link and choose Save Target As or Save Link As from the shortcut menu.

➤ **Save inline images in graphics files.** You can copy images you see in Web pages directly to your hard drive. Right-click an image and choose **Save Image As** or **Save Picture As**.

➤ **Save the document background.** Internet Explorer even lets you save the small image that is used to put the background colour or pattern in many documents. Right-click the background and choose **Save Background As**.

➤ **Create Windows wallpaper.** Internet Explorer also lets you quickly take an image or background from a document and use it as your Windows wallpaper image. Right-click the picture or the background and choose **Set as Wallpaper**.

➤ **Copy images to the Clipboard.** With this neat Explorer feature, you can copy images directly to the Clipboard. Right-click and then choose **Copy** or **Copy Background** from the shortcut menu.

➤ **Print the document.** Most browsers have a **File**, **Print** command and maybe even a **Print** button. Likewise, you'll often find a Page Setup command that lets you set margins and create headers and footers.

➤ **Save URLs to the Clipboard.** You can save URLs to the Clipboard, so you can copy them into another program. Copy the URL directly from the Address or Location text box, or right-click a link and choose **Copy Shortcut** or **Copy Link Location**. Some versions of Netscape also allow you to drag a link onto a document in another program; the link's URL will appear in the document.

➤ **Grab files directly from the cache.** Remember that the cache is dynamic; the browser is constantly adding files to and removing files from it. If you have something you want to save, you can copy it directly from the cache. Internet Explorer makes this easy; you simply click the **View Files** button in the Options dialog box. With Netscape, you can view the directory holding the files. However, Netscape renames files, making them hard to identify.

➤ **Save computer files referenced by links.** Many links do not point to other Web documents; they point to files of other formats – which opens a whole can of worms that we'll explore right now.

Grabbing Files From The Web

I like to group these nondocument files into the two following types:

➤ **Files that you want to transfer to your hard disk.** A link might point to an .EXE or .ZIP file (a program file or a .ZIP archive file) that contains a program you want to install on your computer. Chapter 14, 'What On Earth Are All Those File Types?' deals with the file formats.

➤ **Files that you want to play or view.** Other files are not things you want to keep; instead, they are files containing items such as sound files (music and speech), video, graphics of many kinds, word processing documents and so on, that are part of the Web site you are viewing.

These types of files are the same in one way: whatever you want to do with them – whether you want to save them or simply play them – you *must* transfer them to your computer. However, the purpose of the transfer is different and the way it's carried out is different.

In the second case (when you want to play or display a file), you might have to configure a special viewer, helper application, or plug-in so that when the browser transfers the file, it knows how to play or display it. We'll look at such things in detail in Chapter 7. For now, we're only interested in the first type of file – a file that you want to transfer and save on your hard disk.

Web authors can distribute computer files directly from their Web documents. A couple of years ago, pretty much the only file libraries were FTP sites (covered in Chapter 11). Now, though, many Web sites have links to files. Companies that want to distribute their programs (shareware, freeware, or demo programs) and authors who want to distribute non-Web documents (PostScript, Word for Windows, Adobe Acrobat and Windows Help documents, for example) can use Web sites to provide a convenient way to transfer files.

Files Can Be In Both Categories

Files can be in both the first and second categories. What counts is not so much the type of file, but what you want to do with the file and how your browser is configured. If you want to save the file on your hard disk, perhaps for later use, it would fall into the first category: save on your hard disk. If you want to view the file right now, it would fall into the second category: view in a viewer or plug-in.

Which category a file fits into also depends on the manner in which the file was saved. In its normal format, for instance, an Adobe Acrobat file (a .PDF file) could fall into either category. In some compressed formats, it would fall into the first category only because you'd have to save it to your hard disk and decompress it before you could view it. (Compressed formats are explained in Chapter 14.)

Save It

To see how you can save a file, go to TUCOWS (The Ultimate Collection of Winsock Software at **http://www.tucows.com/**). (Its logo is, as you may have guessed, two cows.) This site contains a fantastic library of Internet software for Windows and Macintosh computers.

Techno Talk

Winsock?

What's this Winsock thing? Winsock is a contraction of Windows Sockets, the name of the TCP/IP 'driver' used to connect Windows programs to the Internet's TCP/IP system. Just as you need a print driver to connect a Windows program to a printer, you also need a special driver to connect a program to the Internet. The term Winsock refers to programs that can connect to a TCP/IP network.

Suppose you find a link to a program that you want to transfer. You click it as usual, and what happens? Well, if you're using Netscape and if the file is an .exe or .com file, you'll probably see a File Save box. If so, choose the directory into which you want to save the file (by the way, we'll discuss download directories in Chapter 14). However, you might see the Unknown File Type dialog box (shown in the next figure). This box appears whenever Netscape tries to transfer a file that it doesn't recognize; Netscape wants you to tell it what to do. You can click the **Save File** button to get to the Save As dialog box and then you can proceed to tell it where you want to save the file.

Explorer uses a slightly different method. First it displays a dialog box showing that a file is being transferred. After a moment or two, you'll see another dialog box (you can see both in the following figure).

Netscape doesn't know what to do with this file type, so you have to tell it.

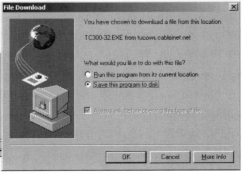

Internet Explorer uses a slightly different system for managing file transfers.

You now have two choices:

> ➤ You can tell Explorer to open it, in which case Explorer transfers the file to your desktop and runs the file. This is actually a pretty lousy idea, for a couple of reasons. First, if it's a compressed archive file, you'll be expanding all files held by the archive onto the desktop, making a huge mess and mixing them in with all the other files already there. Second, the file may be a program file that will run automatically. If by chance it contains a virus, you could be in trouble. You should check program files with virus-check software before running them. (You'll learn more about that subject in Chapter 14.)

> ➤ You can **Save it to disk**. This is the preferable option. Choose this and click **OK** and the transfer will continue. Once the file has been transferred to your hard disk, you'll see a Save As dialog box in which you can choose where to place the file.

Notice the check box entitled 'Always ask before opening this type of file'. If you clear the check box, the next time you download a file, Explorer will automatically transfer it and open it, even if you chose the Save it to disk option button the first time. (To recheck this check box, go to Windows Explorer and choose **View**, **Options** – or **View**, **Folder Options** – and click the **File Types** tab. Click the file type in the list box, click the Edit button, click **Confirm open after download** and then click **OK**.)

The Least You Need To Know

> ➤ If your computer has enough memory, you can open a second Web document in a new window and keep the current window open.

> ➤ You'll probably end up saving Web documents on your hard disk; you can reopen them using the **File**, **Open** command.

> ➤ The cache stores documents you've seen on your hard disk. The browser can get those documents from the cache the next time you want to see them, which speeds up work tremendously.

> ➤ Reload (or Refresh in Internet Explorer) throws away the version of the page held in the cache and grabs a new one from the Web site. You can configure the cache to do this automatically once every session.

> ➤ You can copy, print, and save all sorts of things: document text, the document source file, images, background images, and more.

> ➤ If you click a link to a nondocument file, your browser may ask you what to do with it. You can save it to your hard drive if you want.

Chapter 6

Forms, Applets, And Other Web Weirdness

In This Chapter

➤ Unexpected things you'll run into on the Web

➤ Using tables and forms

➤ Getting into password-protected sites

➤ Using frames and secondary windows

➤ Web programming: Java, JavaScript and ActiveX

➤ Pushing, pulling and multimedia

Not so long ago the Web was filled with static documents that contained pictures and text – originally Web documents didn't even have pictures. But the Web has changed and is still changing; no longer is it just a static medium that you read. In this chapter, you're going to take a quick look at some weird and wonderful things you might find on the Web, such as tables, forms, password-protected sites, secondary or targeted windows, and frames. You'll also learn about Java, JavaScript, and ActiveX applets, as well as push and pull commands and multimedia.

Working With Tables

A *table* is … well, you know, a table. It's a set of columns and rows in which you organize text and (sometimes) pictures. Virtually all browsers these days can display tables. So if you are using a recent one (such as Netscape or Internet Explorer), you'll have no problems. Tables are often used to display, well, tabular data. But they can also be used as a simple page layout tool, to get pictures and text to sit in the correct places. (The following figure shows a table being used in this way.) And recent improvements to the way that HTML handles tables allow authors to use different background and border colours in each cell.

The Discovery Channel (http://www. discovery.com/) page formatted using the table feature.

Interactive Web Pages – Using Forms

A *form* is a special *interactive* Web document. It contains the sorts of components that you've become familiar with while working in today's graphical user interfaces: text boxes, option buttons, command buttons, check boxes, list boxes, drop-down list boxes and so on. You'll find forms at the search sites (see Chapter 16). You use them just like you would a dialog box: you type a search word into a text box, select any necessary options by clicking option buttons and then click a command button.

Forms are also used to collect information (you might have to enter your name and address when downloading demo software) and make sales. You can choose the products you want to buy and enter your credit-card information into a form. The next figure shows an example form that lets you search for flights at Virgin Atlantic (**http://www.virgin-atlantic.com**).

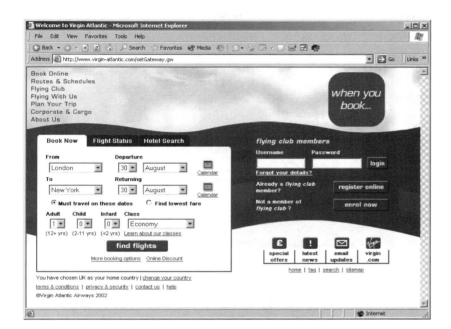

Enter details of the flight you want to find, then click the Find button.

Playing It Safe: Secure Sites

When you enter information into a form and send that information back to the Web server, there is a slight chance that it could be intercepted by someone and read. (It's not very *likely* that your information will be intercepted, but that's another story – which I'll get to in Chapter 17, 'Staying Safe On The Internet'.) Netscape, Internet Explorer, and some other browsers provide a way to send information *securely*. If the form you are viewing comes from a special https:// server (a secure server), the information is *encrypted* before it's sent back from the form to the server. When the server receives the information, it decrypts the information. While the encrypted data is between your computer and the server, the information is useless; anyone who intercepted the information would end up with a load of garbled rubbish.

In most browsers, you know when you are at a secure site. In Internet Explorer, the little padlock icon in the lower right corner is locked (in some versions of Explorer, no lock appears until you're displaying a secure page; in others, the lock's always there, but it's open when you're at a page that is not secure). Some versions of Netscape Navigator have a key in the lower left corner of the window; the key is whole at a secure page (it's broken on pages that are not secure). These versions of Navigator also display a blue bar just below the toolbars when the site is secure. Navigator 4 browsers don't have the blue bar or the key. Instead, they use a padlock icon which is closed. You'll see the padlock icon in the lower left corner of the browser and in the toolbar; the Security button is a padlock that changes according to the type of document

79

Browsers use
various indicators
to show that a site
is secure

The https:// URL, shown
on all browsers

Navigator 4 has a Security button; the
padlock's locked at a secure page.

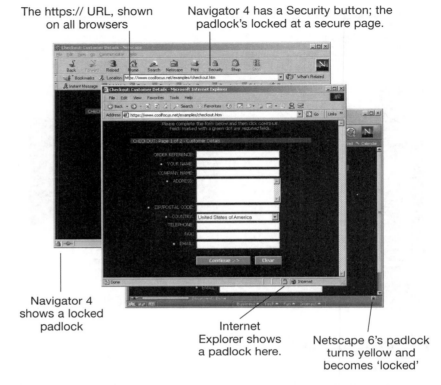

Navigator 4
shows a locked
padlock

Internet
Explorer shows
a padlock here.

Netscape 6's padlock
turns yellow and
becomes 'locked'

displayed. In Netscape 6, the padlock icon in the bottom-right corner becomes locked
and turns yellow at a secure site. Other browsers use similar but slightly different
methods to indicate that you are at a secure page.

One indicator of a secure site is visible in any Web browser. As you can see in the
figure above, the URL of a secure Web page begins with https:// instead of http://. If
you send information to this site or receive information from it, you can be sure that
the information will be transmitted in a secure, encrypted manner.

Secure Pages In Frames

There's one exception to the visible security indicators listed above.
If a site uses frames (explained over the page) to display multiple
pages at once, it's quite possible for one page to be secure while the
rest are not, and in some browsers you won't see any of these
indicators. It's easy enough to find out, though. If you're at a framed
site that asks for your credit card details or other personal information, right-click
the page containing the form and choose Properties (in Internet Explorer) or View
Frame Info (in Netscape) and look for https:// in the URL of the page.

For Your Eyes Only: Password-Protected Sites

Many Web sites are password-protected or have an area that is password-protected. You can't enter a password-protected Web site or area unless you enter a password, which is given to you when you go through a registration process (which often, though not always, includes payment of some kind).

Why do sites use passwords? They may be selling information or some other kind of data (the single most common form of sold data, and in general the most profitable, is pornography). They may have private areas for employees of a particular company or members of a club or association. But sometimes free sites that are open to the public require that you log in. This requirement is often because these sites create an account for you and save information about you. To access that account, you have to log in. For instance, Expedia (**http://expedia.com/**), Microsoft's travel Web site, creates accounts for people that save information about them: their email address, postcode, the airport they generally fly from, and a subscription to an email notification of travel promotions.

Dealing With Secondary Windows

I should know better, but once or twice I've been confused when I've suddenly discovered that Netscape's history list has disappeared. What happened? I clicked a link and then looked away for a moment. While my eyes were averted, another browser window opened automatically. I continued, unaware of what had happened.

Public Letter To Web Authors

Dear Web authors: it's bad interface design to open a secondary window full-screen. Please open your windows slightly less than full screen, so it's obvious to your users what's going on! Signed, Confused in Cardiff.

If they want to, Web authors can set up a link so that when you click it a new window opens and the referenced document appears in that window. It's a very handy feature when used properly. These windows are called *targeted* windows. (I prefer to use an older hypertext term: *secondary* windows.)

When a targeted window opens in Netscape Navigator, the history list from the previous window disappears because the history list is linked to a particular window. In newer versions of Navigator, you *can* still use the history list from the Go menu, though the Back button won't work. That's how it works in all versions of Internet Explorer: although the Back and Forward commands stop working in the new window, you can still access the full history list and get back to a previous page.

Panes Or Frames

Another new feature you may find while browsing on the Web is *frames*. (In other earlier hypertext systems, these were sometimes known as *panes*). The following figure shows an example of frames. When you open a framed document, you find that it displays two or more documents, each within its own pane. Frames can be a good way to organize a lot of information. For example, you might find a table of contents in one frame; clicking a link in the table of contents would load the specified document into the other frame.

The Mystical Universe site (http:// mysticaluniverse. com) shows a good use of frames. Click a heading in the left frame to view that page in the right frame.

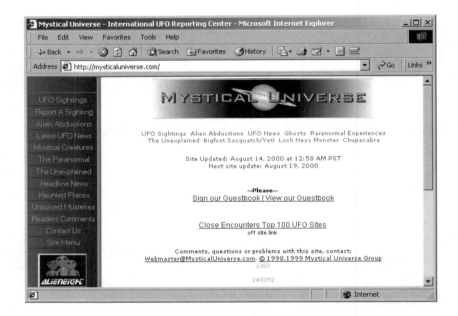

Some browsers have a special reload command for frames: click inside a frame and then choose **View**, **Reload Frame** to reload the contents of that one frame. Some versions of the Netscape browser also have a **Back in Frame** command with which you can move back to the previously viewed document within the frame. Navigator Version 2 had a real problem with frames, though; using the Back command took you all the way out of the frames, perhaps many steps back, rather than showing you the previous document you viewed within the frames. Internet Explorer and Navigator version 4 have no Back in Frame command; instead, they assume that if you're using the Back command, you want to go back step by step, not all the way out of the frames.

Frames are one of the most hated features on the Web. Although they can be very useful when designed properly, too many Web authors misuse them; they put too many frames into a window or lock frame contents so you can't scroll down the page within the frame. Such authors are often working with very high-resolution monitors on which everything works fine, but things get totally messed up on lower-resolution monitors.

Animated Icons

Animated icons are becoming popular these days. These are little pictures embedded into Web documents that appear to be in motion. They are relatively easy for Web authors to create, so you can expect to see many more of them appearing on the Web. They add a little motion to a page (this is known in Web jargon as 'making a page more compelling'), without causing a lot of extra stuff to be transmitted to your computer.

If you find large and complicated things in motion, you've stumbled across some kind of video or animation file format (see Chapter 7) or perhaps an actual Web program created in Java or ActiveX.

Web Programs: Java, JavaScript, And ActiveX

You may have heard of Java by now. I'm not talking about a chain of coffee bars; I'm talking about a programming language that will (if you believe the hype) make the Web more exciting, make every appliance from toasters to dishwashers talk to you in Swahili, bring about world peace, and lead to a complete and total eradication of body odour.

Java has been hyped for a few years, but I think it's finally becoming useful. A number of sites now have Java applets that do something useful (in the early days Java was a toy, and the average Java applet was nothing more useful than a picture of bouncing heads). The Expedia site mentioned earlier, for instance, has Java-based maps. You can select an area to see a map showing a few hotels, and then zoom in on a particular area, or find information about one of the hotels. Java is also used to create moving banners, automatically scrolling text boxes, chat programs (see Chapter 12, 'Online Chat Rooms And Instant Messaging'), and many other useful and not-so-useful things.

Java Interpreters

Java-compatible browsers are Java 'interpreters'. In effect, an interpreter is a program that can run another program, coordinating between the computer's operating system and the program. So a Java applet can run on any operating system (Windows 3.1, Windows 95 and later, Macintosh System 7, and UNIX of various flavours) as long as there is an interpreter created for that operating system. Both Netscape Navigator and Internet Explorer are Java interpreters.

Expedia's Java maps help you find a hotel.

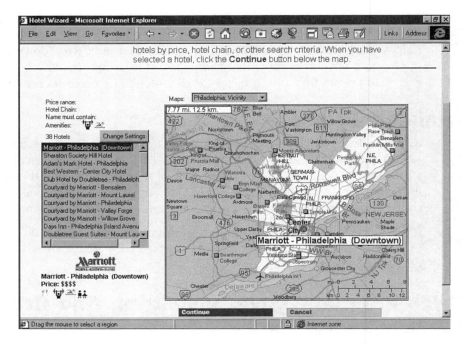

For these programs to work, you must be using a Java-compatible Web browser – and even then they may not work. Netscape 2.0 and later versions, and Internet Explorer 3.0 and later versions, are Java-compatible. The later the version, the more likely that the Java applet will function (Netscape Navigator 2, for instance, doesn't handle Java applets very well). But even if you have the very latest browser, you may still run into problems.

When you reach a Web page that has an embedded Java applet, the Java program is transmitted to your computer, and the browser then runs the program. The program may be a game of some sort, a multimedia display, a financial calculator of some kind, or just about anything else. The figure above shows one of the Java maps at Expedia.

Applications Across The Net

You may have heard the theory that pretty soon, instead of buying software and installing it on your hard drive, you'll 'rent' programs across the Internet, paying for the time you use. If this *ever* happens (and there are good reasons to suspect it won't), it will be a very long time from now. Internet connections are currently about as reliable and efficient as a drunk at a beer tasting, and until they are as reliable as the electricity supply, this system won't work. I've added this projection to my 'yeah, right, don't hold your breath' list.

What About JavaScript And ActiveX?

JavaScript is Java's baby brother. It's a scripting language in which programs are written within the Web page. In other words, a JavaScript-compatible browser reads the Web page, extracts the JavaScript commands, and runs them. JavaScript is not as powerful a programming language as Java, but it's easier to create programs using JavaScript, so it's more common. You can find loads of JavaScript programs at JavaScripts.com (**http://www.javascripts.com**). The following figure shows an example of a JavaScript application, taken from a book I wrote on the subject.

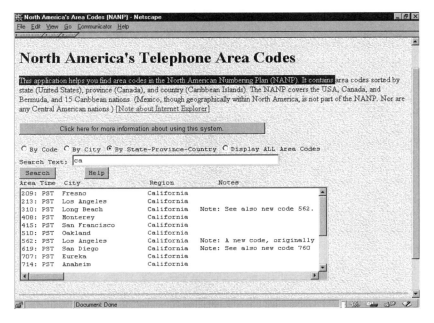

My Area Code program, written in JavaScript (http://www. topfloor.com/java script/areacode. htm).

A competitor to Java, ActiveX is a system from Microsoft, designed to allow Web authors to easily incorporate multimedia and programs into their Web pages. Currently, the only ActiveX browser is Internet Explorer, and you can probably expect it to stay that way for a while. While Netscape was the more popular of the two browsers, Netscape Communications had litle incentive to help their major competitor. These days, with their share of the browser market languishing around the 12% mark, ActiveX is unlikely to figure strongly in their recovery strategy.

Another Programmer's Toy: Dynamic HTML

There's another way to make Web pages move, and that's with a toy called Dynamic HTML (also called DHTML) and layers. A Web designer can now create different layers of information – pictures and text – and then shuffle these layers around on the page, making them visible and then invisible, to create an animation effect and even let people move things around on the page (see the alien head in the following illustration). People define Dynamic HTML differently; layering is a feature that's often used in conjunction with Dynamic HTML, although the purists

Create your own alien head through the wonders of DHTML. (You'll have to use Internet Explorer, though.)

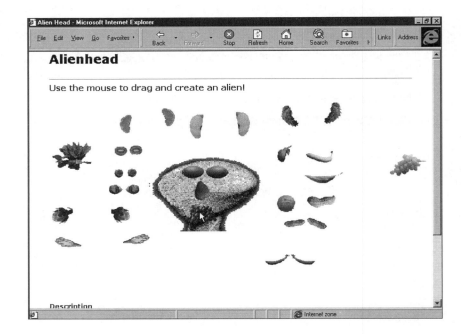

may say it's a different thing. Microsoft and Netscape regard Dynamic HTML and layers as different things, too.

Dynamic HTML means Dynamic HyperText Markup Language. You may remember from Chapter 4, 'Working On The World Wide Web,' that HTML is HyperText Markup Language and is the coding used to create Web pages – you'll see it in action in   Chapter 8, 'Setting Up Your Own Web Site'. So DHTML is sort of like HTML in motion. That's the theory, but advanced DHTML also requires programming skills, not just Web-authoring skills.

Just A Little Shove: Pushing And Pulling

Information generally arrives at your screen because you've directly requested it by clicking a link or entering a URL. However, Web authors can set up their Web pages to use server push and client pull so you can get information without doing a thing.

The first of these, *server push*, occurs when the Web server continues sending information even though you haven't requested it. Suppose you click a link to display a Web page, and just a few minutes later, the Web page changes. Even if you don't request more information, the server sends updated information and continues to send periodic updates until you close the page.

Client pull is similar, except that the request for updates comes from the browser. For instance, you open a page. At the same time the server sends the page, it sends a special program (you don't see this; it all happens in the background). This program tells the browser when to request updates. After the defined interval, the browser sends a request to the server asking for the information. Again, these updates will continue until you leave the page.

These systems work so similarly that you usually won't know which method is being used. They are very useful when you're viewing information that changes rapidly, such as stock quotes, weather reports, news headlines, or auctions.

The Web Gets More Complicated

As you'll see in Chapter 8, creating a simple Web page is quite easy; even many of the more advanced Web-authoring techniques are not particularly complicated. Sure, there are special codes to learn, but it's all reasonably straightforward.

But the latest technologies are things that the average Web author will find much more complicated to use. Technologies such as Java, JavaScript, ActiveX, and Dynamic HTML require programming skills. As a result, it's becoming harder for Web authors to keep up with the Joneses (technologically speaking), which may be a good thing. Now they can concentrate on function instead of form, forget about the glitz, and compete by making their Web sites interesting and content-rich instead of just trying to be cool.

The Multimedia Experience

You'll find all sorts of file formats on the World Wide Web, including still pictures, video and animations, sounds, electronic documents and 3D images. Any file format that you can play or display on your computer can be linked to a Web page.

When you click a link that takes you to one of these file formats, your browser handles the file, if it can. It displays the document or picture in the window in the normal way. If the file is a format that your browser can't handle, it has two options. Your browser may send the file directly to a program that *can* handle it (known as a *plug-in*, *viewer*, or *helper*), or it may ask you what to do. Chapter 7 deals with this topic.

Before I move on, though, here's a quick thought related to this issue:

The Internet is not a multimedia system!

Remember that, and you'll be saved from a lot of frustration. This statement may seem a little strange after you've been bombarded by several years of advertising and media hype about the Internet. We've all seen the TV ads in which video rolls across a computer screen within a Web browser, as quickly as if it were being displayed on a TV screen. But the Internet does *not* work that quickly, and many of its problems seem to arise from people trying to treat it as if it does.

As a multimedia system, the Internet is primitive, mainly because it's so slow. If it's 'lights, cameras, action' that you're after, use the TV or go see a movie; the Internet can't compete. The Internet, despite what you may have heard, is primarily a text-based system. (What's the fastest growing area on the Internet? Email publishing!) Even the Web is primarily text. All the hype in the world won't change that. What will change that is much faster connections from people's homes to the Internet, faster Web servers, and faster and more reliable backbone connections across the Internet. But don't hold your breath, because you'll turn blue before these things appear on the scene.

The Least You Need To Know

➤ The Web is far more diverse than it was a few years ago; it's much more than just text with pictures.

➤ You'll find lots of tables and forms.

➤ Framed documents allow an author to split a document into multiple pieces, each of which is displayed in its own frame.

➤ Java, JavaScript, and ActiveX are Web programming languages that enable authors to bring their pages to life. The latest programmer's toy is Dynamic HTML.

Web Multimedia

In This Chapter

➤ How does a browser handle different file formats?

➤ Finding plug-ins and viewers

➤ Types of plug-ins and viewers you may want

➤ Installing plug-ins

➤ Installing viewers in Netscape

➤ Installing viewers in Internet Explorer

As the Web gets older, and as people start using it more, it's storing more and more types of computer files. You'll find animations, videos, pictures of various formats, sounds that play once they've transferred to your computer, sounds that play as they transfer to your computer, 'slide' presentations, and all sorts of other weird and wonderful things. Think of these formats as the multimedia content of the Web – literally 'multiple media'. For some of us, those with fast connections, the Internet is finally turning into a true multimedia system; that is, one that can work with various types of media without causing great frustration.

For most of us still accessing the Internet through slow modem lines, the full potential has yet to be reached. If *you* are still stuck with a slow connection, some of the things I'll talk about in this chapter will be things you might try now and then, but won't want to put up with very often.

What do I mean by slow connections? Pretty much any kind of telephone modem – it really doesn't matter whether it's a 'fast' modem (a 56 Kbps modem, for instance), all phone modems are slow. It's not until you have the speed of a cable, ADSL or satellite connection – or faster – that you'll find multimedia works well.

How Browsers Deal With Different Files

Today's Web browsers are designed to handle any computer file format. When you click a link to a file, that file is transferred to your computer, and your browser can then use it in one of three ways:

➤ **On its own.** The file format may be one that the browser can handle directly. Web browsers can play or display Web pages (.HTM or .HTML), text documents (.TXT), some graphics formats (.GIF, .XBM, .JPG, and .JPEG), and some sound formats.

➤ **With a plug-in.** The browser may open a *plug-in*, a special add-on program that plays or displays the file within the browser window.

➤ **With a viewer (or helper).** The browser may send the file to a *viewer* or *helper*, which is a separate program that recognizes the file format. That program then opens a window in which the file is played or displayed.

When you first get your browser, it probably won't recognize all the file formats you'll encounter. When the browser comes across a file format that it doesn't recognize, it will ask you what to do; you can then install a new plug-in or viewer to handle that file type, or simply save the file on your hard disk.

Two Types Of Multimedia Inclusions

There are basically two ways to include a multimedia file in a Web page. The author may include the file as a *live, embedded*, or *inline object* (a file that is automatically transferred to your computer along with the Web page). For instance, an embedded file may play a background sound or display a video within the Web page. On the other hand, the author can include the file as an *external file*; you click a link, and that file alone (without a Web page) is transferred to your computer.

What's Available?

Scores of plug-ins and viewers are available; you just have to know where to find them. A good starting point for Netscape Navigator plug-ins is the Netscape Navigator Components page; select **Help**, **About Plug-ins**, and then click the **For More Information on Netscape Plug-ins, Click Here** link near the top of the page, or go to **http://home.netscape.com/plugins**. For Internet Explorer, choose the **Help, Product Updates** options (in older versions) or visit the Windows Updates site. You can also find many viewers at the sites discussed in Appendix C, 'All The Software You'll Ever Need'.

About now you're probably wondering whether you should use a plug-in or a viewer. In general, you'll probably prefer working with plug-ins because they allow the browser to display or play the file. In effect, a plug-in extends the capabilities of the browser, allowing it to work with a file type that it couldn't use before. A viewer, on the other hand, is a completely separate program; the Web browser remains at the previous Web page while the multimedia file is sent to the viewer. Of course, there may be cases in which a viewer is a better program and has more features than the equivalent plug-in. You may want to experiment and find out which is the more capable of the two.

Which Plug-Ins Are Installed?

In Netscape Navigator, you can quickly find out which plug-ins are installed by choosing **Help**, **About Plug-ins**. You'll see a page showing you each plug-in and its filename. You'll also find a link to the Inline Plug-Ins page, where you can download more. In older versions of Internet Explorer, you can select **Help**, **Product Updates**, and you'll see a Web page that lists a number of recommended plug-ins and shows you whether those plug-ins are already installed. This feature is not in Internet Explorer 5 or 6, though. Instead, select **Tools, Windows Update** to go to the Microsoft site and find out which updates are available.

Which Do You Need? Which Do You Want?

You don't need all the available viewers and plug-ins. There are hundreds already – almost 160 plug-ins for Netscape Navigator alone – and more are being added all the time. So unless you are independently wealthy and don't need to waste time working, you probably won't have time to install them all (and you probably don't have the disk space you'd need). To help you determine which plug-ins and viewers you should get, I've broken them down into a few categories and the most common file formats. You may not want to get them until you need them, though.

Music And Voice (Very Useful)

Some of the most useful plug-ins and viewers are those for music and voice. In particular, you may want RealAudio, TrueSpeech, and StreamWorks. (RealAudio is the most popular, and therefore the most useful, of these sound formats.)

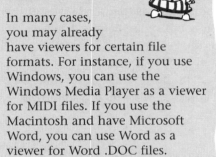

You Already Have Viewers

In many cases, you may already have viewers for certain file formats. For instance, if you use Windows, you can use the Windows Media Player as a viewer for MIDI files. If you use the Macintosh and have Microsoft Word, you can use Word as a viewer for Word .DOC files.

Most sound formats can't play until they have been completely transferred to your disk drive (you twiddle your thumbs for ten minutes, and then listen). The RealAudio, TrueSpeech, and StreamWorks formats play sounds as they are being transferred, though. They're used by radio stations and music libraries, for example, so you can listen to the news from National Public Radio (**http://www.npr.org**) or music from the Internet Underground Music Archives

(**http://www.iuma.com**). The following illustration shows Internet Explorer using RealAudio to play a broadcast from the Virgin Radio web site.

During your Internet travels, you are likely to come across these other sound formats:

➤ **.AU, .AIF, .AIFF, .AIFC, and .SND**. These common sound formats are used on UNIX and on the Macintosh. Your browser can probably play these formats without an additional plug-in or viewer.

➤ **.WAV**. This is the Windows sound format. Your browser can probably play files in this format without an additional plug-in or viewer.

The RealAudio plug-in playing a live broadcast from Virgin Radio, www.virginradio.co.uk

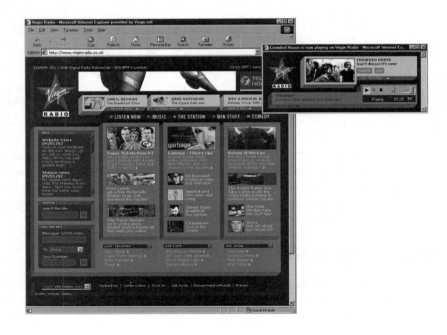

> ➤ **.MID and .RMI**. These are MIDI (Musical Instrument Digital Interface) formats. You may need to add a plug-in or viewer for these. (Netscape Navigator, since version 3, comes with a preinstalled plug-in that will work with MIDI files.)

The MIDI formats are not common, but they are of interest to people who, well, are interested in MIDI. Many MIDI sites on the Web have sound clips. (MIDI is a system used to create music using computers and other electronic toys.)

MP3

MP3 is another important sound format you should know about. What's so special about MP3? Well, MP3 files are CD-quality, and take up relatively little room. One minute of music takes up just 1MB, more or less, of disk space (the format used on audio CDs requires almost 10MB for each minute). MP3 is very popular, and it has the music business terrified; in fact the Recording Industry Association of America has even tried to have an MP3 player banned.

MP3 can be used in many different ways. You can store all your music on your computer, then create playlists. Having a weekend party? Set up a playlist to run all weekend, click the start button, and forget about the music for the next 72 hours.

You can also create custom CDs. Pick the tracks you want, convert them to audio CD, and cut your own CD. Or play the music through an MP3 player, such as Rio from Diamond Multimedia – plug the player into your computer, load the music, and away you go. Create custom cassette tapes and DAT tapes. Send your friends tracks across the Internet, and so on.

The two most popular MP3 players are WinAmp (**http://www.winamp.com**) and MusicMatch (**http://www.musicmatch.com**). MusicMatch has the advantage of including a 'ripper', software that can take tracks off your audio CDs and save them in MP3 format (WinAmp may include a ripper soon, too).

To find music, and learn about all the neat MP3 tools, visit MP3.com (**http://www.mp3.com**, of course), or one of these sites:

> ➤ MP3 Sound at **http://www.mp3sound.com**

> ➤ MP3 2000 at **http://www.mp3-2000.com**

> ➤ MP3 Now at **http://www.mp3now.com**

> ➤ MPEG.ORG at **http://www.mpeg.org**

> ➤ Dimension Music at **http://www.dmusic.com**

Oh, and don't forget to check out a book I've just published, *MP3 and the Digital Music Revolution: Turn Your PC into a CD-Quality Digital Jukebox* (**http://topfloor.com**). It comes with the MusicMatch software and hours of music.

What's the music business doing about all this? They're trying to come up with their own sound formats, such as Liquid Audio and A2B. Of course the problem is that most people won't want to use these sound formats, because the entire purpose of these formats is to make moving your music around *inconvenient*, to discourage piracy. But if it's inconvenient for software pirates (the music business has finally come to the realization that music is a form of software), then it's inconvenient for the rest of us, so the music business will find it hard to get people to switch. (Try this test; visit one of the search sites we discuss in Chapter 16 and search for the word 'MP3'. Then search for 'Liquid Audio'; you'll quickly see which is the most popular!)

Flash And Shockwave

There are two very popular media formats that you're almost certain to run into: Flash and Shockwave, from Macromedia. You might think of Flash as Shockwave's little brother. Shockwave has been around for a few years, and can be used for interactive games, animations, and applications. Flash is not quite as flexible as Shockwave, but very popular for animations. There are two players for these programs; you can install the Flash Player, or the Shockwave Player, which also includes the Flash Player (**http://www.macromedia.com**).

Macromedia claims that 96% of all Internet users have the Flash Player installed, and certainly many Web designers are integrating these formats into their Web sites. If you would like to take a quick look at what Flash – and Shockwave – can do, visit **http://www.flash.com**.

An Adobe Acrobat file in Internet Explorer.

Other Document Formats (Also Very Useful)

Viewers and plug-ins are also available for a number of document formats that you'll find on the Web. In particular, the Adobe Acrobat Reader is useful. You'll also find viewers and plug-ins that display Microsoft Word, Envoy, and PostScript documents.

Adobe Acrobat is a hypertext format that predates the Web. It enables an author to create a multipage hypertext document that is contained in a single .PDF file and that can be read by any Acrobat Reader, regardless of the operating system it is running on. Many authors like to use Acrobat because it gives them more control over the layout than they get when creating Web pages. It's also often used by companies that want to allow people to download forms from their Web sites; you can open the form in Adobe Acrobat Reader and then print it, and it will look exactly as the company intended (it's difficult to create high-quality forms using Web pages). You can see an example of an Acrobat file in the figure on the previous page.

3D Worlds (Greatly Overrated!)

VRML

These 3D images are in a format known as VRML: Virtual Reality Modeling Language.

There are a number of viewers and browsers that display 3D (three-dimensional) images. Netscape Navigator has a plug-in called Live3D or Cosmo Player (depending on the version of Navigator that you are using), which may have been installed when you installed the browser. Internet Explorer has a plug-in called Microsoft VRML Viewer, which probably won't be installed with the browser – you'll have to add it later. You can download other 3D plug-ins or viewers, too.

Do you need a 3D plug-in or viewer? Probably not. Once you've seen a couple of 3D sites, the novelty will quickly wear off. This is another of those much-touted technologies that hasn't yet lived up to the hype. Three-dimensional images load slowly and move slowly. They are, in my opinion, unnecessary gimmicks. Perhaps one day they'll be an integral part of the Web, but for now they're little more than toys.

Still, if you want to experiment, visit one of the following sites, download a viewer, and play…

➤ The Web 3D Repository at **http://www.web3d.org/vrml/vrml.htm**

➤ Aereal Instant VRML Home World at **http://www.aereal.com/instant**

➤ Cosmo Software at **http://www.cai.com/cosmo**

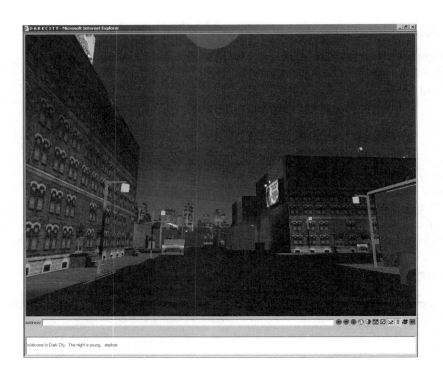

You can walk around these buildings and maybe even into them. This technology is cute, but slow.

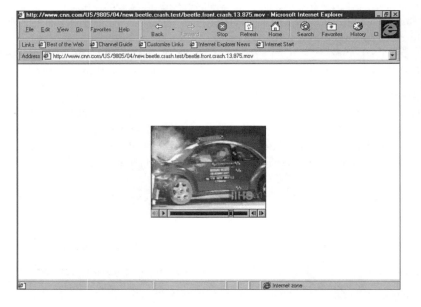

A VW Beetle crash test video from the CNN news site, displayed in the QuickTime viewer inside Internet Explorer.

Video (If You Can Wait)

Video is fairly popular on the Web, but it has serious drawbacks. The main problem is speed. It can take hours for anything big to transfer, and if it's small, what's the point? After waiting an eternity to watch a five-second cut from a movie, I was left with the question, 'Was that really worth it?' ringing in my head. However, now that I have fast access, I really do watch videos more often – news videos at the CNN site, for instance (**http://www.cnn.com**).

Video is another of those things that requires a fast connection. If you are on a corporate network you are probably okay – assuming the video clip is stored on a fast server and the Internet is not as sluggish as molasses on a cold day – but if you are using a modem to connect to a service provider, you'll find video to be very slow.

Still, if you want to try video you can find many viewers and plug-ins. The most common formats are the Windows .AVI and QuickTime formats (which may be built into your browser already) and MPEG. A new format, .VIV, is a compressed .AVI file that provides streaming video. Recently, a video format from RealNetworks has become popular (RealNetworks is the RealAudio company), too, with some news sites using it. Netscape 3.0 comes with a built-in .AVI plug-in, but other .AVI plug-ins and viewers have more features. Another popular player is the VivoActive player from **http://www.vivo.com**.

Streaming Video

I mentioned RealAudio earlier; RealAudio is a streaming audio format, which means it plays as it transmits. That's the new thing in video, too. Not too long ago, you'd have to wait for a video file to transfer completely before you could play it. Now streaming video viewers and plug-ins are turning up; these viewers and plug-ins play the video as it transmits.

GIF Animations

Another very common form of animation is GIF animation. In fact, it's probably the single most common form of animation; those little moving pictures and icons you see are generally GIF animations. The GIF format is one of the basic image formats used on the Web. GIF animations are created by layering several images, and the browser simply displays one image after another. These animations require no plug-in or viewer; if a browser can display images, it can probably display GIF animations.

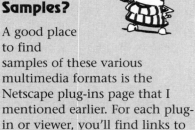

Looking For Samples?

A good place to find samples of these various multimedia formats is the Netscape plug-ins page that I mentioned earlier. For each plug-in or viewer, you'll find links to Web sites using the file format handled by that program.

Other Weird File Formats

You'll find plug-ins and viewers available for all sorts of unusual file formats. Some plug-ins are not programs designed for handling particular file formats that you may come across while cruising the Web – they are more like special utilities designed to extend the features of the Web browser. For instance, there are Netscape plug-ins available for these tasks:

➤ **Carbon Copy.** This Netscape plug-in lets you control a PC across the Internet.

➤ **Chemscape Chime.** This is a plug-in for 2D and 3D chemical models.

➤ **EarthTime.** This plug-in displays eight different times from cities around the world.

➤ **ISYS Hindsight.** This plug-in keeps a record of every Web page you've seen and even allows you to search the text in those pages.

➤ **Look@Me.** This plug-in allows you to view another user's computer screen across the Web and see what's going on. (Assuming that person *wants* you to see what's going on, of course.)

➤ **Net-Install.** This plug-in is designed to automate the transfer and installation of software across the Internet.

➤ **Post-it Notes.** Lets you view and drag Post-it Notes attached to Web pages and drop them onto your desktop. Clicking a Post-it Note later will open your browser and load that page. Very useful, except that you're very unlikely to run into many pages with Post-it Notes attached.

As I mentioned earlier, any file type can be sent to a viewer of some kind. However, only a handful of file types are commonly used (the ones I mentioned earlier as the common formats). You'll only want to install other plug-ins and viewers if the particular file type happens to be used at the Web sites that you frequent.

You don't necessarily need to install these plug-ins or viewers right away. You can wait until you stumble across a link to one of the file formats. If your browser doesn't recognize the format, it will ask you what to do with the file. If you want to access the file, you will need to install the appropriate viewer or plug-in at that time.

Installing A Plug-In

Installing a plug-in is easy. Simply transfer the installation file from the Web and place it in a download directory (see Chapter 16, 'Finding Stuff On The Internet'). Then run the file (double-click it, for instance) to run the installation program. The installation program may run immediately, or you may find that a series of files are extracted from the one you downloaded, in which case you have to run a SETUP.EXE file to start the installation program. Follow the instructions to install the file. After you have installed the plug-in, your browser will be able to automatically call the plug-in any time it needs it.

By the way, your browser may sometimes tell you when you need a plug-in. For instance, if you see the dialog box shown in the following figure (or something similar), you have displayed a Web page with an embedded file format that requires a plug-in. You can click the **Get the Plugin** button, and the browser will open another window and take you to a page with information about plug-ins.

This Netscape dialog box opens when you click a link that loads a file requiring a plug-in you don't have.

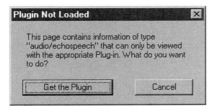

Automatic Installation of Plug-ins

Installing a browser plug-in can be very simple. If you try to load a file type that your browser cannot handle, you may simply have to follow a series of quick steps to automatically install it. If you're lucky, you'll see something like the box in the figure below, asking whether you want to install and run the plug-in. All you need to do is click the Yes button and the plug-in is installed. (It's up to you to decide whether you want to take the security risk implied by the message in the dialog box. There's no easy answer here; all I can say is that in the vast majority of cases it's going to be safe to download and install the software – but that doesn't mean it isn't possible for someone to create a plug-in that is designed to do bad things to your computer!)

Unfortunately, installing plug-ins and viewers is not always this simple. Although it doesn't have to be rocket science, it often takes a few more steps

Installing the iPix viewer (http://www.ipix. com) was as easy as clicking the Yes button.

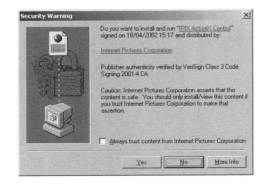

Installing A Viewer

Installing a viewer is a little more complicated than installing a plug-in, but it's still not rocket science. There are generally two different types of viewer installations. One is the type used by the early versions of Netscape and by the Macintosh and UNIX versions of Netscape. In this type of installation, you tell the browser which viewer to work with for each file type. You also add information about a particular viewer to a list of viewers that the browser refers to when it needs to handle the appropriate file type.

The other method is that used by the Windows versions of Internet Explorer and by the Windows versions of Netscape Navigator 4 and later. These use the Windows file associations to set up viewers. For instance, by default Windows associates .WAV files with the Windows Media Player program. That means if you double-click a .WAV file in Windows Explorer, the Windows Media Player opens and plays the file. Internet Explorer and Navigator 4 use the same system-wide file-association system to determine which program should be used when it comes across a file type.

The next section gives you a look at installing a viewer in a Windows version of Internet Explorer, which is very similar to what you would do in the Windows version of Netscape Navigator 4 or 4.5. The section after that covers installing a viewer in a Windows version of Netscape Navigator 3, which is similar to the way installation is handled in other, non-Windows, versions of Navigator and in some other browsers.

Installing A Viewer In Internet Explorer

When you install a viewer in Internet Explorer, you're not merely modifying Internet Explorer's internal settings; you are modifying the Windows file-association settings. When you click a file type that Internet Explorer doesn't recognize, it opens the dialog box shown in the following figure. (This dialog box is similar to what you saw from Netscape.) Because Explorer doesn't recognize the file type, you have to tell it what to do. Click the **Open this file from its current location** option button, and then click **OK.** Explorer transfers the file and then tries to open it.

If Explorer doesn't recognize a file, you will see this dialog box.

102

You'll then see the Open With dialog box, shown next. Type a name for this type of file into the text box at the top. Then, if you can find the viewer you want to use in this list, click it and click **OK**. If you can't find it, click the **Other** button. In the Open dialog box that appears, select the viewer you want to use.

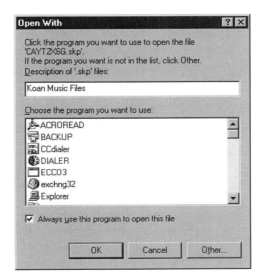

Enter a name for the file type, and then choose the application you want to use as a viewer.

Installing A Viewer In Explorer Beforehand

You can also install an Internet Explorer viewer before you need it. You do this using the File Types system, which you can access from the Windows Explorer file-management utility or, in some versions of Internet Explorer and in Netscape Navigator 4, from within the browser.

Open Windows Explorer, and then select **View**, **Options** (or **View**, **Folder Options** in some versions), and then click the **File Types** tab. You'll see an Options dialog box similar to that shown in the following figure. (In some versions of Internet Explorer you'll be able to access this dialog box in the same way, though more recent versions don't allow this. In Netscape Navigator 4 for Windows, select **Edit, Preferences**, and then open the **Navigator** category and click the **Applications** subcategory. The Navigator dialog boxes will be slightly different from those shown here, but similar enough for you to be able to follow along.)

To add a new viewer, click the **New Type** button, and then fill in all the information in the dialog box that appears. Enter the description (whatever you want to call it), the file extensions used by that file type, and the MIME type. Click the **New** button and type **open** in the first text box you see. Then click the **Browse** button and find the application you want to use as the viewer.

You can add viewers to Internet Explorer using the Folder Options dialog box.

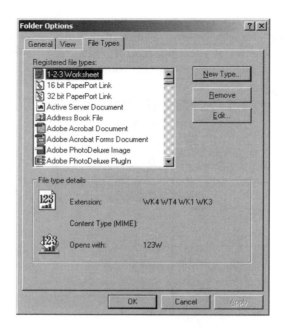

What's MIME?

MIME stands for multipurpose Internet mail extensions. Although originally intended for email transmission of files, MIME is used on the Web to identify file formats. You can find detailed information about MIME and a large list of MIME types at **http://www.cis.ohiostate.edu/hypertext/faq/usenet/ mail/mime-faq/top.html** or at **http://home.netscape.com/ assist/helper_apps/mime.html**.

Installing A Viewer In Netscape 3

This section explains how to configure a viewer in the Windows version of Netscape Navigator 3. The process is similar in other versions of Netscape and even in other browsers. Rather than modifying the list of Windows file associations, you're modifying a list belonging to the browser. (For Netscape 4 and 4.5, go back and read the Internet Explorer instructions; these versions of Netscape use a similar method.)

Suppose you came across a link that looked interesting, and you clicked it. Netscape displayed the Unknown File Type dialog box, shown next. This means that Netscape doesn't recognize the file, so you have to tell it what to do.

*The Unknown
File Type dialog
box opens if you
click a link to a
file that Netscape
doesn't recognize.*

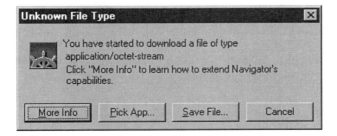

If you want, you can click the **More Info** button. Netscape will open another
browser window and display an information document with a link to a page from
which, perhaps, you can download a plug-in. Let's assume that you already know
there is no plug-in for this particular file type or that for some other reason you want
to configure a viewer. Click the **Pick App...** button, and you'll see the dialog box in
the following figure.

Click the **Browse...** button and then find the program that you know can handle
this type of file. (Remember, you can find viewers at the sites listed in Appendix C.)
Double-click the program, and it is placed into the Configure External Viewer dialog
box. Then click **OK**. That's it! You've just configured the viewer. The file referenced by
the link you clicked will now be transferred to your computer and sent to the
program you defined as the viewer. The viewer will then display the file (assuming, of
course, that you picked the right viewer).

*The Configure
External Viewer
dialog box lets
you define which
viewer should
handle the file
type.*

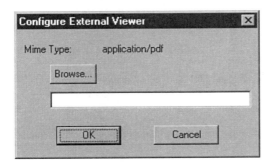

Setting Up Netscape Navigator Beforehand

You can also set up Netscape Navigator's viewers before you ever get to a site that
uses unusual file formats. Choose **Edit, Preferences**, and then open the
Navigator category and click the **Applications** subcategory. Or, if you're using an
early version of Navigator, choose **Options, General Preferences**, and then click
the **Helpers** tab. You'll see the dialog box shown below.

105

The big list shows all the different file types (well, most of them; you can add more using the **Create New Type** button). To configure a viewer for one, click it in the list and then click one of the **Actions.** You can tell Netscape to **Save to Disk** if you want, but if you intend to configure a viewer, click **Launch the Application** instead. Then click the **Browse** button to find the application you want to use as the viewer.

What's That Button For?

In case you're wondering, the Unknown: Prompt User option button is the default setting for formats that haven't been set up with a viewer. If you click a file for which you've configured this setting, Netscape will ask you what to do with the files of this type when they are transferred to your browser.

You can preconfigure viewers in Netscape's Preferences dialog box.

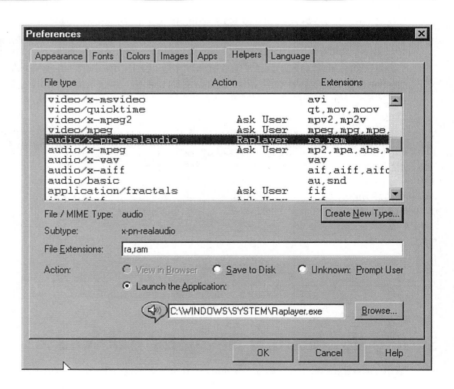

The Least You Need To Know

➤ A browser can handle many file formats: HTML, text, graphics, and sounds of various kinds. If a browser encounters a file format that it can't handle, it tries to pass the file to a viewer or plug-in.

➤ Viewers and plug-ins are designed to play or display file types that browsers can't handle. The difference between the two is that a plug-in temporarily converts the browser window into a viewer, but a viewer is a completely separate program that opens without changing the browser window in any way.

➤ There are hundreds of viewers and plug-ins for scores of file types. Most of these file types are rarely used, however.

➤ Plug-ins are more convenient than viewers. However, if you find a viewer that has more features than the plug-in, use it.

➤ If your browser comes across a file type that it doesn't recognize, it asks you what to do. You can then install a plug-in or specify a viewer.

Chapter 8

Setting Up Your Own Web Site

In This Chapter

➤ Your ten-minute Web page

➤ Setting a page as your home page

➤ Why create your own Web pages?

➤ All about HTML

➤ Adding links

➤ Creating a hierarchy of pages linked to the home page

➤ Shortcuts to grabbing links

➤ Where can you put your Web site?

A few years ago I would never have considered putting a chapter about creating Web pages in an introduction to the Internet. But times change. Many newcomers to the Internet are setting up Web sites – in fact, many people get onto the Internet so they can set up a Web site.

Luckily, setting up a basic Web site is very easy. A Web site is just a collection of Web pages, and creating a single Web page is quite simple – so simple that I'm betting I can teach you to create a simple Web page in, oh, one chapter. No, I take that back! I'll bet you can create a very simple customized Web page in about ten minutes. I'll cheat a little, though, by giving you a template, in which you can fill in the 'blanks'.

My Fill-In-The-Blanks Web Page

I've created a Web page for you below; just type the following lines into your text editor exactly as they appear here.

If you use a word processor instead of a text editor, you'll have to remember to save the file as a text file instead of as a normal word processing file when you finish working with it. As you'll learn later in this chapter, Web pages are simple text files. In many cases, using a word processor is not a great idea because word processors often automatically insert special characters such as curly quotation marks and em dashes, characters that can't be converted to plain text. Therefore, you're better off using a text editor.

```
<HTML>
<HEAD>
<TITLE>My Very Own Web Page--Replace if You Want</TITLE>
</HEAD>
<BODY>
<H1>Replace This Title With Whatever You Want</H1>
Put whatever text you want here.<P>
This is another paragraph; use whatever text you want.
<H2>First Subcategory: Replace this With Whatever Title You Want</H2>
<A HREF="http://www.pearsoned.com">The Pearson Education Web Site</A><P>
<A HREF="url_here">Another link: replace this text</A><P>
<A HREF="url_here">Another link: replace this text</A><P>
<A HREF="url_here">Another link: replace this text</A><P>
<A HREF="url_here">Another link: replace this text</A>
<H2>Second Subcategory: Replace this With Whatever Title You Want</H2>
Put more text and links here.
<H2>Third Subcategory: Replace this With Whatever Title You Want</H2>
Put more text and links here.
<H2>Fourth Subcategory: Replace this With Whatever Title You Want</H2>
Put more text and links here.
</BODY>
</HTML>
```

110

The following figure shows you what this file looks like when displayed in a Web browser. For now, don't worry if you don't *understand* what is going on here; you're trying to break a speed record, not actually learn right now. In a few moments, I'll explain how this whole Web-creation thing works.

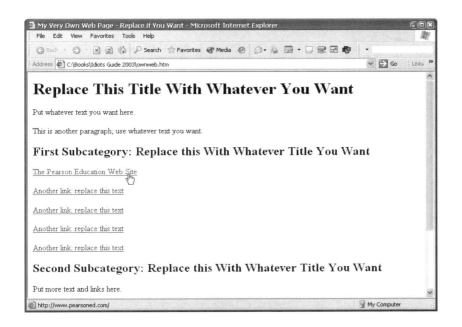

This is what the Web page template looks like in a Web browser.

First, I want you to replace some things. You can start with the text between the <TITLE> and </TITLE> *tags*. Whatever text you type between those tags will appear in the browser's title bar (as you can see in the figure), so replace the text that's there by typing your name, or **My Home Page**, or whatever you want. When you finish doing that, replace the text between the <H1> and </H1> tags. The text you type here will be a heading – the top-level heading, as a matter of fact. You can use the same text that you entered as the title if you want (that's what Web authors often do).

Now, save your work, but don't close the text file. Use your Web browser to open the file; you can double-click the file in Windows File Manager or Windows Explorer, or use the browser's **File**, **Open** command. You can see the changes you've made.

Next, add some text to the file if you want. Replace the text immediately below the <H1></H1> heading, or remove it if you don't want it. (Notice, by the way, that you must end each paragraph with the <P> tag.) After that, replace the next headings with names of categories that describe the sort of links you want in your page. If you have favourite music sites that you visit, you might make the first heading Music.

Check This Out...

What's A Tag?

Text that has a less-than symbol (<) in front of it and a greater-than symbol (>) after it is known as a tag. The tags tell your Web browser how to display the text in an HTML file.

Another heading might be Financial, and another might be Goofing Around. It's your page. Use whatever categories you want. You can quickly see your changes by saving the file and clicking the browser's **Reload** (Netscape Navigator) or **Refresh** (Internet Explorer) button.

Before you change the 'Another link ...' lines, take a close look at the links I've created. The first one is a link to the Pearson Education Web site. (This book is published by Alpha Books, a division of Pearson Education.)

```
<A HREF="http://www.pearsoned.com">The
Pearson Education Web Site</A><P>
```

The words *The Pearson Education Web Site* appear on the Web page as the actual link text; you can see those words in the figure. The URL for the linked page goes between the quotation marks, as in `"http://www.pearsoned.com"`. Keeping that in mind, go ahead and modify the links I've provided. For instance, you might change this:

```
<A HREF="url_here">Another link: replace this text</A><P>
```

to this:

```
<A HREF="http://www.iuma.com">Internet Underground Music
Archive</A><P>
```

Check This Out...

Be Careful

Make sure that you don't remove any of the < or > symbols. If you do, it can really mess up your page.

Replace all the generic links with links to Web sites you like to visit. As a shortcut, you can copy a link, paste it a few times below each category heading, and then modify each of the copied links so that they point to more Web sites. When you finish making your changes, save the page and click the browser's **Reload** or **Refresh** button. Right before your very eyes, you'll see your brand new ten-minute Web page. Didn't I tell you it was easy?

Make It Your Home Page

Once you've created a home page, you need to tell your browser to use it as the home page. In Internet Explorer, begin by displaying your new page in the browser window. Then, in Internet Explorer 5 or 6, select **Tools, Internet Options**, and click the **Use Current** button to set the page in the browser as the home page. In Explorer 3 choose **View, Options**, and click the **Start and Search Pages** tab; in Explorer 4 it's the **Navigator** tab, or maybe the **General** tab. Then you might have to choose **Start Page** from the Page drop-down list.

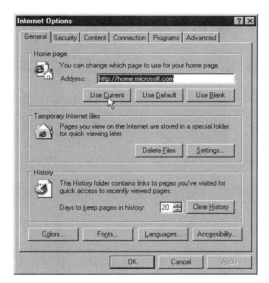

In Internet Explorer, you can click the Use Current button to select the currently displayed page as the home page.

To make your Web page the home page in Netscape Navigator 4 and Netscape 6, load the page into the browser, and then choose **Edit**, **Preferences**, click the **Navigator** category, and click the **Use Current Page** button. In Navigator 3, choose **Options**, **General Preferences**, and click the **Appearance** tab. Look for the **Browser Starts With** text box. You have to type the path and filename of the page you want to open. (For instance, in Windows 95, you would type **c:\program files\netscape\navigator\ownweb.htm** for a file named ownweb.htm that's in the \PROGRAM FILES\NETSCAPE\NAVIGATOR\ directory on drive C:.) Then click the **OK** button.

The next time you start your browser, you'll see your very own home page. And the next time you click the **Home** button, up pops your home page.

Setting the home page in Netscape Navigator 4.5 is similar to doing so in Internet Explorer (and much easier than in Netscape Navigator 3).

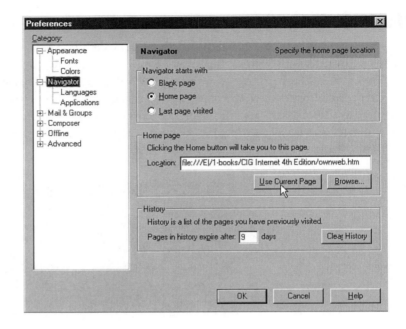

Your Web Page: What's It Good For?

Why bother creating your own page? There are a few reasons. First, telling your browser to view a home page on your hard drive will speed up loading the program. Most browsers these days are configured to use a home page at the browser publisher's Web site, but it's much quicker to load from a 'local' drive than to transfer a page from across the Internet. If that were the only reason, though, you could just copy an HTML document from the Web somewhere and put it on your hard drive.

The second reason has to do with the fact that everyone uses the Internet in a different way. The home page someone else has created won't have all the links you want and will contain plenty of links that you don't want. So you might as well customize your home page to work the way you want it to work and include links to sites you want to go to. You can also create a home page that has a series of documents linked to it (such as one for work, one for music, one for newsgroups, and so on).

Another reason (if you still need coaxing) is that you might want to put information about yourself or your business on the World Wide Web. You're not limited to creating a Web page for your own use and saving it on your hard drive. You can create a Web page that the world can read by saving it on your service provider's system so that it's available to the Internet at large.

HTML Basics

You've already seen how simple Web authoring can be. Now you're going to learn a bit more theory about *HTML* (HyperText Markup Language). HTML is the language of the Web, and all those *<xxx>* tags you looked at are HTML tags.

HTML files are not very complicated. They're in a simple text format. The nice thing about a simple text file is that it's widely recognized by thousands of programs and many types of computers.

Rendering

This term is used to describe the action carried out by the browser when it looks at the HTML codes and formats the text according to the instructions within those codes. It strips the codes from the text and displays the resulting text in the browser.

It's important to understand that although text editors (such as Notepad and SimpleText) create text files, word processors do not. A word processor is like an advanced text editor. It formats the text in many ways that simple text files cannot. It adds character formatting (italic, bold, underline, and so on), special characters (curly quotation marks, copyright symbols, em and en dashes, and many others), and formats paragraph spacing, for example. That's why you have to be careful when creating HTML files in a word processor; you must save the file as text instead of in the word processor's file format.

HTML files are text files that have been specially designed to be read by Web browsers. They use the same characters as any other text file, but they use a special convention that all Web browsers understand. That convention is this: 'If you see anything in brackets like these < >, you know it's a special code'. When Web browsers are rendering the HTML document into normal text so that they can display the document on the screen, they look for these brackets and follow the instructions inside them.

You've already created a Web page, so you know what tags look like. But take a minute to go back and examine the tags you used.

➤ <TITLE> </TITLE>. The text between these tags is the title of the document. You won't see this text in the document; it's simply an identifier that the browsers use. For instance, Netscape and Internet Explorer would put the text in the title bar. In addition, this title is used in bookmark and history lists, and if you've put the page out on the Web, the title may be used by Web search sites

Does It Have To Be Upper-case?

Don't worry about the case of the tags. You can type <TITLE>, <TITLE>, <Title>, <TItlE>, or <TiTlE> – whatever tickles your fancy.

(see Chapter 16, 'Finding Stuff On The Internet') to help them index or categorize your site.

➤ <H1> </H1>. These particular tags mark the first-level heading. You can include up to six levels using the tags <H2> </H2>, <H3> </H3>, <H4> </H4>, <H5> </H5>, and <H6> </H6>. Experiment with these tags in your own Web page.

➤ <P>. This tag is used at the end of a paragraph. Simply typing a carriage return in your HTML file will *not* create a new paragraph in the final document that appears in the browser. You must use the <P> tag instead. Without the tag, the paragraphs will run together.

Anchors

The <A HREF="url"> tags are often called anchors. For this reason, many people refer to the actual links in the Web documents as anchors.

Notice that, in most cases, tags are paired. There's an opening and a closing tag, and the closing tag is the same as the opening tag with the exception of the forward slash after the left angle bracket. <H1> and </H1> form a pair, for instance. The <P> tag is one exception to this. You only need the <P> tag, and it appears after the paragraph.

Finally, there's an *anchor* tag, which is used to create a link:

<A HREF="http://www.mcp.com">The Macmillan Web Site</A><P>

Notice that the URL is included within the angle brackets and within quotation marks. A *link tag* (a tag that you use to create a hypertext link in your document) consists of <A, followed by a space, followed by HREF=". After that tag, you enter the URL. You've looked at URLs before; these are the same URLs that you can use to tell a browser to go to a particular Web site. At the end of the URL, you add ">, followed by whatever text you want. (That text is going to appear on the finished Web page as the link text.) Following the text, you use the closing tag </A>. In the preceding example, I also used the <P> tag to start a new paragraph; I wanted to make sure that the link would appear on its own line.

A Word About Paragraphs

Web browsers don't deal with paragraphs in the same way that word processors do. If the browser finds several spaces, including blank lines, it will compress all the space into a single paragraph unless it sees the <P> tag somewhere. When it finds the <P> tag, it ends that paragraph and starts a new one below it, generally leaving a blank line between the two. If for some reason you want to move text down to the next line but you don't want a blank line between the two lines of text, you can use the <BR> tag instead of <P>. The <BR> tag inserts a line break without starting a new paragraph.

116

<P> and </P>

You've already learned that the <P> tag doesn't have to have a matching code to make a pair. Actually, you can use <P> and </P> as a pair if you want. <P> marks the beginning of a paragraph, and </P> marks the end. However, this is not necessary, and few Web authors do so unless they want to add certain 'attributes' to the <P> tag – but that's further into HTML than we'll go in this book.

Don't Stop At One: Multiple Pages

You can easily create a hierarchy of documents. Why not have a document that appears when you open the browser, with a table of contents linked to several other documents? In each of those documents, you can then have links related to a particular subject.

Say you want to set up a document for the music sites you are interested in. Call it rnr.htm, or music.htm, or whatever you want. Create that document in the same way you did the first one, and put it in the same directory. You can then create a link from your home page to the rock 'n' roll document, like this:

```
<A HREF="rnr.htm">Rock 'n' Roll</A>
```

Although rnr.htm is a filename, you can use it in place of the URL. In fact, rnr.htm is a URL: it's what's known as a *relative URL*. This link tells a Web browser to look for the rnr.htm file. Although it doesn't tell the browser where to look for the file, the browser makes a basic assumption. Because the URL doesn't include the hostname or directory, the only place the browser can look is in the same directory as the original file. (And that's just fine because you are going to place the rnr.htm file in the same directory, right?)

This is really simple, isn't it? You create a home page (called home.htm) with links to any number of other documents in the same directory. You might have links to sites for rock 'n' roll, art, music, conspiracy theories, or whatever sort of information you are interested in and can find on the Web. Then you fill up those documents with more links to all those interesting sites. Whad'ya know? You're a Web publisher!

Finding URLs

There are shortcuts to creating the links in your home page. Who wants to type all those URLs, after all? One way to grab the URLs is to visit the Web page you are interested in and copy the text from the Location or Address text box at the top of the browser window. To do that, you can highlight the text, and then press **Ctrl+C** or select **Edit**, **Copy**. (Most browsers have some method for copying the URL.) Then you can just paste it into your home page.

You can also grab URLs from links on a document. Right-click a link to see a pop-up menu (if you're using a Macintosh, try clicking and holding the mouse button down for a second or two). Click the **Copy Shortcut** option in Internet Explorer, or click the **Copy Link Location** option in Netscape.

You can also grab information from the bookmark list or, in some cases, the history list. In Internet Explorer, you can open Favorites (that's the name it uses for its bookmark system). Choose **Favorites**, **Organize Favorites** (or **Favorites**, **Open Favorites Folder** in earlier versions), right-click an item, and choose **Properties**. Then click the **Internet Shortcut** tab and copy the URL from the **Target URL** text box.

In Netscape, you can open the Bookmarks window (**Window, Bookmarks** or perhaps **Communicator**, **Bookmarks**, **Edit Bookmarks**) and do much the same thing. Right-click an item, select **Properties**, and then copy the URL from the box that appears. (Or click the item and select **Edit**, **Properties**.) You can also choose **File**, **Save As** to save the entire bookmark system in an HTML file. Then you can open that file in a text editor and pick and choose which URLs you want.

Publishing On The Web

If you want to publish on the Web – that is, take the pages you have created and make them available to anyone on the Web – you have a two-step process to go through. First, you create the page. But then you have to place it somewhere that is accessible to the Internet. It has to be put on a Web server.

Most online services and Internet service providers allow their subscribers to post their own Web pages. Some of these services even allow each subscriber to post a megabyte or two, sometimes as much as 50MB, of Web pages, graphics, and so on. Check with your service to find out how much data you can post and where to put it. But a service provider isn't the only place to put a Web site. You have a variety of additional choices:

➤ **On your own Web server.** You can buy your own Web server (you need a computer, connection hardware, and Web-server software), connect it to the Internet, and place your Web site on that server. This is what I call the 'open your wallet' method. It's expensive and complicated, and few people should try it.

➤ **At a free-page Web site.** There are organizations and individuals who provide free Web space to anyone who asks. Visit **http://www.yahoo.com** and search for 'free web pages', which will lead you to a list of dozens.

➤ **At a cybermall.** You can sign up with a Web mall. In general, however, Web malls tend to be expensive and often not very high quality.

> **Getting A Domain Name**
>
> To register a .com, .net, .org, or .edu domain name, go to **http://www.worldnic.com/**. For other domains, try a commercial service such as NetNames: **http://www.netnames.co.uk**.

➤ **At a Web store.** A number of stores allow companies to place pages in the Web store. For instance, a number of book sites sell space to small publishers.

➤ **At a Web host's site in a sub-directory or subdomain.** A Web host is a company that sells space on its Web server to companies that want a Web site. The cheapest way to do this is to use the hosting company's URL and have your Web site as a subdirectory: **http://www.verybigwebhost.com/yoursite**, for instance.

➤ **At a Web host's site as a virtual host.** You place your Web pages on a Web host's server, but you use your own domain name: **http://www.yoursite.com/**.

Finding A Web Host

A free Web site, or the space available at an online service or service provider is fine for most people. But if you're serious about setting up a Web site for a small to medium company or for some kind of club or organization, you'll probably want to use a Web-hosting company, for several reasons:

➤ You need your own domain name. It will be easier for your clients or members to remember, easier to get listed at Yahoo! (the single most important search site on the Internet; they have a bias against sites placed in a subdirectory of an online service or service provider), and you won't have to change your Web site's URL each time you move your Web site. Most online services or service providers won't let you use your own domain name with your basic Internet access account, although some domain-name registration companies will redirect visitors to this account. without charging any extra for doing so.

119

➤ Most online services and service providers don't provide the sort of services that a Web site needs, such as the capability to run scripts (the things that make Web forms work).

Where can you find a low-cost hosting company? A good place to start is Yahoo!'s UK site at **http://www.yahoo.co.uk**. Type **web hosting** into the text box, click the **Search** button and you'll find links to UK hosting companies charging as little as £50 a year. For a little extra, many companies will also handle the spadework of registering your domain name. It's also worth looking at the advertisements in the back of Internet and computer magazines.

There's a problem, though. Selecting a hosting company can be rather complicated. There are so many things to consider, you shouldn't choose one until you understand what you're looking for. I'll provide a little help, though. At my Web site, you'll find a free report called *20 Questions to Ask a Web-Hosting Company* (**http://www.poorrichard.com/freeinfo/special_reports.htm**), which should give you enough information to get started.

Posting Your Web Pages

Once you have a Web site, how do you get the pages from your computer to the Web site? Generally, you'll have to use FTP, which you will learn about in Chapter 11, 'Downloading Files With FTP'. This system enables you to transfer files from your computer to another computer on the Internet. Some of the online services use a different system, though; check with your online service for more information.

If you're using an HTML authoring program, though, you may have a transfer utility built in. These programs are like word processors for HTML. You type your text, format the text using normal word processing tools, and the programs create the HTML for you. Many of these tools are available, and they can greatly simplify Web creation. See **http://www.yahoo.com/computers_and_internet/software/internet/world_ wide_web/html_editors/** for links to some of these programs.

Using Web Templates

Now that you've learned a little about HTML, I suppose I should mention that you might not need to know anything about it at all! Many Internet service providers have templates you can use to create your Web pages. In other words, you can go to a service provider's Web site and follow through a series of forms in which you enter your information, pick colours and backgrounds, upload images, and so on. All the HTML coding is done for you and the page is automatically posted at the service provider's Web site. Check at your service provider's site to see whether such templates are available to you.

There are even sites that provide these sorts of tools for free. You get a free Web site, and you get templates to help you build the pages. Tripod (**http://www.tripod.com**) and GeoCities (**http://www.geocities.com**) are two of the biggest such sites.

Nifty Web Site Tricks

The first thing people want to know after creating a few simple Web pages seems to be... How can I add cool stuff to my Web pages?

The answer is don't. Or, at least, think carefully before you do. Let me explain...

Don't Overdo It

Remember the days of 'kidnap-note desktop publishing'? When desktop-publishing programs first became widely available, the standard of printed materials in the Western world plummeted, as millions of people with all the design skills of the average turnip suddenly realized they could create 'professional-looking' documents cheaply and easily. They could select different fonts, different font sizes, and even different colours. They could place them left justified and right justified and centred. They could wrap words around pictures, and pictures around words. So, they did it all, often on the same page. The result was... a design disaster.

Well, we've reached a similar point on the Web. You can do all sorts of things to 'spliff up' your Web pages. But should you? In most cases, not.

There's another problem. Unfortunately, a lot of people who *do* have design skills have led the way on the Web, creating beautiful and very cool Web sites. But these Web sites are often pointless, expensive, and don't serve any real purpose.

A few years ago, the mantra on the Web was 'make it cool, and they will come.' Make your Web site exciting and entertaining, and people would visit the site. This is complete nonsense. Sites need to be *useful*, not cool. Think about why someone would visit your site. Because of your 'beautiful' design work? Probably not.

So, some of the information we're about to cover is dangerous stuff. I'm going to explain how to add certain things to your Web site, but before you do so, consider whether you really should! We'll look at some useful-if-not-abused stuff, too, such as pictures and frames. Oh, and we'd better not forget tables, a tool that is very handy for getting things to sit in the right place on a Web page.

121

Adding Pictures

Of all 'multimedia' content placed into Web pages, pictures are the most innocuous (so much so that most people don't even think of them as coming under the multimedia umbrella). Don't be fooled, though – some of the most irritating content online is pictures. Don't simply create an image and upload it – check the size first! For instance, if you take a picture of the family with a digital camera, and then upload it right to your Web site, you may find that Aunt Edna, dialing in from Scotland, gets tired of waiting for the image to download.

Inserting an image into a page is very easy. Do it something like this:

```
<img height="51" width="187" src="logo.gif" alt="Company Logo">
```

Size Does Matter

How big should the images in your pages be? Assume that every 10 KB of image size is about 10 or 12 seconds of download time using a 28.8 Kbps Internet connection. That doesn't mean using a 28.8 Kbps modem, though, because actual connections are usually slower than the maximum modem speed.

It's a good idea to put the `height` and `width` attributes, although not essential. Doing so can speed up the loading of the page, though, because even if the image has not yet transferred, the browser knows how much space to leave for it. (How do you know the image size? Any good image-editing program should have a command somewhere that will display image 'attributes' or 'properties'.)

The `src` attribute is the name of the file you want to appear in the Web page (or the path to the file, if it's not in the same directory as the page). And the `alt` attribute is another optional attribute; this is the text that pops up over the image when someone points at the image with the mouse pointer. (It's also displayed in place of the image if someone is viewing the page with images turned off in the browser.)

For The More Advanced Stuff...

I'm explaining the very simple stuff here. There are many more attributes that I'm not covering, things such as the ability to put borders around images or flow text around the image in a specific way. For the details, get a good HTML book (there are only about 100,000 in print, it seems), or visit one of the HTML reference sites online. One of my favourites is the **Index dot HTML** site, at **http://www.blooberry.com/indexdot**.

Positioning Things With Tables

Tables are very handy tools. But let me tell you a secret; although I sometimes work in the raw code of a Web page – work directly on the HTML code in a text editor – I rarely do so for tables. Tables can be very confusing, so I generally use an HTML editor to create them for me.

Tables are created using a variety of HTML tags; the `<table>` and `</table>` tags enclose the entire table; the `<tr>` and `</tr>` tags are used to configure rows within the table, and the `<td>` and `</td>` tags enclose information in a particular table cell (the tag is `td`, not `tc`, meaning table data).

The following HTML code shows a table with two rows and two columns; I created this using Microsoft FrontPage.

```
<table border="1" width="100%">
    <tr>
    <td      width="50%">Cell 1</td>
    <td      width="50%">Cell 2</td>
    </tr>
    <tr>
    <td      width="50%">Cell 3</td>
    <td      width="50%">Cell 4</td>
    </tr>
</table>
```

Frames Are Okay (Sometimes)

A frame configuration is one in which two or more Web pages are displayed in a Web browser at the same time, each in its own portion of the browser window. Frames can be very useful, particularly to display a navigation panel in one frame – clicking on a link in the navigation panel in one frame can load a page into the other frame.

Frames should be used carefully, though. Some earlier browsers simply don't work well with frames. The first frame-enabled browser, Netscape Navigator 2, was only partly frame-enabled. It often crashed when encountering frames. And although newer browsers work well with frames, they can still be a nuisance, especially for users using screens with low video resolutions (not only people with old computers, but those with bad eyesight, too). I'd also recommend that you never use more than two frames in a window, three at the absolute maximum. The more frames in a window, the less room in each frame.

Don't Make This Frame Mistake

If you do create frames, don't make the mistake of omitting the scrollbars without checking to see whether the configuration works in low-resolution screens! (The advanced attributes let you configure various characteristics related to the scrollbars and border.) I often run across frame configurations without scrollbars that were created by Web authors using high-resolution monitors; but in low resolutions some of the text is not visible, and there's no way to scroll down to view it.

Frames are created using what is sometimes called a *frame-definition document,* or a *frames page.* Here's an example of the *frameset* inside such a document:

```
<frameset cols="150,*">
<frame name="contents" target="main" src="contentspage.htm">
<frame name="main" src="mainpage.htm">
<noframes>
<body>
<p>This page uses frames, but your browser doesn't support them.</p>
</body>
</noframes>
</frameset>
```

The `<frameset>` tag defines the overall look of the browser and its internal frames. In this case, it's saying that there will be two columns, with the first one 150 pixels wide. (The second one will take up as much room as is left over after 150 pixels have been assigned to the first column.)

Each column, starting on the left side of the browser, has its own `<frame>` tag; each tag defines the frame name, and the source (`src`), which is a document that will be loaded into the frame. In this case, the frame named `contents` also has a `target` attribute, which is named the same as the name of the second frame. This means that if you put any links into the document loaded into that frame, when the user clicks on the link the referenced page will load not into the same frame, but into the target frame – the `main` frame.

What about the `<noframes>` and `</noframes>` tags? Everything between this text is displayed if the browser the page is loaded into is one that cannot handle frames.

Frames are actually quite easy to work with, but still, you may want to use an HTML editor to help you create them (if you can find one; most HTML editors do not create frame-definition documents).

124

Adding Java Applets

You can insert Java applets – little Java programs – into Web pages using the `<applet>` tag. Will you ever? Probably not, if the average Web-page author is anything to go by. Java applets are much hyped, but the average person will never install one (and very few will ever actually create their own Java applets; this is a realm for programmers, not computer neophytes). On the other hand, there are libraries of Java applets in which you can find applets you *may* want to install on your site, so perhaps you should take a look.

For instance, I found a simple little text scroller called DanScroller at JavaBoutique (**http://javaboutique.internet.com**). I simply downloaded the files to my computer, put them into the same directory as the page I wanted to place the scroller into, and then added this text (I copied the text from the library page at JavaBoutique):

```
<APPLET archive="Scroller.jar" code="Scroller.class" width=450 height=20>
<PARAM NAME="copyright" value="(c) 1999 Dan MacFarlane.
http://www.dancity.com/">
<PARAM NAME="text" value="This is the new scroller applet from DanCity.
You can easily specify your own scroll text and even incorporate
hypertext links (mailto or http) and images into it! You can also drag
the text forwards or backwards for your viewing convenience!">
<PARAM NAME="background" VALUE="#FFFFFF">
<PARAM NAME="textcol" VALUE="#330000">
</APPLET>
```

It took about five minutes to take this applet from the JavaBoutique library and install it in a Web page.

125

The `<applet>` tag is used to insert the applet into the page, but you'll notice that there are associated `<param>` (parameter) tags that pass information to the applet. In this case, you can change the second `<param>` tag to modify the text that appears in the scroller, and the last two change the background and text colors.

You can find more Java libraries by searching at Yahoo! for *java applets.*

Linking To Images And Sounds

You can very easily create links to images and sounds from your Web pages. Remember earlier in the chapter, when I talked about linking from one page to another? Well, use the exact same type of tag, but simply provide the name of a multimedia file rather than a Web-page file.

What kinds of images? The two most common formats are GIF and JPG (sometimes using the .jpeg extension). You may see PNG files mentioned here and there, but most browsers in use today do not work well with these types of images right now, so I'd limit myself to the GIF and JPG formats, if I were you. As for sounds... we'll look at them in more detail now.

Adding Background Sounds

Here's a truly obnoxious use of Web multimedia, adding background sounds to a Web page. Actually I have seen examples where it made sense, or was in some way funny or entertaining (see the HampsterDance site, at **http://www.hampsterdance2.com/ hampsterdance.html**, and **http://www.NuttySites.com** for a few examples).

Luckily, most people don't know how to add sounds to a Web page – at least, sounds that play automatically when the page loads. The competition between Microsoft and Netscape ensured that adding background sounds is not a simple matter – each browser handles background sounds in a different way, and not always correctly. (In fact, most authors of HTML books have given up in frustration and simply ignore this issue entirely, or cover it incompletely.)

What Sound Files?

What types of sound files can you use? Common formats are .wav (Windows 'wave' files), .snd (a Macintosh format), and .mid (MIDI – Musical Instrument Digital Interface – files). Most recent computers can also work with .mp3 (a CD-quality audio format) and .ram (RealAudio) files.

So, in the interest of seeing a more diverse and obnoxious Web, I'm going to release this information into the Web community, and help you and your friends do what so many millions of other Web-page creators have had the sense not to do. Here's a simple way to add sounds to your Web pages. Add these two lines to the top of your Web age:

```
<embed src="filename" hidden autostart="true" loop="TRUE">
<noembed><bgsound src="filename" loop="infinite"></noembed>
```

This should cover both browsers; the sound should play in both early versions of Internet Explorer (using the `bgsound` tag) *and* Netscape Navigator or more recent versions of Internet Explorer (using the `embed` tag). Note that where I've put *filename*, you should put either the filename of the sound file (if the file is in the same directory as the Web page), or the full or relative path to the file. As for the other "attributes" in these tags, here's what they mean:

> `hidden` – The `embed` tag is really intended to place an object directly into the Web page. But for a background sound you don't really want anything visual to appear in the page, so place this word into the tag to make it hidden. (You can also put `hidden="true"`, as some HTML authors do.)

> `autostart` – You guessed it; this makes the sound start playing automatically.

> `loop` – Putting `"true"` after `loop` in the `embed` tag makes the sound play continuously; in the `bgsound` tag it should really be `"infinite"` (although `"true"` seems to work, too). Or put a number to specify how many times the file should play.

> `<noembed></noembed>` – If the page is loaded into Netscape Navigator, a recent version of Internet Explorer, or any other browser that works with the `<embed>` tag, everything between these two tags is ignored; that is, the `bgsound` tag will not be used. If it's loaded into an early version of Internet Explorer, or any other browser that *doesn't* use the `embed` tag, the text between these tags is not ignored. That is, the `bgsound` tag will be used. This avoids problems that may occur if a browser tries to play the sound using both methods.

The Least You Need To Know

> ➤ Creating a home page is very simple; you can use the template provided to create one in as few as ten minutes.

> ➤ Enclose HTML tags within brackets < >.

> ➤ In most cases, you need an opening tag and a closing tag, such as <TITLE>My Home Page</TITLE>.

127

➤ You use tags to tell your browser which text you want displayed as titles, headings, links, and so on.

➤ To create a link, type `<A HREF="URL">`Your Link Text`</A>`, replacing URL and Your Link Text with those you want to use.

➤ If you use a filename in place of the URL in the link, the browser will look in the same directory as the current document.

➤ You can replace your browser's default home page with your new one.

➤ Once you've created a page, you can post it at your service provider's site so the whole world can see it!

➤ Be careful with multimedia in your Web pages – you generally don't need it.

Part 2
There's Plenty More

The Internet is far more than just the Web, although you might not be able to tell that from the media coverage. The Internet offers tens of thousands of discussion groups (newsgroups and mailing lists), a file-library system called FTP and instant messaging. And, of course, there's chat. No, it's not really chat – instead of talking, you type – but many people find it to be a great way to while away an hour or ten. And how about Voice on the Net? You'll learn about a system that enables you to make international phone calls for just pennies an hour!

Even if you don't use all of the services covered in this part of the book, you're almost certain to find something useful.

Chapter 9

Newsgroups: The Source Of All Wisdom

In This Chapter

➤ What is a newsgroup?

➤ What you can find in newsgroups

➤ Finding out what newsgroups exist

➤ What is Usenet?

➤ Choosing a newsreader

In this chapter, I'm going to introduce you to one of the Internet's most dangerous services: newsgroups. Many people find these discussion groups to be addictive. Get involved in a few groups and if you have an addictive personality, you'll soon find that the rest of your life is falling apart, as you spend hours each day swapping messages with people all over the world, on subjects such as bushwalking in Australia, soap operas, very tall women, or very short men.

But don't let me put you off. If you don't have an addictive personality, newsgroups can be interesting, stimulating and extremely useful. And anyway, it's better than being addicted to booze or drugs. So read on and in this chapter you'll find out what newsgroups are; in the next chapter, you'll find out how to use them.

What's A Newsgroup?

Let's start with the basics: *what is a newsgroup?* Well, are you familiar with bulletin board systems (BBSs)? Electronic BBSs work much like the real corkboard-and-thumbtack type of bulletin board. They're computerized systems for leaving both public and private messages. Other computer users can read your messages and you can read theirs. There are tens of thousands of small BBSs around the world, each of which has its own area of interest. In addition, many computer companies have BBSs through which their customers get technical support and many professional associations have BBSs so their members can leave messages for each other and take part in discussions.

An information service such as CompuServe is essentially a collection of many bulletin boards (called *forums* in CompuServe-speak). CompuServe has a few thousand such BBSs. Instead of having to remember several thousand telephone numbers (one for each BBS), you can dial one phone number and access any number of BBSs in the series.

As you've already seen, the Internet is a collection of networks hooked together. It's huge and consequently it has an enormous number of discussion groups. In Internet-speak, these are called *newsgroups* and there are thousands of them on all conceivable subjects. Each Internet service provider subscribes to a selection of newsgroups – sometimes a selection as large as 50,000!

Check This Out...

Newsgroups Dying Out?

MSN recently announced that it would no longer carry newsgroups. If you are an MSN subscriber, you'll still be able to get them through an independent service, as you'll learn later in this chapter.

But what does MSN's move signify? Perhaps that the days of the newsgroups are numbered, as mailing-list discussion groups and Web-based discussion boards take over their work.

What do I mean by 'subscribe'? Well, these newsgroups are distributed around the Internet by a service called Usenet; consequently, they're often referred to as Usenet groups. Usenet distributes somewhere over 50,000 groups (the number keeps changing), but not all service providers get all of the groups. A service provider can choose which groups it wants to receive, in essence *subscribing* to just the ones it wants. Although more than 50,000 internationally distributed groups exist (along with thousands more local groups), most providers get only a few thousand of them.

If your service provider subscribes to a newsgroup, you can read that group's messages and post your own messages to the group. In other words, you can work only with groups to which your service provider has subscribed. As you'll see, you read newsgroup messages by using a *newsreader*, a program that retrieves messages from your service provider's *news server*.

If you've never used a newsgroup (or another system's forum, BBS, or whatever), you may not be aware of the power of such communications. This sort of messaging system really brings computer networking to life and it's not all computer nerds sitting around with nothing better to do. (Check out the Internet's 'alt' newsgroups; these people are   not your average introverted propeller-heads!) In my Internet travels, I've found work, made friends, found answers to research questions (much quicker and more cheaply than I could have by going to a library) and read people's 'reviews' of tools I can use in my business. I've never found a lover or spouse online, but I know people who have (and anyway, I'm already married). Just be careful not to get addicted and start spending all your time online.

Public News Servers

If your service provider doesn't subscribe to a newsgroup you want, ask the management there to subscribe to it. If they won't, you *might* be able to find and read it at a public news server. Try looking at these sites for information about public servers:

**http://dir.yahoo.com/computers_and_internet/internet/usenet/
public_access_usenet_sites/**

http://www.newzbot.com

You can also read newsgroups through a Web site, at
http://www.supernews.com/.

So What's Out There?

You can use newsgroups for fun or for work. You can use them to spend time 'talking' with other people who share your interests – whether that happens to be algebra (see the **alt.algebra.help** group) or antique collecting (**rec.antiques**). You can even do serious work online, such as finding a job at a nuclear physics research site (**hepnet.jobs**), tracking down a piece of software for a biology project (**bionet.software**), or finding good stories about what's going on in South Africa for an article you are writing (**za.events**).

News?

True to its UNIX heritage, the Internet uses the word 'news' ambiguously. Often, when you see a reference to news in a message or an Internet document, it refers to the messages left in newsgroups (not, as most people imagine, to journalists' reports on current affairs).

The following newsgroups represent just a tiny fraction of what is available:

alt.ascii-art Pictures (such as Spock and the Simpsons) created with ASCII text characters.

alt.comedy.british.blackadder Discussions about Mr Bean's earlier life.

alt.current-events.russia News of what's going on in Russia right now. (Some messages are in broken English and some are in Russian, but that just adds romance.)

alt.missing-kids Information about missing kids.

bit.listserv.down-syn Discussions about Down's syndrome.

comp.research.japan Information about computer research in Japan.

misc.forsale Lists of goods for sale.

rec.skydiving A group for skydivers.

sci.anthropology A group for people interested in anthropology.

sci.military Discussions on science and the military.

soc.couples.intercultural A group for interracial couples.

If you are looking for information on just about any subject, the question is not 'Is there a newsgroup about this?' The questions you should ask are 'What is the newsgroup's name?' And 'Does my service provider subscribe to it?'

Can You Read It?

There are so many newsgroups out there that they take up a lot of room. A service provider getting the messages of just 3000 newsgroups may have to set aside tens of megabytes of hard disk space to keep up with it all. So service providers have to decide which ones they will subscribe to. Nobody subscribes to all the world's newsgroups because many are simply of no interest to most Internet users and many are not widely distributed. (Some are of regional interest only; some are of interest only to a specific organization.) So system administrators have to pick the ones they want and omit the ones they don't want. Undoubtedly some system administrators censor newsgroups, omitting those they believe have no place online.

I've given you an idea of what is available in general, but I can't specify what is available to *you*. You'll have to check with your service provider to find out what they offer. If they don't have what you want, ask them to get it. They have no way of knowing what people want unless someone tells them.

I Want To Start One!

Do you have a subject about which you want to start a newsgroup? Spend some time in the news.groups newsgroup to find out about starting a Usenet newsgroup, or talk to your service provider about starting a local newsgroup.

Okay, Gimme A List!

The first thing you may want to do is find out what newsgroups your service provider subscribes to. You can do that by telling your newsreader to obtain a list of groups from the news server; we'll talk more about newsreaders in a little while.

What if you don't find what you are looking for? How can you find out what's available that your provider does not subscribe to? There are lots of places to go these days to track down newsgroups. I like Google Groups (**http://groups.google.com**) and Tile.Net (**http://www.tile.net**) which you can see in the following figure.

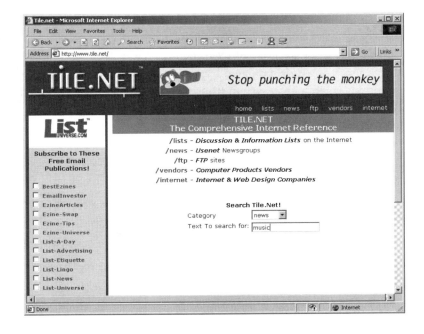

Tile.Net is a good place to find out what's available on UseNet.

Tile.Net also list thousands of mailing lists (see Chapter 10), and FTP sites (see Chapter 11). In addition to Tile.Net, you can try the Usenet Info Centre (**http://sunsite.unc.edu/usenet-i/**) or the Finding Newsgroups and Mailing Lists page (**http://www.synapse.net/~radio/finding.htm**). And of course you can search at any Web search site (which you'll learn about in Chapter 16).

Moderated Groups

As you'll see from the lists, some newsgroups are *moderated*, which means someone reads all the messages and decides which ones to post. The purpose is to keep the newsgroup focused and to prevent the discussions from 'going astray'. Of course, it may look a little like censorship – depending on what you want to say.

Where Does It All Come From?

Where do all these newsgroups come from? People create newsgroups from their computers all over the world. Any system administrator can create a newsgroup and many do. Each host has newsgroups of local interest – about the service provider's services, local politics, local events and so on.

A large number of newsgroups – though not all of them – are part of the Usenet system. Like the Internet, Usenet is intangible – a network of networks. No one owns it and it doesn't own anything itself. It is independent of any network, including the Internet (in fact, it's older than the Internet). Usenet is simply a series of voluntary agreements to swap information.

What's In A Name?

Now let's take a quick look at how newsgroups get their names. Newsgroup names look much like host addresses: a series of words separated by full stops. This is because, like host names, they are set up in a hierarchical system (though instead of going right-to-left, they go left-to-right). The first name is the top level. These are the primary top-level UseNet groups:

comp Computer-related subjects.

news Information about newsgroups themselves, including software you can use to read newsgroup messages and information about finding and using newsgroups.

rec Recreational topics, including hobbies, sports, the arts and so on.

sci Discussions about research in the 'hard' sciences, as well as some social sciences.

soc A wide range of social issues, such as discussions about different types of societies and subcultures, as well as sociopolitical subjects.

talk Debates about politics, religion and anything else that's controversial.

misc Stuff. Job searches, things for sale, a forum for paramedics. You know, *stuff.*

Not all newsgroups are true Usenet groups. Many are local groups that Usenet distributes internationally (don't worry about it, it doesn't matter). Such newsgroups are known as Alternative Newsgroup Hierarchies. They comprise other top-level groups, such as these:

alt 'Alternative' subjects. These are often subjects that many people consider inappropriate, pornographic, or just weird. In some cases, however, it's simply interesting reading, but someone created the newsgroup in an 'unauthorized' manner to save time and hassle.

bionet Biological subjects.

bit A variety of newsgroups from BITNET.

biz Business subjects, including advertisements.

clari Clarinet's newsgroups from 'official' and commercial sources; mainly UPI news stories and various syndicated columns.

courts Related to law and lawyers.

de Various German-language newsgroups.

fj Various Japanese-language newsgroups.

gnu The Free Software Foundation's newsgroups.

hepnet Discussions about high energy and nuclear physics.

ieee The Institute of Electrical and Electronics Engineers' newsgroups.

info A collection of mailing lists formed into newsgroups at the University of Illinois.

relcom Russian-language newsgroups, mainly distributed in the former Soviet Union.

uk Groups covering subjects of interest to UK Internet users.

vmsnet Subjects of interest to VAX/VMS computer users.

You'll see other groups, too, such as the following:

brasil Groups from Brazil (Brazil is spelled with an 's' in Portuguese).

Birmingham Groups from Birmingham, England.

podunk A local interest newsgroup for the town of Podunk.

thisu This university's newsgroup.

137

Okay, I made up the last two, but you get the idea. Seriously, though, if you'd like to see a list of virtually all of the top-level group names in both Usenet and 'Alternative' newsgroups, go to **http://www.magmacom.com/~leisen/mlnh/**.

Reaching The Next Level

The groups listed in the previous section make up the top-level groups. Below each of those groups are groups on another level. For instance, under the **alt.** category is a newsgroup called **alt.3d** that contains messages about three-dimensional imaging. It's part of the alt hierarchy because, presumably, it was put together in an unauthorized way. The people who started it didn't want to go through the hassle of setting up a Usenet group, so they created an alt group instead – where anything goes.

Another alt group is **alt.animals**, where people gather to talk about their favourite beasties. This group serves as a good example of how newsgroups can have more levels. Because it's such a diverse subject, one newsgroup isn't really enough. So instead of posting messages to the alt.animals group, you choose your particular interest. The specific areas include:

>   **alt.animals.dolphins**
>
>   **alt.animals.felines.lions**
>
>   **alt.animals.felines.lynxes**
>
>   **alt.animals.felines.snowleopards**
>
>   **alt.animals.horses.icelandic**
>
>   **alt.animals.humans**

And there are many more. If you're into it, chances are good there's a newsgroup for it.

All areas use the same sort of hierarchical system. For example, under the bionet first level, you can find such newsgroups as **bionet.genome.arabidopsis** (information about the Arabidopsis genome project), **bionet.genome.chrom22** (a discussion of Chromosome 22), and **bionet.genome.chromosomes** (for those interested in the eucaryote chromosomes).

I'm Ready; Let's Read

Now that you know what newsgroups are, you'll probably want to get in and read a few. Newsgroups store the news messages in text files – lots of text files. You'll read the messages using a *newsreader* to help you sort and filter your way through all the garbage.

If you are with an online service, you already have a built-in newsreader. These range from the good (MSN's newsreader is pretty capable) to the absolutely awful (CompuServe's was horrible last time I looked; maybe its next software upgrade will fix that). If you are with a service provider, they may give you a newsreader or it may be already installed on your computer. For example, Netscape Navigator and some versions of Internet Explorer have built-in newsreaders, and Windows 98 comes with Outlook Express (see the following figure), which includes a newsreader. Or you may have one of many other newsreaders, such as WinVN, Gravity, Free Agent, or OUI (on Windows), or NewsWatcher and Nuntius (on the Mac). Note, though, that there are far fewer newsreaders available now than there used to be. As with some other forms of Internet software (push programs and VRML viewers are examples), there was a kind of bandwagon that every software producer jumped onto which lost a wheel or two along the way.

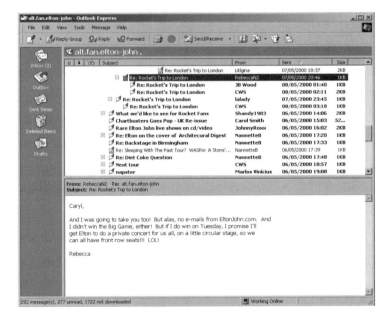

Outlook Express, which is included with Windows 98, Me, 2000 and XP, displays the list of messages in the top pane and the selected message in the lower pane.

I'm going to use the Outlook Express newsreader for my examples in the next chapter. If you have something different, the actual commands you use will vary, but the basic principles will remain the same. Of course, different programs have different features, so you might want to try out a few programs to see what you like (see Appendix C for information about finding software).

The Least You Need To Know

➤ A newsgroup is an area in which people with similar interests leave public messages – a sort of online public debate or discussion.

➤ There's a newsgroup on just about every subject you can imagine. If there isn't, there probably will be soon.

➤ Newsgroup names use a hierarchical system and each group may have subgroups within it.

➤ The major online services have built-in newsreaders. If you are with a service provider, it may have given you a newsreader. If for any reason you're looking for a newsreader, try the software 'libraries' listed in Appendix C.

➤ Some available newsreaders include Gravity, Free Agent, WinVN and OUI on Windows, or NewsWatcher and Nuntius for the Mac.

Chapter 10

Your Daily News Delivery

In This Chapter

➤ Starting your newsreader

➤ Reading and responding to messages

➤ Marking messages as read

➤ ROT13: encoded messages

➤ Sending and receiving binary files

➤ Special newsreader features

➤ Mailing lists – have your news delivered by email

This chapter explains how to work in the newsgroups. As I mentioned in the preceding chapter, I'm going to use the Outlook Express newsreader for my examples, but many other newsreader programs are available. Although each program is a little different, they all share certain characteristics. Check your program's documentation for the specific details and to learn about any extra features it includes. Even if you don't have Outlook Express, I suggest that you read this information because it provides a good overview of the functions available in most newsreaders.

If you are using an online service, you may be using that service's system to work in the newsgroups. The most recent MSN software uses the Outlook Express newsreader or the Microsoft Internet News newsreader (an earlier version of Outlook Express). In CompuServe, use **GO INTERNET**; in AOL, use the keyword **Internet** to find more information about starting the newsreaders.

A Quick Word On Setup

I want to quickly discuss setup and subscribing. If you are with an online service, there's nothing to set up; it's all done for you. If you are with a service provider, though, you may have to set up the newsreader.

First, your newsreader must know the location of your news server. Ask your service provider for the hostname of the news server (the news server is the system the service provider uses to send messages to your newsreader); the hostname may be **news.big. internet.service.com**, or **news.zip.com**, or something like that. Then check your newsreader's documentation to see where to enter this information.

The other thing you may have to do is subscribe to the newsgroups you are interested in. I've already said that your service provider has to subscribe to newsgroups; that means that the provider makes sure the newsgroups are available to its members. However, the term *subscribe* has another meaning in relation to newsgroups. You may also have to subscribe to the newsgroup to make sure that the newsgroup you want to read is available to your newsreader. Not all newsreaders make you subscribe in order to read a newsgroup. For instance, you don't have to worry about subscribing if you use MSN's newsreader or if you are reading newsgroup messages through a newsgroup 'gateway' Web site such as Super-news (**http://www.supernews.com/**). Many newsreaders, however, require that you fetch a list of newsgroups from your service provider (the newsreader has a command you'll use to fetch and display the list and may even offer to do so the first time you start the program) and then subscribe to the ones you want to read. Subscribing is no big deal; you simply choose which ones you want. Until you subscribe, though, you can't see the messages.

Pick Your Own Newsreader

Some of the online services have rather weak newsreaders. But if your online service allows you to get to the Internet through a TCP/IP connection, you may be able to install another newsreader, such as Gravity, Free Agent, NewsWatcher, or Nuntius. However, to do so, you may have to connect to one of the public news servers that I mentioned in Chapter 9, 'Newsgroups: The Source Of All Wisdom'. The online services often have special news servers that are not designed to be accessed by TCP/IP; they're designed to be accessed with the service's own program. Check with your service's technical support staff.

Starting And Subscribing

The following figure shows the Outlook Express newsreader, which comes with all Windows versions since 98. The first time you use the program a dialog box opens, asking for all the configuration information. Then the Newsgroups dialog box opens (shown in the following figure) and begins grabbing a list of newsgroups from your service provider's news server.

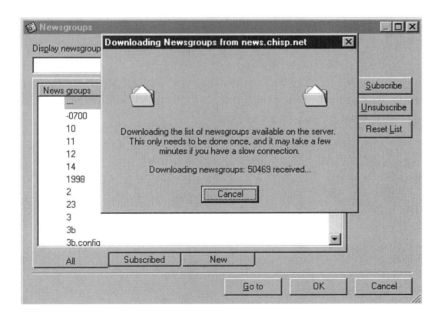

The Outlook Express Newsgroup dialog box, where you can view a list of all the newsgroups your service provider has subscribed to; at the moment, the system is downloading a list of newsgroups from the server.

Once you have the list, you can decide which newsgroups you want to read. (Remember that this is a list of only the newsgroups that your service provider has subscribed to, not a full list of all the groups distributed by Usenet. For information about finding newsgroups not included in this list, see Chapter 9.) In Outlook Express, you click the group you want to read, and then click the **Subscribe** button, or simply double-click the name. (You can also use the text box at the top; type a name or part of a name to move to that part of the list.)

Where Are The Alt. Groups?

If you are with an online service, you may find that you can't initially read the alt. groups and perhaps some others as well. Your online service may regard these groups as a trifle 'naughty', in which case you have to apply for permission to read them. Go to your online service's Internet forum or BBS to find out how to activate these groups, or refer to the parental control information.

When you close the dialog box, you'll see a list of the newsgroups you subscribed to in a pane on the left side of the window. You can subscribe to more later by clicking the **Newsgroup** button or by selecting **Tools, Newsgroups** to see the dialog box again (to refresh the list, click the **Reset List** button). You can also open the dialog box, click the **New** tab, and then click the **Reset List** button to see a list of newsgroups that your service provider has added since you last collected the list.

Click one of the newsgroups you've subscribed to in the left pane, and the top pane will display a list of messages from that newsgroup (see the next figure). It may take a little while for these messages to transfer, especially if your service provider is using the dynamic sucking feed I mentioned in the last chapter. (If so, you'll see a message header that says **Group download in progress**.)

Many newsgroups are empty – they rarely, if ever, contain messages – so you won't always see message 'headers' in the top pane. Most newsreaders will have some kind of indicator showing how many messages are in the newsgroup (see the numbers in parentheses in the following illustration). If there are only a few messages, it's quite possible that all the messages are promotional messages completely unrelated to the subject of the newsgroup, perhaps advertising get-rich-quick schemes or pornographic Web sites.

Messages in the selected newsgroup

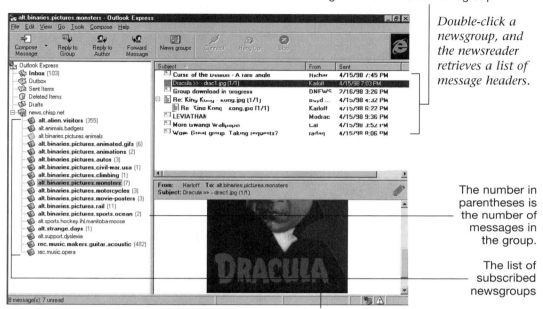

Double-click a newsgroup, and the newsreader retrieves a list of message headers.

The number in parentheses is the number of messages in the group.

The list of subscribed newsgroups

The selected message is displayed here.

Not All The Messages

You may not see all the messages listed at once. Some newsreaders enable you to specify a number to retrieve each time (in the program's Options or Preferences dialog box). So if the newsgroup is very busy, only a portion of the messages will be listed; you'll have to use another command to retrieve the rest.

Taking A Look

Notice that some messages are indented below others, and that there's a small – icon next to the messages. This icon indicates that the message is part of a *thread* (known as a *conversation* in some newsreaders). So what's a thread? Suppose you post a message to a newsgroup that isn't a response to anyone; it's just a new message. Then, a little later, someone else reads your message and replies. That message, because it's a reply, is part of the thread you began. Later, someone else sends a response to *that* message, and it becomes part of the thread. (Note, however, that there's generally a long lag time – a day or more – between the time someone

145

sends a message to a newsgroup and the time that message turns up in everyone's newsreader.)

If you click the little – icon, the thread closes up, and you see only the message at the beginning of the thread. The icon changes to a + icon. Click the + icon to open up the thread again. (A message that has a – icon but does not have messages indented below it is not part of a message thread.) Most newsreaders (but not all) support threading and many other functions in a very similar manner.

To read a message, click the message's header (some newsreaders make you double-click). The newsreader retrieves the message and places it in the bottom pane of the window, as you can see in the figure at the bottom of this page.

The Messages Are Gone!

The first time you open a newsgroup, all the messages from that newsgroup currently held by your service provider are available to you. How long a message stays in the newsgroup depends on how busy that newsgroup is and how much hard disk space the service provider allows for the newsgroup messages. Eventually all messages disappear. You don't necessarily see all the newsgroup's messages the next time you use your newsreader, though. When you return to the newsgroup later, you may see all the messages *except* those marked as read.

This message is from the alt.alien.visitors newsgroup.

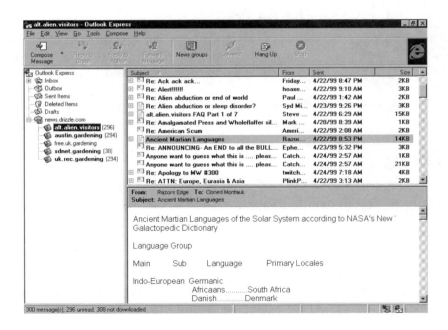

Why didn't I just say 'all the messages except those that you have read?'. Well, the newsreader has no way of knowing which messages you've read – it can't see what you are doing. Instead, it has a way of marking messages that it thinks you've read, and it generally provides you with a way to mark messages as read, even if you haven't read them (in effect, providing a way for you to tell the newsreader that you don't want to see the messages).

Marking Your Messages

Most newsreaders mark a message as read when you open the message. Some newsreaders enable you to quickly scan messages without marking them as read. Outlook Express, for instance, has a setting in the Options dialog box labelled **Message is read after being previewed for x second(s)**. So you can set this option to, say, 10 seconds, allowing you to read a little bit of a message and move on, leaving the message marked as unread.

In addition, newsreaders often allow you to mark the messages as read even if you have not read them. This capability might come in handy to tell the newsreader that you don't want to see certain messages when you come back to the newsgroup in a later session. Suppose you get a couple of messages into a conversation and realize that it's pure rubbish (you'll find a lot of messages that have virtually no usefulness to anyone!). Mark the entire thread as read, and you won't see the rest of the messages the next time you open the newsgroup window. Or maybe the messages are worthwhile (to someone), but you quickly read all the messages' Subject lines and find that nothing interests you. Mark them all as read so you see only new messages the next time.

You can generally mark messages as read in several other ways as well. Here's what you can do in Outlook Express, for instance:

➤ Click a message header and select **Edit**, **Mark As Read**.

➤ Click a message header and select **Edit**, **Mark Conversation As Read** to mark the entire thread as read. (I recently noticed that Outlook Express uses the term 'conversation' in place of 'thread'.)

➤ Right-click a message header and select **Mark As Read** or **Mark Conversation As Read** from the shortcut menu.

➤ Choose **Edit**, **Mark All Read** to mark all the current newsgroup's messages as read.

Articles

In keeping with the 'news' metaphor, newsgroup messages are often known as *articles*.

Different newsreaders handle read messages differently. Some newsreaders remove them from the list, so you only see the unread messages listed. Gravity, an excellent and popular Windows newsreader (**http://www.microplanet.com/**), does this. If you don't want the newsreader to remove the read messages, you can change the view by choosing **Newsgroup**, **Filter Display**, **Read Articles** to see just messages you've read, or **Newsgroup**, **Filter Display**, **All Articles** (or by selecting these from the drop-down list box in the toolbar) to make Gravity show the read message headers in grey text. Other newsreaders might use special icons or grey text to indicate messages that you've read.

Outlook Express, on the other hand, displays all the messages, read and unread. But you can select **View**, **Current View**, and then choose an option. Choosing **Unread Messages**, for instance, would make Outlook work like Gravity; it would display only the messages you haven't yet read.

I Want The Message Back!

If you need to bring a message back, your newsreader probably has some kind of command that enables you to do so. For example, Gravity has the **Newsgroup**, **Filter Display**, **Read Articles** command that I just mentioned. But if your service provider no longer holds the message you want to see – that is, if the message has been removed from the service provider's hard disk to make more space for new messages – you're out of luck. So if you think there's a chance you may want a message later, save it using the **File**, **Save As** or equivalent command.

Many newsreaders even have commands for marking messages as unread. Perhaps you've read a message, but want to make sure it appears the next time you open the newsgroup. You can mark it as unread so that it will appear in the list the next time you open the newsgroup. In Outlook Express, for instance, select **Edit, Mark As Unread**.

Moving Among The Messages

You'll find a variety of ways to move around in your messages. As you already know, you can double-click the ones you want to view (some newsreaders use a single click). In addition, you'll find commands for moving to the next or previous message, the next or previous thread, and, perhaps, the next or previous unread message or thread. In Outlook Express, these commands are on the View, Next menu.

Many newsreaders also provide a way for you to search for a particular message. Outlook Express has several Find commands in the Edit menu, which allow you to search for a message by the contents of the From line or the Subject line. Outlook Express also enables you to search through the text of the currently selected message. Some other newsreaders have much more sophisticated utilities. In Gravity, for example, select **Search**, **Search** to access a dialog box in which you can search for text in the From or Subject lines or even within the text of the messages; you can also specify whether to search the selected newsgroup or all the subscribed newsgroups. You can even tell Gravity whether to search only those messages already transferred to the newsreader or to search messages still held by the news server.

Saving And Printing

If you run across a message that you think might be useful later, you can save it or print it. Simply marking it as unread isn't good enough because newsgroups eventually drop all messages. So sooner or later it won't be available.

Most newsreaders have a File, Save As (or File, Save) command or toolbar button. Most also have a File, Print command or button. Of course, you can always highlight the text, copy it to the Clipboard, and then paste it into another application, such as a word processor or email program.

Your Turn: Sending And Responding

There are several ways to send messages or respond to messages. For example, you can use any of the techniques listed here in Outlook Express. (Although Outlook Express is typical, and many newsreaders use these same command names, some newsreaders may use different names.)

➤ You can send a message that isn't a response (that is, you can start a new thread). In Outlook Express, for instance, select **Message, New Message** or click the **New Post** toolbar button.

➤ You can reply to someone else's message (the reply is often known as a follow-up). Choose **Message, Reply to Group** or click the **Reply Group** button.

➤ You can reply to someone privately via email (that is, send a message that *doesn't* appear in the newsgroup). Select **Message, Reply to Sender** or click the **Reply** button.

➤ Reply to both the author and the newsgroup at the same time. Select **Message, Reply to All**.

➤ You can send a copy of the message to someone else. Select **Message, Forward** or click the **Forward** button.

Sending messages to a newsgroup – or via email in response to a message – is much the same as working with an email window. You type the message and then click some kind of **Send** or **Post** button.

What's This Gibberish? ROT13

Now and again, especially in the more contentious newsgroups, you'll run into messages that seem to be gibberish. Everything's messed up, and each word seems to be a jumbled mix of characters, almost as if the message is encrypted. It is.

What you are seeing is *ROT13*, a very simple substitution cypher (one in which a character is substituted for another). ROT13 means 'rotated 13'. In other words, each character in the alphabet is replaced by the character 13 places further along. Instead of A you see N, instead of B you see O, instead of C you see P, and so on. Got it? So to read the message, all you need to do is substitute the correct characters. Easy. (Or *Rnfl*, as I should say.)

For those of you in a hurry, there is an easier way. Most newsreaders have a command that quickly does the ROT13 for you. For instance, in Outlook Express,

*An example of a
ROT13 message.*

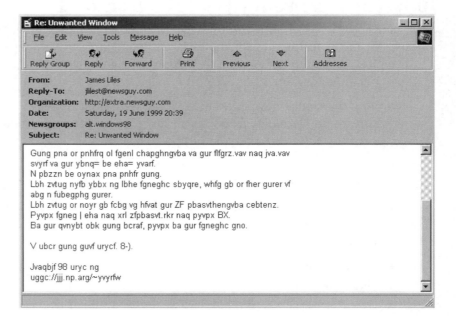

you can select **Message**, **Unscramble (ROT13),** and, like magic, the message changes into real words. If you don't run across ROT13 messages and want to see what ROT13 looks like, use the command to take a normal message and convert it to a ROT13 message (which is what I did for the figure above). How do you create one of these messages to send to a newsgroup? You'll often find a ROT13 command in the window in which you create a message. For instance, in Gravity's message composition window, there's an **Options, Scramble (ROT13)** command. For some reason, Outlook Express, although it can unscramble messages, doesn't let you use ROT13 when sending messages.

You might be wondering why a person would encode a message with a system that is so ridiculously easy to break. People don't ROT13 (if you'll excuse my use of the term as a verb) their messages as a security measure that's intended to make them unreadable to anyone who doesn't have the secret key. After all, anyone with a decent newsreader has the key. No, using ROT13 is a way of saying 'if you read this message, you may be offended; so if you are easily offended, *don't read it!*' ROT13 messages are often crude, lewd, or just plain rude. When a message is encoded with ROT13, the reader can decide whether he wants to risk being offended.

Pictures (And Sounds) From Words

The newsgroups contain simple text messages. You can't place a character into a message that is not in the standard text character set. So if you want to send a computer file in a newsgroup message – maybe you want to send a picture, a sound, or a word processing document – you must convert it to text. Some of the newer newsreaders help you do this, either by automating the process of attaching MIME-formatted files to your messages or by uuencoding files and inserting them into your messages. Some newsreaders will even convert such files on-the-fly and display pictures inside the message when they read the newsgroup messages; others will automatically convert the file to its original format.

If you were using Outlook Express, for example, you could follow these steps to send a file:

1. Open the message composition window using the **Message, New Message** command or the **Message, Reply to Group** command.

2. Choose **Insert, File Attachment** or click the **Attach** toolbar button (the little paperclip). You'll see a typical File Open dialog box, from which you can choose the file you want to send.

3. Select the file and click **OK**. The name of the attached file appears in a new **Attach** field at the top of the message window (see the following figure).

4. Send the message (click the **Send** button or select **File, Send Message**). The name of the file appears in the message header when you view the messages in that particular newsgroup.

What method was used to send this message? MIME or uuencode? Outlook Express doesn't make this clear. Some newsreaders let you quickly specify which method to use; Gravity, for instance, enables you to select **uuencode** or **MIME** from a drop-down list box at the top of the window. In Outlook Express, the method of transmission is hidden away. By default, the program uses uuencode when sending to newsgroups (that's the standard method of sending files to newsgroups). If you want to use MIME, you have to go back to the main Outlook Express window, choose **Tools, Options**, click the **Send** tab, click the **Plain Text Settings** button next to **News Sending Format: Plain Text**, and click the **MIME** option button.

When a message with an attached file is posted to a newsgroup, what do participants of that newsgroup see? If the attached file is an image, as many are, some newsreaders will display the picture inside the message. Others may display the message text, something like that shown in the following figure.

Most newsreaders let you send uuencoded or MIME files to a newsgroup.

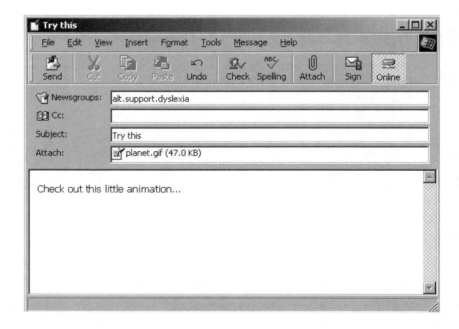

No Built-In Converter

If you are using a newsreader that doesn't have a built-in conversion system, you can save the message on your hard disk and then use a conversion program such as Wincode (a Windows program that converts uuencode), munpack (a DOS program that converts MIME), or Yet Another Base64 Decoder (a Macintosh program that converts both uuencode and MIME).

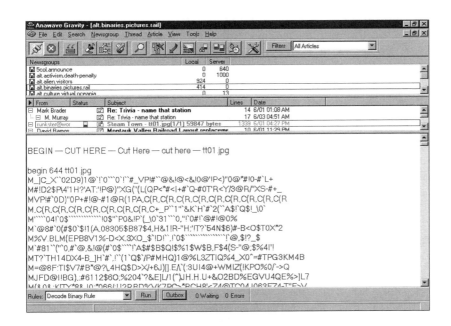

This message contains an attached file. The jumbled text is the file, converted to text. The text must be converted back before you can view the file.

Even if your newsreader doesn't initially display the image within the message, it may be able to convert the image file. In particular, newsreaders can often convert .GIF, .JPEG, and perhaps .BMP files to their original formats. In the case of Gravity, for instance, you can click the **View Image** button or select **Article, View**, and Gravity converts the file for you and then places it in a viewer window (as you can see in the following figure). Outlook Express will display the image by default.

A few newsreaders can even decode several messages together. If someone posts a large picture split into several pieces, for instance (as people often do), the newsreader may automatically retrieve all the pieces and paste them together.

The Fancy Stuff

Some newsreaders have useful extra features. For example, the newsreader may be able to automatically 'flag' messages if the header contains a particular word. Or you may be able to set up the newsreader to automatically remove a message if the header contains a particular word. Outlook Express has a filtering system that you can use to automatically throw away some messages, depending on who sent the message or what the subject is, if it's older than a specified time, or if it's longer than a specified length (choose **Tools**, **Newsgroup Filters**). Some other newsreaders have much better filtering systems. Gravity, for instance, can throw the message away, display a special alert message, or save the message in a text file according to what appears in the header or body text.

Many newsreaders display links in the newsgroup messages. You can click email addresses or Web URLs that appear in messages to automatically open the mail window or your browser. Outlook Express can set up a little slide show, displaying one image after another in messages that contain multiple images.

In this case, the message window displays an image that's been inserted into a message.

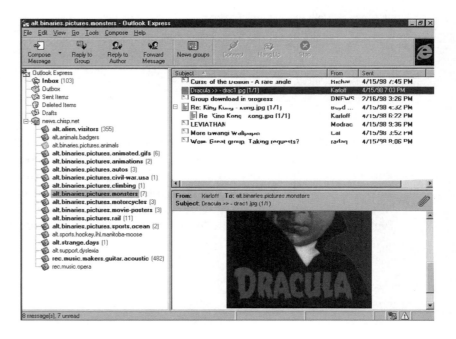

Newsreaders can do a lot of different things, so you may want to experiment to find out what's available in the newsreader you have; if you spend a lot of time in newsgroups, you may want to go searching for the most capable newsreader. (Check out Appendix C for information about finding software.)

A Word Of Warning

Newsgroups can be addictive. You can find messages about anything that interests you, angers you, or turns you on. If you are not careful, you can spend half your life in the newsgroups. You sit down in the morning to check your favourite newsgroups, and the next thing you know you haven't bathed, eaten, or picked up the kids from school.

Hang around the newsgroups, and you'll find people who are obviously spending a significant amount of time writing messages. These people are usually independently wealthy (that is, they work for large corporations who don't mind paying for them to talk politics over the Internet or who don't know that they are paying them to do so). If you have a job, a family, and a life, be careful!

Mailing Lists – More Discussions

You might feel that a choice of several tens of thousands of discussion groups is about enough and I wouldn't disagree. But there's a slightly different system that can add another few thousand to that total, **mailing lists**.

A mailing list is like a newsgroup that arrives by email: once you've subscribed, all the messages from the group are delivered automatically to your mailbox for you to down-load when you like. In most cases, you can opt to receive a *digest* version which gives a single, large daily or weekly message rather than a constant stream of separate ones. To subscribe to a mailing list takes a single email message, as does unsubscribing.

Mailbox Mayhem

Be very wary of mailing lists – if you like the general idea, start by subscribing to one and see how things go. Popular lists generate a huge amount of email and it's not a good idea to be subscribed to half-a-dozen of those while you're still finding your feet!

Mailing lists come in many shapes and forms, but the two primary systems are **LISTSERV** and **Majordomo**. Like most mailing list systems, these are automatic, run by a program on a computer which reads the email you send to subscribe and adds your email address to its list. For automatic lists, your email message must be constructed in a certain way.

LISTSERV Mailing Lists

LISTSERV is one of the major automated systems and requests for information and subscriptions are made by sending an email message to one of the computers on the LISTSERV system. All LISTSERV computers are linked together, so it doesn't matter which one you use for requests; if you don't know of any other, send your messages to **listserv@listserv.net**.

The request message you send needs nothing in the **Subject** line, although if your email program insists you enter something, just type a dot. The message itself must contain nothing but the request (so make sure you turn off your email program's Signature option!).

To do this message	Type this request in your email
Subscribe to a list	**SUB *listname your name***
Unsubscribe to a list	**SIGNOFF *listname***
Get information about a list	**INFO *listname***
Receive the digest version of a list	**SET *listname* DIGEST**
Get a list of request commands	**HELP**
Find all the lists on this system	**LIST**
Find all LISTSERV lists in existence	**LISTS GLOBAL**

Be a bit wary of that last option – the message you'll receive containing a list of all the mailing lists available will be about half a megabyte in size! Most LISTSERV lists can also be read using your newsreader – you'll find them in the **bit.listserv** hierarchy.

To send messages to a list you've subscribed to, you'll need to know which computer runs that list (the **sitename**, which should be in the details that are returned to you). You can then take part in the discussion by sending messages to ***listname@sitename***. Make sure you don't get these two addresses confused. The first address I gave above is only for making requests and queries about lists and this second address is only for messages that you intend every subscriber to read. If you send your requests to the second address, a copy will be sent to everyone on the list, but the request itself won't be processed!

More Mailbox Mayhem

If you're going on holiday for a while and won't be able to download your email, consider unsubscribing from your mailing lists while you're away. Otherwise you might be faced with a barrage of email when you next log on!

Majordomo Mailing Lists

The Majordomo system is similar to LISTSERV, but each computer on the system is independent so you need to know which computer handles the list you're interested in (the **sitename**). Armed with this information, send an email message to **majordomo@ *sitename*** containing one of the following requests:

To do this	Type this request in your email message
Subscribe to a list	**subscribe *listname***
Unsubscribe to a list	**unsubscribe *listname***
Find all lists on that computer	**list**

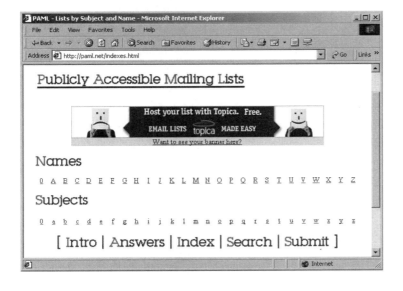

Pick one of hundreds of subjects to choose from thousands of lists.

There May Be An Easier Way ...

I mentioned a moment ago that you can get a flavour of some of the LISTSERV lists before subscribing by using your newsreader. Many mailing lists also have their own page on the World Wide Web giving information about the list and a simple form you can fill in online if you want to subscribe. To find lists of mailing lists on the Web, use your browser to go to Topica at **http://www.topica.com** (where you can search for a mailing list by typing in a keyword) or **http://paml.net**, shown in the screenshot on page 157.

Using The Web Forums

Web forums are discussion groups associated with a particular Web site. They're often technical support forums, forums set up by a company to help provide information to their customers, but you might run into forums about many subjects and for many purposes.

Finding Web forums is a little difficult; they're the sort of thing you run into, rather than go looking for. Probably the best way to find them is at a search engine. I haven't yet been able to track down a good Web forum directory.

To use a Web forum, click the appropriate links at a Web site. You'll use forums to read messages and to respond to them; you can see an example in the figure below.

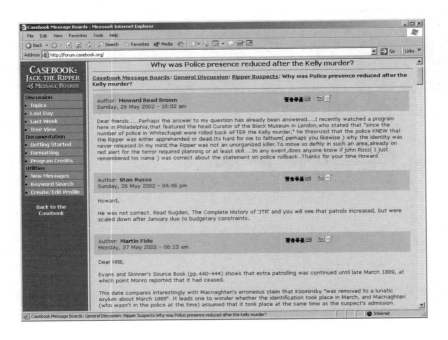

A Jack-the-Ripper discussion, an example of a Web-based discussion forum.

The Least You Need To Know

➤ Start your newsreader and then download a list of newsgroups from the server. You may also have to subscribe to the groups you want to read; each newsreader does this a little differently.

➤ A good newsreader lets you view a 'thread' or 'conversation', which shows how messages relate to each other.

➤ ROT13 is a special encoding system that stops people from accidentally stumbling across offensive messages. Many newsreaders have a ROT13 command that converts the message to normal text.

➤ You can include binary files in messages using uuencode or MIME.

➤ Many newsreaders these days can decode uuencode and MIME attachments. If your newsreader doesn't, you'll need a utility such as Wincode or munpack (for Windows and DOS) or Yet Another Base64 Decoder (for the Macintosh). Or you can get another newsreader!

➤ A mailing list is a discussion group in which messages are exchanged through the email system. Mailing lists may be administered manually, or run by a program such as LISTSERV or Majordomo.

➤ Subscribe to a LISTSERV group by including the command **subscribe *listname* *your name*** in the body of an email message and sending it to **listserv@ *sitename*** (if you know the sitename) or **listserv@listserv.net** (if you don't).

➤ To subscribe to a Majordomo list, send a message saying **subscribe *listname*** to the Majordomo address (such as **majordomo@bighost**).

➤ Thousands of Web forums are available, but they're hard to track down. Search for **'web forum'** at AltaVista.

159

Chapter 11

Downloading Files With FTP

In This Chapter

➤ What is FTP?

➤ FTP can be difficult, but it can be easy

➤ Ftping with your Web browser

➤ Clues that will help you find files

➤ Ftping with true FTP programs

➤ Dealing with compressed files

➤ Protecting yourself from viruses

The Internet is a vast computer library. Virtually any type of computer file imaginable is available somewhere on the Internet. You'll find freeware (programs you can use for free) and shareware (programs you must pay a small fee to use) in almost all types of files: music, pictures, video, 3D images, and many types of hypertext documents. You'll probably find every file type you can possibly name on the Internet.

Where are these files? You looked at the World Wide Web in Chapters 4–8 and you know that you can download plenty of files from the Web. But there's another system that predates the Web: FTP.

To give you a little bit of history, FTP is one of those quaint old UNIX-geek terms. It stands for *file transfer protocol* and it's an old UNIX system for transferring files from one computer to another. In fact, FTP is really the original core of the Internet: the whole purpose of the Internet was to allow the transfer of computer files between research institutions. Even email came later; it was reportedly slipped into the Internet by geeks who didn't keep the bureaucrats fully apprised. (The geeks feared that the managers would think email would be misused; from what I've seen of electronic communications, the managers would have been right!)

Can't Get In?

Like Web sites, FTP sites can only cope with a limited number of users at once, and for some FTP sites that number can be quite small. If you can't connect to a particular site, it may be that the site is currently too busy. Some sites don't allow anonymous logins (see page 163) during their local business hours, so try again later. Of course, you might just have typed the address wrongly – always a good place to start!

There are FTP sites all over the Internet, containing literally millions of computer files. And although some of these sites are private, many are open to the public. With FTP, it's very possible that you might discover a fascinating file on a computer in Austria (or Australia, or Alabama, or anywhere). You might have checked it out because someone told you where it was, or because you saw it mentioned in an Internet directory of some kind, or because you saw a message in a newsgroup about it. The file itself could be a public domain or shareware program, a document containing information you want for some research you're working on, a picture, a book you want to read, or just about anything else.

Suppose then that you're searching for one of the files described above. You might be told to 'ftp to such and such a computer to find this file'. That simply means 'use the FTP system to grab the file'. Of course, you don't know what that means either, so you find yourself asking, 'how do I get the file from that computer to my computer?'.

In some cases, you may have specific permission to get onto another computer and grab files. A researcher, for instance, may have been given permission to access files on a computer owned by an organization involved in the same sort of research – another university or government department, perhaps. (I have private FTP directories on various publishers' FTP sites, so I can upload Web pages, or chapters for a book, or whatever.) To get into a directory that requires special permission, you need to use a login name and a password.

In other cases, though, you'll just be rooting around on other systems without specific permission. Some systems are open to the public; anyone can get on and grab files that the system administrator has decided should be publicly accessible. This type of access is known as *anonymous ftp*

Tracking Down A File With Archie

What if you know the file you want, but you have no idea where to look for it? A quick way to track down a file is using Archie. You'll learn about Archie later in this chapter.

because you don't need a unique login name to get onto the computer; you simply log in as *anonymous* and you normally enter your email address for the password. If you are working at the UNIX command line, as many unfortunate people still do, you have to type this information. However, the rest of you are using a program that will enter this information for you.

Different Flavours Of FTP

FTP was originally a command-line program in which you had to type commands at a prompt and press the Enter key. Information would then scroll past on your screen, perhaps too fast for you to read (unless you knew the secret command to make it slow down or stop). You'd have to read this information and then type another command. Although UNIX geeks got some sort of strange masochistic pleasure out of that sort of thing, real people found early FTP to be a painful experience – and most people avoided it.

However, for about seven or eight years now there have been graphical FTP programs, Windows and Macintosh programs using familiar point-and-click (and even drag-and-drop) tools. Most of these graphical FTP programs enable you to see lists of files and use your mouse to carry out the operations. Using FTP with these systems was a pleasure; all of a sudden FTP became easy.

Of the many graphical FTP programs available, the best I've seen are CuteFTP and WS_FTP (Windows shareware programs) and Fetch and NetFinder (Macintosh shareware programs); see Appendix C, 'All The Software You'll Ever Need' for information about finding all these programs. Another FTP program is Anarchie, a shareware program that melds FTP with Archie (which I'll mention later). But many others are available, particularly for Windows.

163

Finally, FTP has been incorporated into Web browsers. You can now go to an FTP site using your Web browser – and usually without a special FTP program. Because the FTP site appears as a document with links in it, you can click a link to view the contents of a directory, to read a text file, or to transfer a computer file to your computer.

We'll look first at running FTP sessions with a Web browser – for a couple of reasons. First, it's a very easy way to work with FTP. Second, you probably already have a Web browser. However, there are some very good reasons for getting hold of a true FTP program; I'll discuss this issue towards the end of this chapter.

Hitting The FTP Trail

To work through an FTP example, go to **ftp://sunsite.org.uk/**. This is one of the best and fastest FTP archives in the UK. (If you prefer to visit another FTP site, you can follow along and do so; the principles are the same.) You can find a list of FTP sites to play with by visiting **http://tile.net/ftp/** and choosing either **Country** or **Site Name**.

What's In A Name?

Take a minute to analyse a site name. First there's the **ftp://** part. This simply tells your browser that you want to go to an FTP site. Then there's the FTP site name (or host name): **sunsite.org.uk**. It identifies the computer that contains the files you are after. That might be followed by a directory name. I haven't given you a directory name in this example, but I could have told you to go to **sunsite.org.uk/pub/computing**. The **/pub/computing** bit tells the browser which directory it must change to in order to find the files you want.

To start, open your Web browser. Click inside the **Address** text box, type **ftp://sunsite.org.uk** (or **ftp://** and the address of another site you want to visit) and press Enter. Actually, in most browsers these days, you can omit the ftp:// as long as the site name begins with ftp. For example, if you were visiting another useful UK site, ftp.demon.co.uk, instead of typing out **ftp://ftp.demon.co.uk**, you could get away with typing only **ftp.demon.co.uk**.

In a few moments, with luck, you'll see something like the screen shown in the following figure. Without luck, you'll probably get a message telling you that you cannot connect to the FTP site. If that happens, check to see if you typed the name correctly. If you did, you'll have to wait and try again later; the site may be closed, or it may be very busy.

Notice, by the way, that you didn't have to enter the anonymous login name or your email address as a password. The browser handled all of that for you.

There's another way to get to an FTP site. Many Web authors create links from their Web pages to an FTP site. Click the link and you'll go to that site. The links at Tile Net (mentioned on the previous page) work like this.

Name Or Number

The FTP site or host name could even be a name (leo.nmc.edu) or a number (192.88.242.239).

If you've used command-line FTP, you'll love working in a browser.

* Please note that the fttp://sunsite.org. uk site is due to be upgraded. The images reproduced here do not represent the upgraded site.

Files And Links – What Is All This?

What can you see at the FTP site? Each file and directory is shown as a link. Depending on the browser you are using, you might see information about the file or directory (refer to the previous figure). You might see a description of each item – file or directory, for instance – and the file size, so you'll know how big a file is before you transfer it. You'll often see the file date and little icons that represent the directory or file type. In the previous figure, you can see that there are both files and directories.

Private FTP Sites

If you want to enter a private FTP site, you will have to enter a login ID and a password. You can often enter the FTP site information in the format ftp://*username:password@hostname/ directory/*. For example, if you enter **ftp://joeb:1234tyu@ftp. microsoft.com/t1/ home/joeb**, your browser connects to the ftp.microsoft.com FTP site and displays the /t1/home/joeb directory; it uses the username **joeb** and the password **1234tyu** to gain access. However, in some browsers, using that method causes the browser to save your password in a drop-down list box associated with the Location text box. Therefore, if you want to be really safe, use the format ftp://*username@hostname/directory*. When the browser connects to the FTP site, it opens a dialog box into which you can type your password.

Click a link to make the browser display another Web document that shows the contents of that directory. In most browsers, you'll also find a link back to the parent directory: in Netscape you'll see an 'Up to a higher level directory' link, for instance. The following figure shows what you will find if you click the **pub** link at the **sunsite.org.uk** site. Why pub? Because that's commonly used to hold publicly available files. This time, you can see that there's a file in this directory, along with more subdirectories.

What happens when you click a link to a file? The same thing that would happen if you did so from a true Web document. If the browser can display or play the file type, it will. If it can't, it will try to send it to the associated application. If there is no associated application, it will ask you what to do with it, allowing you to save it on the hard disk. This all works in the same way as it does when you are at a Web site – the browser looks at the file type and acts accordingly. (See Chapters 5 and 7 for more information.)

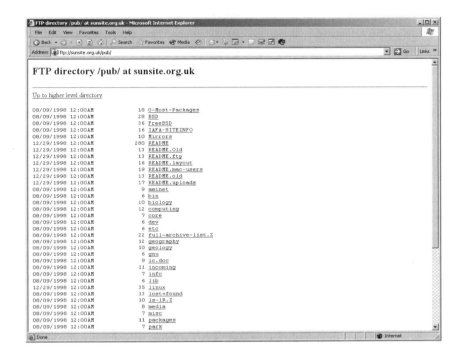

The contents of the pub directory at the SunSite FTP site.

Finding That Pot o' Gold

Now that you're in, you want to find the file that you know lies somewhere on this system. Where do you start? Well, finding files at an FTP site is often a little difficult. There are no conventions for how such sites should be set up, so you often have to dig through directories that look like they might contain what you want, until you find what you want.

Remember, though, that your Web browser can display text files. When you first get to an FTP site, look for files called INDEX, README, DIRECTORY and so on. These often contain information that will help you find what you need. The more organized sites even contain text files with full indexes of their contents, or at least lists of the directories and the types of files you'll find. Click one of these files to transfer the document to your Web browser, read the file and then click the **Back** button to return to the directory.

You'll often find that directories have names that describe their contents: **slip** will probably contain SLIP software, **mac** will have Macintosh software, **xwindow** will have X Window software, **windows** will have Microsoft Windows software, **gif** will contain GIF-format graphics and so on. Directory names often become more specific as you delve deeper. So if you're looking for an email program, for example, you might click on **pub**, then on **computing**, then **internet** and then **email**.

It Looks A Little Strange

You'll often see full FTP site and path information, which takes you straight to the directory you want (such as **ftp.usma.edu/msdos/**). If you're used to working in DOS and Windows, FTP site directory names may seem strange for two reasons. First, you'll see a forward slash (/) instead of a backslash (\), separating the directories in the path. In the DOS world, you use a backslash (\), but in the UNIX world, you use the forward slash character (/) instead – and most Internet host computers still run on UNIX. Second, the directory names are often long. In DOS, you can't have directories with more than 12 characters in the name (including a full stop and an extension). In Windows 95 and later, however, you can. This operating system *and* UNIX computers allow long file and directory names.

Getting The File

When you find the file you want, simply click it and save it in the same way you would save a file from a Web document (see Chapter 5). The following figure shows a file being saved from the SunSite FTP site.

Many files on FTP sites are *compressed*. That is, a special program has been used to 'squeeze' the information into a smaller area. You can't use a file in its compressed state, but if you store it and transmit it in that state, you'll save disk space and transmission time. You can read more about these compressed formats in Chapter 14.

In this case, we are transferring a .zip file that contains several other files. A program such as WinZip can extract the files from within this .zip file (a common format for transferring files across the Internet).

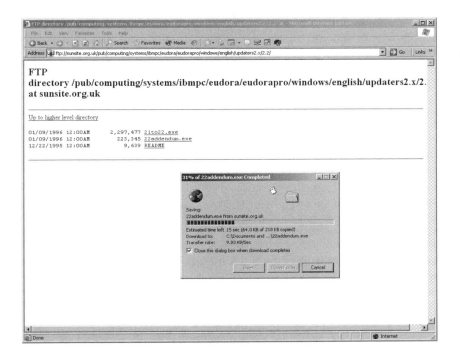

You can save files from FTP sites by just clicking on the filename.

Same Name, Different Extension

While digging around in an FTP site, you might notice that files often have the same name except for the last few characters; you might find THISDOC.TXT and THISDOC.ZIP, for instance. The first file is a simple ASCII text file, and the second is a .ZIP file, which (you'll probably notice) is much smaller than the first. If you know you can decompress the file once you have it, download the compressed version; doing so will save you transfer time.

It's The Real Thing: Using A Genuine FTP Program

There are some very good reasons for using a genuine FTP program instead of making do with your Web browser. First, you may run into FTP sites that don't work well through a Web browser. Some browsers simply don't like some FTP servers. Also, if you need to upload files to an FTP site, you may have problems; more recent browsers, such as Netscape Navigator 4 and Internet Explorer 5, allow you to do this, but many other browsers don't. (In Navigator, you can drag files from, for example, Windows Explorer and drop them onto the FTP site displayed in the browser window to automatically upload those files.)

169

Another reason for getting hold of a true FTP program – a reason that's little under-stood yet very important – is that some good FTP programs (such as CuteFTP) can resume interrupted transfers. For instance, suppose you've almost finished transferring the latest version of your favorite Web browser, which could easily be 15MB (add an MB to that figure for every month that passes), when the transfer stops. Why it stops is not important; perhaps your two-year-old rugrat just reached up and pressed that big red button on the front of your computer. Perhaps your service provider's system just died. Maybe lightning struck the power lines somewhere, and the power went out. Whatever the reason, if you're using a Web browser to transfer that file, you'll have to start all over again. If you were using a good FTP program, though, you could reconnect, go back to the FTP site, and begin the transfer again, but all that the program would need to do would be to transfer the missing part of the file, not all the stuff that had already transferred.

Now, I've heard it said that the Internet represents in some ways a giant step *backward* in technology. Well, okay, I've said it myself a few times. Resumed transfers is one of those cases in which the technology being used on the Internet is way behind what has been used *off* the Internet for years. (Online help is another case.) This technology is just finding its way to the Internet, but for the moment Web browsers cannot resume interrupted downloads. Some FTP programs, although not all, can. (Note that not all FTP servers can resume interrupted transfers, so this feature won't work all the time.)

If you transfer a lot of files across the Internet, in particular large files, you should use a true FTP program. Not only can you use the FTP program when you are working in an actual FTP site, you can also use it at other times. In many cases, when you think you're transferring from a Web site, the file is really coming from an FTP site. For example, the following illustration shows Shareware.com, a large shareware library. Notice that underneath the links to the download files you can see little labels that tell you where each file is stored – ftp.tas.gov.au, for instance. In this case, you can quickly see that the file is coming from an FTP site. However, most Web pages won't be this convenient. You can still figure out if the file is coming from an FTP site, though; point at the link, and in the status bar you'll see the URL of the file, in this case **ftp://ftp.tas.gov.au/pub/ simtelnet/win95/inet/u2n4332f.zip**.

You can quickly copy this information from the link using the browser's pop-up menu (in a Windows browser, right-click on the link and choose something like **Copy Link Location**; in a Mac browser, you'll probably be able to hold the mouse button down for a moment to open the pop-up menu). Then you can paste the information into your FTP program and use that program to download the file.

If that's not enough, here are two more reasons to use a real FTP program. It's often quicker and easier to connect to a site using an FTP program than a Web browser, and you can also set an FTP program to keep trying automatically every few minutes. So if the site's busy, the FTP program can keep trying until it gets through. You also may run into cases in which the browser FTP features are not enough. For those times, you need to get a real FTP program.

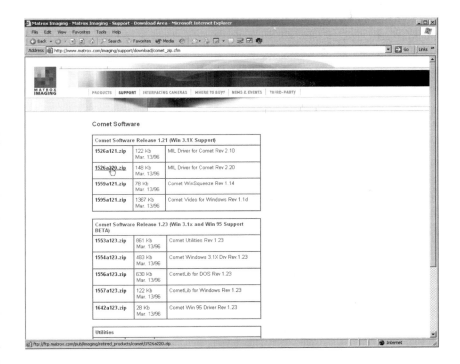

Yes, it's a Web page, but the files the page links to are stored at an FTP site, as you can see by pointing at a link and looking at the status bar.

Which And Where

There are lots of good FTP programs. If you use a Mac, try Fetch or Anarchie. For Windows, try WS_FTP or CuteFTP (my personal favorite). Many good Windows FTP programs are available as freeware or shareware on the Internet. See Appendix C for ideas on where to look for the software you want. (Remember, you need a program that will allow you to resume interrupted downloads, which means you'll probably have to pay the registration fee!)

When you get an FTP program, go through that old familiar routine: read the documentation carefully to make sure you understand how to use it. (FTP programs are generally fairly easy to deal with.) To give you an idea of how FTP programs work, let's take a quick look at CuteFTP. CuteFTP is very easy to use. If you've ever used UNIX FTP, you know that using it is like eating soup with a fork – not particularly satisfying. CuteFTP, on the other hand, is what FTP should be. You have all the commands at your fingertips, plus a library of FTP sites to select from. No more mistyping FTP hostnames!

171

Installing CuteFTP is simple. Just run the installation program. Then start CuteFTP by going through the Windows Start menu or double-clicking CuteFTP's Program Manager icon. CuteFTP has two ways to connect to an FTP site: you can add an entry to the Site Manager (press **F4** to open it, and then click **Add Site**) or use Quick Connect (**Ctrl+C**). Use the Site Manager for FTP sites you expect to visit again (they'll be stored in the Site Manager); use Quick Connect if you *don't* expect to be back.

Adding FTP site information to the Site Manager.

For instance, in the above figure you can see the Site Settings for New Site box, the one that opens when you add a site to Site Manager. Enter the following information:

1. Type a **Label for site** (anything that helps you remember what the site contains). This name appears in the Site Manager's list on the left side.

2. Enter the **FTP Host Address**.

3. If you are going to an 'anonymous' FTP site, leave the **FTP site User Name** and **FTP site Password** boxes empty, and leave the **Anonymous** option button selected at the bottom of the dialog box. You need to enter a **User Name** and **Password** only if you're going to a private FTP site.

4. You can generally ignore the **FTP site connection port** setting, unless you've been told by the site administrator to use something different.

5. Click the **OK** button to save the information.

6. In the Site Manager's list on the left, click the new entry, and then click **Connect** to begin the session.

When you click **Connect**, CuteFTP tries to connect to the FTP site. After it connects, you'll see the FTP site's directories listed on the right and the directories on your computer's hard disk listed on the left (see the following figure). You can move around in the directories by double-clicking folders or by right-clicking somewhere in the right pane and selecting **Change Directory** from the pop-up menu (that feature is handy, because if you know where you want to go it's a lot quicker to type it in than to go through each directory in the path to get there).

Files on your computer

A log window, showing you the funky FTP commands that you don't have to type

Directories on the remote computer

FTP transfers made easy: just drag the files you want onto the directory on your hard disk.

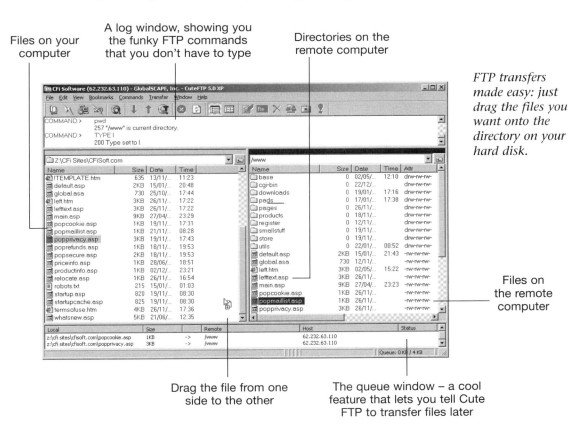

Files on the remote computer

Drag the file from one side to the other

The queue window – a cool feature that lets you tell Cute FTP to transfer files later

To read an index file, right-click the file and select **View**. To transfer a file to your system, just drag it from one side to the other (or if you prefer using menus, right-click and choose **Download**).

173

ASCII Versus Binary

Notice the little ab, 01, and a0 buttons on the right side of the toolbar? These buttons control whether the files are transferred as ASCII (the ab button), as Binary (the 01 button), or whether the program should decide the best way to transfer them (the a0 button). Make sure you select the correct one before transferring a file. Select **ASCII** for files you know to be ASCII text files; select **Binary** for anything else. Remember, word processing files are not ASCII; they're binary; they contain special codes that are used to define the character formatting. You can tell the program to automatically determine a file's transfer type using the **FTP, Settings, Text File Extensions** menu option.

It's Alive! Viruses And Other Nasties

If you haven't been in a cave for the past six or seven years, you've probably heard about computer viruses. A *virus* is a computer program that can reproduce itself and even convince unknowing users to help spread it. It spreads far and wide and can do incredible amounts of damage.

As is true of biological viruses, the effects of a virus on your system can range from nearly unnoticeable to fatal. A virus can do something as harmless as display a Christmas tree on your screen, or it can destroy everything on your hard disk. Viruses are real, but the threat is overstated. It's wise to take certain precautions, though, to ensure that you don't transfer viruses from FTP sites – or Web sites, for that matter – to your computer system. We'll be talking more about viruses in Chapter 17, 'Staying Safe On The Internet'.

Where Now?

Although there are thousands of FTP sites all over the world, FTP generally is either a service of last resort – people go to the Web first and only use FTP if they know exactly where to go to get what they are looking for – or a service that is linked to Web pages. Perhaps you've read in a newsgroup message or a magazine article that a particular file is available at a particular FTP site. You can go directly to the site to find it, but most people don't go looking for things at FTP sites. The Web sites are far more convenient starting points.

However, you might want to see the Tile.Net FTP Reference to Anonymous Sites (**http://tile.net/ftp**), or perhaps the Monster FTP Sites list at **http://hoohoo.ncsa.uiuc.edu/ftp/index.shtml**.

Searching FTP Sites

Let's say you're looking for a particular file. You know it's out there somewhere, and you're pretty sure you know the name of the file. You haven't been able to track it down on the Web, but you also know it's probably something that's been around for a few years and is almost certain to be lurking somewhere on an FTP site. How do you find it?

Start with AllTheWeb.com (**http://www.alltheweb.com**). Click the FTP Files link and you'll see the search boxes below change to allow searching of FTP sites rather than Web pages. Type the name of the file (or a part of the name) into the right-hand box. The drop-down list on the left gives you a number of choices over how your text should be interpreted; the default, 'multiple substrings search' is vague; if you typed the exact filename choose 'exact search'; if you typed only a part of the name choose 'substring match'; if you used wildcard characters to replace unknown characters in the name, choose 'wildcard search'.

You can also try using *Archie*. Archie is the original FTP search system (but I won't go into detail about it because AllTheWeb's search options are much easier). The name comes from the word *archive*, as in file archive. Remove the *v* and what do you have? Archie.

There are Archie programs for both Windows and the Macintosh (one Mac FTP program, Anarchie, has a built-in Archie utility). But there are also Archie 'gateways', Web sites that will help you to search Archie. There aren't many left, though; if you want to find one, I suggest you search for **archie** or **"archie gateway"** at a Web search engine such as Yahoo! or Google.

Download Utilities

There's another way to handle Internet downloads – using various download utilities. The two most popular are probably Netscape's SmartDownload (**http://home.netscape. com/download/smartdownload. html**), and a Windows program called GetRight (**http://www.getright.com**).

SmartDownload's main advantage is that it allows you to resume interrupted downloads, or even to interrupt them yourself and continue later. For instance, you might begin a download and then decide you want to find other information on the Web, *quickly*, without that download stealing your speed. Just stop the download, do what you need to do, and then complete the download later.

GetRight is a much more advanced download utility. In fact, I found it took quite some getting used to. (I've no doubt its many features are very useful, but I'm set in my ways and found it irritating to have GetRight continually taking over downloads for me.) GetRight sits quietly in the background waiting for you to begin downloading a file. When you click on a link in your browser to download a file it grabs the information and, depending on your choice, either downloads it right away or saves it for download later.

You can gather together as many files as you want and 'queue' them in GetRight. When you're ready to download files, you can leave GetRight to transfer them all while you go for lunch. It can even schedule transfers for any time you choose, dial your modem automatically, and disconnect when it's finished. You can also pause and resume downloads, and fetch the missing portion of a file if you got disconnected halfway through the download process.

GetRight has lots of neat features such as a file library that helps you categorize and find files you've downloaded, and a 'segmentation' option that can split files into pieces and fetch the pieces simultaneously, accelerating the download speed.

The Least You Need To Know

➤ FTP stands for file transfer protocol and refers to a system of file libraries.

➤ Anonymous FTP refers to a system that allows the public to transfer files.

➤ Start an FTP session in your Web browser using the format **ftp://hostname** in the Address text box (replacing *hostname* with the appropriate URL) and pressing **Enter**.

➤ Each directory and file at an FTP site is represented by a link; click the link to view the directory or transfer the file.

➤ If your browser can't connect to a particular site, or if you want the capability to resume interrupted downloads, get a true FTP program, such as CuteFTP (Windows) or Fetch (Macintosh).

➤ Protect yourself against viruses, but don't be paranoid. They're not as common as the antivirus companies want you to think.

➤ Download utilities such as SmartDownload and GetRight can make downloading from Web and FTP sites easier.

Online Chat Rooms And Instant Messaging

One of the most important – yet least discussed – systems in cyberspace is *chat*. It's important because its immense popularity has been a significant factor in the growth of online systems (not so much the Internet, but more the online services). It is, perhaps, the least discussed because the fact is that many people use the chat systems as a way to talk about sex and even to contact potential sexual partners.

In this chapter, you'll take a look at chatting in cyberspace – in Internet Relay Chat (the Internet's largest chat system) as well as in the online services. And you'll also learn that there's plenty more than sex-related chat.

Chatting And Talking

What is chat? Well, here's what it's *not*: a system that allows you to talk out loud to people across the Internet or an online service. That sort of system does exist (see Chapter 13), but a chat system does not use voice, it uses the typed word. Communications are carried out by typing messages to and fro.

What's the difference between chat and email, then? With email you send a message and then go away and do something else. You come back later – maybe later that day, maybe later that week – to see if you have a response. Chat is just the opposite: it takes place in *real time*, to use a geek term. (What other kind of time is there but real time, one wonders.) In other words, you type a message and the other party in the chat session   sees the message almost instantly. He can then respond right away and you see the response right away. It's just like, yes, a chat – only you are typing instead of talking.

Chat *Can* Have Voice

That's the problem about the Internet: you make a statement today and tomorrow it's wrong. Right now the use of voice in chat sessions is rare. Voice *is* being added to chat, though, and you can expect chat sessions to gradually come to resemble the real thing, as people type less and talk more. However, as wonderful as that may sound it presents a problem. Many IRC (Internet Relay Chat) users are working at big companies, sitting in their little cubicles, typing away and looking busy. Their bosses may think they are working hard, but they are actually gabbing on IRC and *voices would just give the game away!*

There's also something known as *talk*, which also isn't talking. Talk is a system in which one person can 'call' another on the Internet and, once a connection has been made, can type messages to the other person. You probably know it by its more recent name, *instant messaging*. It's very similar to chat, once the two parties are connected. But the manner in which you connect is different. With chat you have to go to a chat 'room' to chat with people; with talk – instant messaging – you simply open the talk program, enter the email address of the person you want to connect to and click a button to call that person (who may not be available, of course). To further complicate the issue, some Voice on the Net programs (discussed in Chapter 13) incorporate these talk programs, but they sometimes call them chat systems!

Sex?

Should I be talking about sex in this book? It's been suggested by my editors that I should avoid sexual subjects for fear of offending people. Chat, however, is a case in which it's hard to avoid the sexual. Certainly many people go to chat rooms for nonsexual purposes. But be warned that many (possibly most?) are there to meet members of the opposite sex (or the same sex in some cases) for sexual purposes, both real and imagined. (Imagined sex is known, on the Internet, as cybersex. Real sex is known as sex.)

Chat is one of those 'love it or hate it' kind of things. Obviously many people just love it; they even find it addictive, spending hours online each night. Personally, I can do without it. It's an awkward way to communicate. I can type faster than most people, yet I find it rather clunky. Quite frankly, my experiences with chat question-and-answer sessions have not been exactly the high points of my life. I've been the guest in chat sessions in both MSN and CompuServe; the sessions tend to be chaotic at worst, simply slow at best. You run into too many people trying to ask questions at once, lots of typos, long pauses while you wait for people to type and they wait for you and so on. I'm not a chat fan, but chat certainly appeals to millions of people.

Two Types Of Sessions

Chat sessions are categorized into two types: private and group. Generally, what happens is that you join a chat 'room', in which a lot of people are talking (okay, typing) at once. Then someone may invite you to a private room, where just the two of you can talk without the babble of the public room. These private rooms are often used for 'cybersex' sessions, though of course they can also be used for more innocent purposes, such as catching up on the latest news with your brother-in-law in Paris, discussing a project with a colleague, or talking about a good scuba-diving spot in Mexico.

Often public chat rooms are used as sort of auditoriums or lecture halls. A famous or knowledgeable person responds to questions from the crowd. Michael Jackson and Buzz Aldrin, for instance, have been guest 'speakers' in chat forums, as have many other world famous people.

Score One For The Online Services

I'm going to mostly discuss the online services in this chapter because they generally have the most popular, and in some ways the best, chat systems. Chat has been extremely important to the growth of the online services, so they've made an effort to provide good chat services. Chat on the Internet, though, is still relatively little used and in many ways not as sophisticated. (That's changing as many new chat programs designed for the Internet, often running through the Web, are being introduced.)

And the line between online-service chat and Web chat is starting to blur, as the online services move out onto the Web. Both MSN and CompuServe, for instance, now provide their chat rooms through Web-based software, accessible to all.

Chatting In AOL

In AOL, click the **Chat** button in the **People** bar at the top of the window and then choose **Chat Rooms** from the window that opens. (You can also just use the keyword **chat rooms** to reach the same place.) There are well over 160 UK chat rooms listed in about 20 categories, which you can view by topic or by name, or click one of the links in the **Worldwide** list to see chat rooms in the USA, Australia, Canada and Germany. To enter a chat room, just double-click its name.

AOL's chat room system: lots of glitz, very busy.

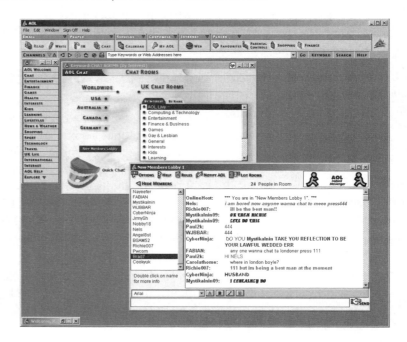

AOL's system enables you to create private rooms so that you and your friends (or family or colleagues) can use that room without interference. If you want to talk to only one person, you just double-click the person's name in the People Here box and click the **Send An Instant Message** button. If the person responds, you get your own private message window for just the two of you. You can see in the following figure that this message box has special buttons that allow you to modify the text format.

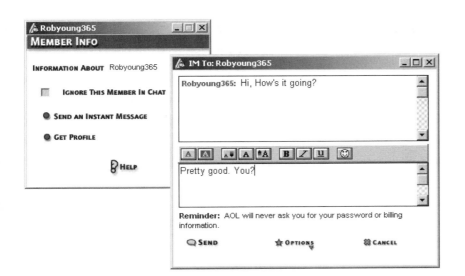

AOL provides you with a little message window in which you can carry on private conversations.

CompuServe's Forums

To use a CompuServe chat room, you can go to just about any Forum. The busiest of these is the UK Chat Forum, where you'll find loads of chat sessions. Most Forums have a number of conference rooms, but unless some kind of presentation has been scheduled, they may all be empty. You can be sure to find people to chat with in the UK Chat Forum, though (**GO UK CHAT**, or click the big **Chat** button in the main menu).

You can also go directly to CompuServe's chat area in a Web browser, using **http://member.compuserve.com/chat**. On your way in, you'll have to enter your Screen Name and password, but there's a handy button you can click to create a free Screen Name.

You can sometimes enter chat rooms directly from a link – clicking on a link opens the program and drops you into the room directly. But in some cases a list of available rooms opens.

Double-click a room to open the chat window, or click a room and then click the **Enter** or **Eavesdrop** button to take part in the chat room's discussion or just 'listen in'. The list of rooms shows you how many people are in each room; this might be helpful if you want to pick a quiet one or get right into the action. You can listen by reading other people's messages; whenever you want to jump in, you can type your own message in the lower panel of the window, then press Enter to send the message or click the **Send** button. You can invite people to private rooms too; just double-click on the name of a participant in the right pane, and a little message window opens up into which you can type a private message.

181

Microsoft Chat and MSN

Like MSN itself, Microsoft's chat options have gone through some major changes to become Web based. The bonus of this approach is that you don't have to be an MSN member to join in: just visit **http://chat.msn.com** to pick from dozens of chat rooms, and sign in as a guest. The first time you use MSN Chat you'll have to wait a minute or two while the chat software is installed on your computer, as with other Web-based chat rooms mentioned later in the chapter.

MSN's chat rooms are Web based and available to all.

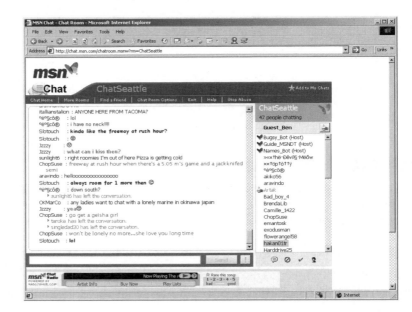

MSN Chat isn't quite as flexible as AOL or CompuServe, but you'll find most of the features you need there somewhere. You can direct a private message to someone in the room by double-clicking their name (known as 'whisper' mode), or click the little person icon to view a user's profile.

Microsoft Chat

If you have Windows 98, you may find that Microsoft Chat is installed on your computer and accessible through a Start menu option (**Start**, **Programs**, **Internet Explorer**, **Microsoft Chat**). However, this program no longer functions, having been superseded by a chat program that is installed from the Web site into your Web browser.

Commands To Look For

Although the details for using each chat system differ, a number of features are similar in most systems. For example, these features are generally similar (even though the names may vary):

➤ **Who** or **People Here** shows a list of people currently participating in the chat session.

➤ **Invite** enables you to invite a participant in the current chat to a private chat room. (On AOL, you send the person an Instant Message.)

➤ **Ignore** or **Squelch** enables you to tell the program to stop displaying messages from a particular user. This command is very useful for shutting up obnoxious chat-room members. (You'll find a lot of them!) It's also a good tool for 'tuning out' conversations you don't want to hear.

➤ **Profile** allows you to view information about a particular participant, including whatever information that person decided to make public. Some systems allow more information than others, but the information might include a person's email address, interests, real name, and even phone number and address in some systems (although most participants choose *not* to include this information).

➤ **Change Profile** or **Handle** gives you access to the place where you'll change your own information. Some systems let you change your profile from within the Chat program, but on others you may have to select a menu option or command elsewhere.

➤ **Record** or **Log** or **Capture** usually lets you record a session. (Of course, in most cases you'll want to forget the drivel – oh, there I go again!)

➤ **Preferences** enables you to set up how the system works: whether to tell you when people enter or leave the room, for example.

➤ **Kick** or **Ban** are available on some systems if you set up the chat room yourself. **Kick** allows you to remove someone from the chat room; **Ban** stops the person from getting back in.

No matter which chat system you use, read the documentation carefully so you can figure out exactly how to get the most out of it.

183

Pick Your Avatar

The latest thing in chat is the use of graphical systems in which you select an *avatar*, an image that represents you in the chat session. The figure on the following page shows a room with several avatars, each representing a real-life person, in Club Chat. Selecting an avatar is a simple matter of clicking a button in the top-left portion of the window, and then choosing from a drop-down list box. Then you can type a message in the text box at the bottom and click the **Send** button. You can also choose from a small selection of sounds ('Aaaah', 'Joy', 'Doh', and other such intellectual utterings).

So far I've heard mixed reactions to these graphical chat systems. Some people say they are awful; some say they're nothing special; some say it's just stuff to get in the way of the chat. Others really like them. Experiment and decide for yourself.

Interestingly, MSN *used* to have avatar chat, in the form of a program called Comic Chat, but the new version of the software does not have this feature. Maybe it will return in a later version, but I suspect that avatars are more of a gimmick than a really necessary feature.

Playing with avatars in SiteSticky.

The best place to start is Worlds.com's 3D portal at **http://www.worlds.net**. Although you can reach this site on the Web, all your chat and exploration takes place using the free WorldsPlayer software. Follow the links on the site to download and install the software, then use the WorldsPlayer to choose the 3D world you want to visit and select your avatar.

Various other avatar chats are available on the Web although they seem to be less common today than a couple of years ago (which seems to indicate that the whole idea is a bit of a gimmick). Try one of these sites, which have links to a number of chat sites that use avatars:

➤ Virtual Places: **http://www.vplaces.net**

➤ Contact Consortium: **http://www.ccon.org/hotlinks/hotlinks.html**

➤ Yahoo!: **http://dir.yahoo.com/Recreation/Games/Computer_Games/ Internet_Games/Multi_User_Games/Virtual_Worlds**

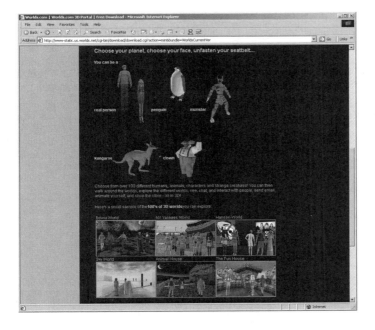

Worlds.com offers hundreds of 3D virtual worlds and a wide choice of avatars.

185

Web Chat's Coming Up Fast

Most chat participants are still using chat systems running on the online services, but it may not always be that way. Hundreds, perhaps thousands, of Web-based chat systems have sprung up and in some cases are quite good. There are chat sites set up for celebrity 'visits', education-related issues, gay chat, skateboarding chat, and more. If you're a chat fan and have been hiding out in the online service chat rooms, perhaps it's time to take a look at the World Wide Web and see what's available. (Here's a good place to start: **http://dir.yahoo.com/computers_and_internet/internet/world_wide_web/chat/**.)

Check This Out...

Chat Versus Discussion Groups

There's a little confusion on the Web about the difference between chat rooms and discussion groups. Some Web sites advertising 'chat' actually have Web forums. If the discussion isn't 'real time' – you type something, someone immediately responds, you type back – then it's not chat.

Freeserve Chat, one of the UK's most popular chat sites.

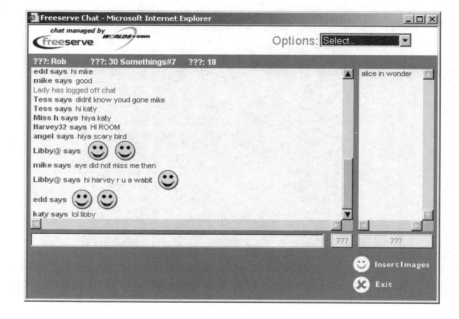

Web chat systems vary from the very clunky – your message is displayed within a Web page, which must be constantly rewritten to see the conversation – to the very good. The better sites, such as Talk City (**http://www. talkcity.com/**) and Freeserve Chat (**http://www.freeserve.com/chat**), have their own chat programs that you must download before you enter the chat room. These are true chat systems, with the same sort of features as the chat rooms in the online services. You can see an example of the Freeserve chat program in the figure on page 186.

Chatting On The Internet

The Internet has its own chat system called Internet Relay Chat, or **IRC**. Like all the other Internet services, you'll need to grab another piece of software to use it. One of the best and the easiest to use is **mIRC** from **http://www. mirc.co.uk**. The first time you run mIRC, you'll see the dialog shown in the following figure into which you can enter the few details needed by the program.

Enter your name and email address in the appropriate spaces and choose a nickname (or *handle*) by which you'll be known in chat sessions. A nickname can be anything you choose: it might give an indication of your hobby or job, or a clue to your (adopted?) personality, or it might just be meaningless gibberish, but it can't be more than nine characters in length. Finally choose a UK server from the list and click **OK**.

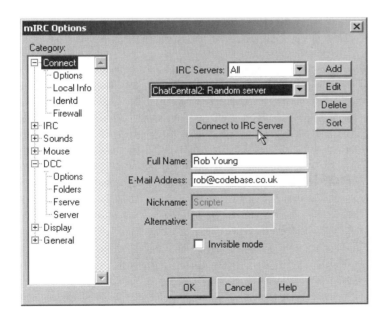

Fill in three boxes, choose a server, and you're ready to start chatting.

Channels

In the weird world of IRC, which bases its jargon heavily on CB radio, a *channel* is the term for a chat room.

Now you're ready to connect and start chatting. Make sure you're connected to your service provider first (mIRC won't start the connection for you) and then click the thunderbolt-button at the extreme left of the toolbar. As soon as you're connected, you'll see a small dialog box listing a collection of channels that mIRC's author thought you might like to try. You could double-click one of these to enter that channel, but now is a good time to use one of the many IRC commands.

Close the little list of channels, type **/list** in the box at the bottom of the main window and then press Enter. A second window will open to display all the channels available on the server you chose (shown in the next figure). There could be several hundred channels, so this might take a few seconds. Beside each channel's name you'll see a figure indicating how many people are on that channel at the moment and a brief description of the channel's current subject of discussion. Choose a channel and double-click its list-entry to enter.

Some long-time IRC users can be a bit scathing towards newcomers, so it's best to choose a beginners' channel while you take your first faltering steps. Good channels to start with are **#beginners**, **#mirc** (for mIRC users), **#irchelp** or **#ircnewbies**. You may see some more channel names that refer to help, beginners or newbies – try to pick a channel that has at least half-a-dozen people in it already so that you won't feel too conspicuous!

After connecting to a server, you can pick from a list of suggested channels.

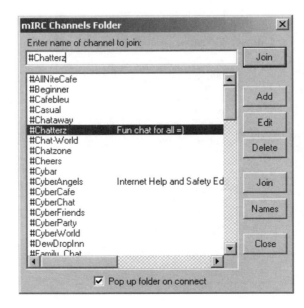

188

When a channel window opens, you'll see your nickname listed among the channel's other occupants on the right, with the conversation taking place on the left. As soon as you enter the channel, your arrival will be broadcast to everyone else (you'll see this happen when others arrive and leave) and you may receive an automated Welcome message, or someone might even say Hello. To join in with the chat, just start typing into the text box at the bottom and press Enter to send. If you want to leave a channel, type the command **/leave** and press Enter.

IRC Commands - Chat Like A Pro

The IRC system has a huge number of commands that you can learn and put to good use if you're really keen and mIRC includes a general IRC help-file explaining how they   work. You certainly don't need to know all of them (and mIRC has toolbar buttons that replace a few), but once you feel comfortable with the system you can experiment with new ones. Here's a few of the most useful to get you started.

Type this	To do this
/help	Get general help on IRC
/list	List all the channels available on the server you connected to
/list -min *n*	List all the channels with at least *n* people in them (replace *n* with a figure)
/join #*channel*	Enter a channel. Replace *channel* with the name of your chosen channel
/leave #*channel*	Leave the specified channel (or the channel in the current window if no channel is specified)
/quit *message*	Finish your IRC session and display a message to the channel if you enter one (see below)
/away *message*	Tell other occupants you're temporarily away from your computer, giving a message
/away	With no message, means that you're no longer away
/whois *nickname*	Get information about the specified nickname in the main window

So what are those *messages*? When you quit, you might want to explain why you're leaving, by entering a command like **/quit Got to go shopping. See you later!** Similarly, if you suddenly have to leave your keyboard, you might type **/away Call of nature. BRB** to indicate that you'll be back in a minute if anyone tries to speak to you. (BRB is a common shorthand for 'Be right back' – turn to Chapter 2 for more of this Internet shorthand.) When you return, just type **/away** to turn off this message again.

An Easy Way To Make A Fool Of Yourself

All commands start with a forward slash. If you type the command without the slash it will instead be displayed to all the participants in your channel and give everyone a good giggle at your expense.

You can also 'talk' privately to any of the participants in a channel. If you want to start a private talk with someone called Zebedee, type the command **/query Zebedee Can I talk to you in private?** (of course, the message you tag on the end is up to you). Zebedee will have the opportunity to accept or decline the talk: if he/she accepts, a separate private window will open in which the two of you can exchange messages.

Easy Window Management

You can keep windows open in mIRC as long as you want to. The program places each new window on a taskbar so that you can switch between open channels and lists to your heart's content. Many people even keep several 'chats' going at once in this way!

Starting Your Own IRC Channel

If you always connect to the same server and always use the /list command to get a list of channels, you might notice that the number of channels varies. Channels are dynamic – anyone can create a new one and when the last person leaves that channel it ceases to exist. Here's how to create your own channel.

1. Pick a channel name that doesn't already exist and enter it. To create a channel called Skylight, type **/join #Skylight**.

2. To put yourself in charge of this channel you have to promote yourself to *channel operator* status. Do this by typing **/op *nickname*** (entering your own

nickname). As operator, your nickname will be displayed with an '@' prefix to indicate your status to anyone who enters your channel.

3. Now set a topic that will displayed in the channel list and (with luck!) attract some passers-by. Type **/topic** followed by a description of what your channel would be discussing if there was someone else to discuss with. As people join your channel and the discussion moves to different areas, use the **/topic** command to update the description every so often.

As channel operator you are all-powerful: you can invite people into your channel using /**invite** followed by their nickname and the name of your channel (for example, **/invite Zebedee #Skylight**) and you can kick someone out if their conduct is offensive or disruptive using **/kick #Skylight Zebedee**. You can also use the **/op** command to promote other visitors to channel operator status if you wish to.

What Is It Good For? Real Uses For Chat

It could be argued that chat systems are a complete waste of perfectly good electrons. (*I* wouldn't claim that, of course, but I'm sure many people would.) The chat is often little better than gibberish. ('Hey, dude, how goes it? … Cool, man, you? … Yeah, doing well; you chatted with that babe CoolChick, yet? … No, she cute?' … blah … blah … blah.) This is neither educational nor particularly interesting.

I should note that not all chats are quite so inane. Chats allow people of like interests to get together in cyberspace, literally reaching across continents, across the entire globe, to discuss issues that interest them in a way that would be prohibitively expensive using any other technology. (Actually, I've proposed a *stupidity-tax* to make the totally stupid chats prohibitively expensive again.)

There are other worthwhile uses, too. This list points out a few such scenarios:

➤ Technical support can be given using chat rooms. This will become more important as more software is distributed across the Internet. For instance, a small company that, in the past, might have provided support only within the USA can now provide support to any nation with an Internet account.

➤ Companies can use chat systems for keeping in touch. An international company with salespeople throughout the world can arrange weekly 'meetings' in a chat room. Families can do the same so that family members can keep in touch even when they're separated by thousands of miles.

➤ Groups that are planning international trips might want to try chat rooms. For instance, if a scout group is travelling to another country to spend the summer with another group, a chat room could provide a way for the leaders to 'get together' beforehand to iron out final details.

➤ Colleges can use chat. Many colleges already provide courses over the Internet, using the Web to post lessons and using email to send in completed assignments. In addition, teachers can use chat to talk with students, regardless of the geographic distance between them.

However, having said all that, chat may eventually be superseded by what's known as Voice on the Net (VON), a system that allows you to place 'phone calls' across the Internet and even have conference calls (see Chapter 13).

International phone rates have dropped tremendously in the last couple of years, making connecting by typing less attractive than it used to be.

Instant Messaging

Earlier in this chapter, I talked briefly about *talk*, a system that's now known as *instant messaging*. This is a system that allows two people to get together and chat privately online; no need to go to a chat site, you just open your program, choose the person you want to talk to, and begin typing.

There are a lot of instant messaging (IM) programs around, but almost all users are working with one of the following programs (and by far the most are using the first one):

➤ AOL Instant Messenger: **http://www.aol.com/aim**

➤ MSN Messenger/Windows Messenger: **http://messenger.msn.com**

➤ Yahoo! Messenger: **http://messenger.yahoo.com**

➤ ICQ: **http://web.icq.com**

You may run into various others:

➤ Netscape Instant Messenger: **http://home.netscape.com/aim**

➤ CompuServe Instant Messenger: **http://www.compuserve.com/csim**

➤ Lycos Messenger: **http://www.messenger.lycos.com**

➤ Odigo: **http://www.odigo.com**

➤ EveryBuddy: **http://www.everybuddy.com**

➤ Jabber: **http://www.jabber.com**

and many more. But in some cases these programs are merely re-branded versions of one of the others (Netscape Instant Messenger, for instance, is actually AOL Instant Messenger, and EveryBuddy is a special program that combines the AOL, Yahoo!, ICQ and MSN programs).

I used to recommend that people try out a few of these programs and see which they prefer, and then tell their friends to download the same one. But it's probably a good idea to work with one of the major systems, such as AOL Instant Messenger (AIM) or Windows Messenger, because they're in such wide use. Windows Messenger, for instance, is installed automatically with Windows XP, giving it a place on millions of desktops. Likewise, AIM is included with the America Online software and some versions of the Netscape Web browser.

The IM War And IM Interoperability

In 1999, Microsoft and AOL went to war over IM (instant messaging). In the summer Microsoft launched its own IM service, MSN Messenger... and made it compatible with the AOL IM service. That is, people using MSN Messenger could send messages to people using AOL Instant Messenger. At the same time Microsoft called for complete IM interoperability – all IM services should be able to communicate with each other, they said.

AOL didn't much like that. They had a monopoly in instant messaging, and decided to block access, so that other IM companies couldn't send messages into their system. So for months a back-and-forth struggle went on: AOL blocking access, other companies finding a way around the blocking, AOL blocking access again, other companies (including Microsoft and Yahoo!) complaining to the Federal Communications Commission, AOL blocking someone else, another group complaining to the Senate Commerce Committee.

I should note that AOL claims that it's blocking access for security and privacy reasons. On the other hand, these seem like excuses, buzzwords guaranteed to give people pause but actually non-issues. There's no reason that interoperability has to be insecure or require the release of private information.

At the time of writing, almost three years after it all began, the war continues. It seems, however, that over the long term interoperability is inevitable, and that most IM systems will communicate with each other. With or without AOL Instant Messenger, the other guys will get together and make their programs talk to each other, and there's a very good chance that some court or government department will eventually force AOL to open its system up.

For now, though, you may find that if you want to communicate with friends using different IMs, you'll have to install all those different systems (or perhaps use a program such as EveryBuddy).

Using IM

So, make your choice. Pick a system; but how? I'd suggest that you check with the people with whom you want to communicate, to see which system they're using. Note, by the way, that just because you're *not* an AOL member doesn't mean you can't use AOL Instant Messenger. Even if you're not an MSN member, you can use MSN Messenger or Windows Messenger. These companies are distributing their programs to anyone who wants one, so if you have AOL friends using AOL Instant Messenger, yet you're with some little Internet service provider, don't worry – you can still download and use that program.

So, what features does the world's most popular IM program, AOL Instant Messenger, have?

➤ Keep a list of people you commonly communicate with – your Buddy list. Then, double-click on a person to send that person a message. If the person's available, he can instantly reply.

➤ Change text colour, size, text-background colour, and style (bold, italic, underline).

➤ Create links in the messages; when the recipient clicks on a link, the referenced Web pages open in his Web browser.

➤ Place image 'smileys' into messages.

➤ Insert text from a file into a message.

➤ Send 'warnings' to people who have sent you obnoxious messages. If enough people send warnings, that person will be temporarily blocked from sending messages to *anyone*.

➤ Permanently block people from sending messages to you.

➤ View the person's profile.

➤ Select a 'Buddy Icon', a picture to represent you, displayed when someone's viewing your messages (you can even use your own photograph).

➤ Create an 'away message', displayed when someone tries to contact you and you are unable to respond.

➤ Transfer files to someone you're communicating with.

➤ Send pictures to people.

➤ Talk to people – yes, using your voice and a microphone.

➤ Play games with your IM buddies.

➤ All sorts of other configuration options: setting up the ticker displayed at the bottom of the Buddy list; modify alerts; set privacy options; and lots more.

The Enemy: MSN Messenger

It's not as widely used as AOL Instant Messenger (though its inclusion in Windows XP as Windows Messenger has increased its usage dramatically), but MSN Messenger is preferred by many people, and has some interesting features. It has built-in voice-on-the-net that allows you to call from your computer to any telephone in the world at a lower rate than most phone companies charge (U.S. for free) (we'll look at voice-on-the-net in more detail in Chapter 13).

It has built-in stock tracking, can send messages to pagers and cell phones, play games, and control whether your kids can use the program. Of course, it has instant messaging features, too – some unusual features such as an indicator showing when the person you're communicating with is typing, about to send something back to you, so that you can pause and wait for the response. It has more advanced text and messaging formatting, too. (Some very cute little smileys.)

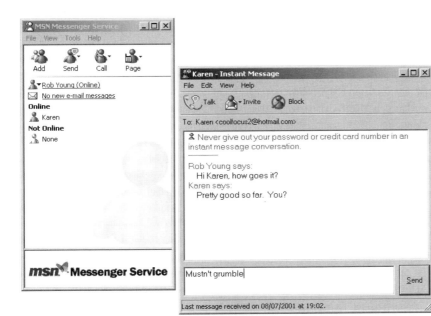

MSN Messenger, more than just IM. You can send pager messages or text messages to mobile phones, and even dial phone calls.

ICQ (Figure It Out)

ICQ is an instant messaging phenomenon in its own right. Started by a small group of Israeli programmers, in 1998 ICQ was bought by AOL for $287 million, with productivity bonuses that reportedly were potentially as much as $110 million or so.

It certainly is a great program, but it's far more than just an instant-messaging program. It allows both instant messaging and chat – you can have private or public communication sessions. But it also allows you to send notes that will pop up on people's screens, send files – simply drag a file and drop it onto the recipient's name, and away it goes – launch other programs when files arrive, tell people to telephone you, and so on.

It's a fantastic 'collaboration tool', an ideal program for when you're working with people and need to be in constant contact, yet they're somewhere else. You can create a sort of virtual office, with people spread around the world, and constantly share information and ideas. You can even see whether your colleagues are available, as you can set an indicator to show whether you're out for lunch, currently at your computer, or whatever.

It works like this. When you get an ICQ account, you add other ICQ users to your list – you'll add the ICQ accounts of the other people you plan to work with, for instance. Then, you'll see little indicators in the ICQ window showing the status of these other ICQ accounts. Sally might have set her ICQ program to show that she's **Away**; Fred might have set his to show **Extended Away**; John might have set his to **Occupied (Urgent Messages)**, so he doesn't want to be disturbed by trivia, but he's there if you really need him; Gill might not have logged on yet, so she's shown as **Offline**, and so on.

So, you can see exactly who's available, and what you can do. By clicking on their names and selecting actions, you can send them messages, initiate a chat (or talk) session, transfer files to them, send notes asking them to call you, and various other things. In fact, there are so many features in this thing that the company even publishes a book explaining how to use it all – this is no dumb chat program.

The product's free, too. (I haven't quite figured out what sort of productivity bonuses you can have when the product doesn't cost anything, and there's no advertising being sold on the system. That's Internet economics for you.) You can download it from **http://www.icq.com**. A great system, well worth a look.

Oh, before we leave this chapter – have you figured out what ICQ stands for? Say the letters slowly, and then try them fast. Listen to the words that the letters seem to represent, and you'll figure it out.

The Least You Need To Know

➤ A *chat* system allows participants to take part in public discussions or to move to private 'rooms' if they prefer. A *talk* system is a direct link between participants in a conversation, without the need for a public chat room.

➤ Neither chat nor talk uses actual voices; you type messages and send them to and fro.

➤ Chat sessions are often very crude and sexually orientated; so if you're easily offended, pick your chat room carefully.

➤ All the online services have popular chat systems. Many Web sites have chat rooms, too.

➤ If you want to use Internet Relay Chat, you'll have to download an IRC program from a shareware site and then connect across the Internet to a server.

➤ You can use chat rooms to keep in touch with friends, family, or colleagues – or to meet new people.

➤ There are many instant messaging (IM) systems, but only a handful of popular ones.

➤ Right now, IM programs don't operate with each other, but may soon. Find out which IM systems your friends are using, and get the same.

➤ ICQ is an IM system on steroids, a real collaboration tool.

Chapter 13

Voice On The Net, White Boards, And More

In This Chapter

➤ International calls for a penny per minute ...

➤ Calls routed to domestic phone systems

➤ Where do you get phone software?

➤ Connecting to a 'server' and finding someone to talk to

➤ Text transmission, white boards, conferencing, and more

➤ Video conferencing and other weird stuff

You've already seen a few ways that the Internet allows you to communicate with friends, family and colleagues. You can use email (Chapter 2), and you can use chat and instant messaging (Chapter 12). But these systems are a little clunky. Most people alive today grew up in the telephone age; we're used to picking up the phone and talking to people. And although Internet programmers like to use terms like 'chat' and 'talk', these programs don't use *real* chat and talk, they use typing.

So now I have some good news for you (and some bad news). The good news is that there's a system that allows you to really talk across the Internet. The bad news? There's a good chance that you'll never use it (at least, not any time soon) because of its disadvantages. A couple of years ago, talking on the Internet – known as **VON**, or Voice On The Net – was set to be the Next Big Thing. But as we've seen elsewhere in this book, Next Big Things don't always work out, and VON is one that hasn't. Still, it's available and some people do use it, so let's take a closer look.

Voice On The Net – Talk Really Is Cheap!

So how does VON differ from an ordinary telephone conversation? First and foremost, the price – because you're only dialling in to your local access provider, you're only paying for a local phone call although you may be speaking to someone in Australia. But it's the extra goodies that VON programs offer that make them valuable. Depending on the program you use, you can send computer files back and forth, hold conferences, use a whiteboard to draw sketches and diagrams, and you can even take control of programs on the other party's computer. If you connect a Webcam (a small, cheap movie camera) to your computer, recent programs can make use of this to make the fabled 'video phone' a reality at last. Admittedly the pictures are small and rather jerky, but you can finally see and be seen while you talk.

Will They Be Online?

You can only talk to someone else if they're online and have their VON software running. Many US users have access to free local phone calls and can stay online all day, but if you want to contact another UK user you might still have to arrange to be online at a pre-specified time.

Sounds Good, What's The Catch?

The downside is that the other party must also be online to receive the 'call', so you'll both pay phone charges, but even added together these should amount to less than the price of an international call. In fact, some of these systems can even dial someone's *phone number* rather than email address, making it possible to make these cheap international calls to someone who doesn't even have an Internet account!

A second catch is that you probably have to be using the same program as the person you want to talk to. (Although there's a standard VON system available called H.323, which many Internet phones support, it only provides the bare bones and isn't easy to work with.) If you talk to a lot of people, you might need several different programs that do the same job just because *they* all use different programs. Fortunately some of these programs are free, so it's probably easiest to pick a free one and then convince your friends to grab a copy themselves!

What Do I Need?

Unlike the other services you use on the Internet, VON programs have some definite hardware requirements. To begin with, you'll need a fairly new computer. Not necessarily top of the line, but not an old piece of junk, either. If you have a PC it should be at least a 486DX, and preferably a Pentium. If you have a Mac you'll probably need a Performa or Power PC (some of these programs run only on the Power PC). On any platform you'll need a reasonable amount of RAM, probably a bare minimum of 8MB, preferably 16MB or more. But, as I always say, you can never have too much money, too much time off, or too much RAM.

You need a soundcard too, of course, and you'll need a microphone and speakers (or perhaps a headset) plugged into it. Be sure that it's a 16-bit soundcard or better, and that it also allows you to record (some don't). Ideally you need a full-duplex card. And then there's your Internet connection and modem to consider. You might just get by with a 28.8 or 33.6Kbps modem, but you'll get much more useable results from a 56Kbps modem or one of the recently-introduced digital access methods.

Full Duplex

There are two choices: full duplex and half duplex. A full duplex card can record your voice while playing the incoming voice so that you can both talk at the same time if you want to (ideal for arguments, for example!). With a half duplex card you can either talk or listen, but not both – you'd normally switch off your microphone after speaking as an indication you'd finished (rather like saying 'Over' on a walkie-talkie).

Finally, of course, you need the software. Some of the top products are Microsoft's NetMeeting and Windows Messenger, MediaRing Talk and Video VoxPhone Gold. Not surprisingly, the Microsoft offerings are the most popular, partly by virtue of being installed automatically with Windows. Follow these directions to get your hands on one or all of these products, or update an older version:

➤ **MediaRing Talk.** A stylish free program that lets you make PC-to-phone or PC-to-PC calls, available from **http://www.mediaring.com**.

➤ **Video VoxPhone Gold.** Along with PC-to-phone and PC-to-PC calls, this commercial program lets you use text chat and video chat. You can download a trial version from **http://www.voxphone.com**.

➤ **Microsoft NetMeeting.** Microsoft's Internet phone system is included with Windows 98/Me/2000 and some versions of Internet Explorer, and allows PC or phone calls, text and video chat, conferencing, and quite a lot more. You can download it as a separate item from **http://www.microsoft.com/netmeeting**.

➤ **Microsoft Windows Messenger.** A new replacement for NetMeeting and the MSN Messenger program mentioned in Chapter 12, which combines the best features of both into a simpler and more compact program. Windows Messenger is included with Windows XP Home and Professional editions.

You can find other VON products by searching for **internet voice** at any good search engine (see Chapter 16), or by visiting the Internet section at Tucows (**http://tucows.mirror.ac.uk**). Many such programs are available as shareware, commercial products, or completely free 'give-it-away-ware'. However, it's worth noting that this is another area of the Internet that is actually shrinking as companies stop developing products due to the overwhelming lack of interest in VON by the general public.

Don't Be Out When The Call Comes In!

To get the most from *any* chat, talk, or VON program, make sure you run it every time you go online; if you don't, it's like leaving your phone permanently off the hook – no-one will be able to contact you! Even if you just plan to do a bit of Web-surfing, run the program and then minimize it. If someone wants to talk, a dialog will appear to ask if you'd like to accept.

Working With Your Phone Program

Let's take a look at how to work with one of these systems. I'll assume that you have your soundcard and microphone properly installed – that's one can of worms I'm *not* crawling into! I'll also assume that you've installed some sort of phone program and have run through the setup (so it already has all of your personal information that it needs, such as your name, email address, and so on).

The next question is, to quote Ghostbusters, *Who ya gonna call?* Yes, I know … you were so excited about the idea of making phone calls on the Internet that you went ahead and installed everything you need. But you haven't quite persuaded your siblings or your mad Aunt Edna to do the same. So you actually have *nobody* to call.

Not so long ago, that wouldn't have been a problem. All the software companies used to set up their own servers to which you could connect and find someone else who, just like you, was all dressed up with nowhere to go. Every user who was online with their VON software running was automatically logged in to this directory server and shown in a list of active users. To start chatting, you just picked a name from the list and clicked the **Call** button (or, of course, someone picked your name and called you).

Nothing Better To Do?

If your VON program uses the directory server system, connect to one of these servers and just wait. Every now and then you'll get a call. It's a kind of magical mystery phone session, not knowing who's going to call next. Where does she live? What does he do? Can she get her microphone working?

These days, as part of the general demise of VON, most of these companies have gone off to do different things, and their directory servers have gone too. One of the few programs that still uses this system is Video VoxPhone Gold's PC-to-PC service: click the **Call** button, and a list of users will be shown in a choice of categories such as Family, Business and Casual. Select a name and click the **Dial** button.

MediaRing Talk uses telephone numbers to make PC or phone connections. MediaRing.com Ltd. A company headquartered in Singapore.

If you're using one of the other programs, things work rather differently: you have to know in advance who you want to talk to and how to contact them:

➤ If your program uses phone numbers, as MediaRing Talk does, type the user's phone number to make the call. For PC-to-PC calls, this must be the number of the phone line to which the user's modem is connected.

➤ If you want to call mad Aunt Edna, and you both have H.323-compliant programs, you can get in touch by entering her IP address into the program. The problem is that you need to *know* Aunt Edna's IP address: if she has a permanent connection to the Internet, the address will always be the same and you can just add it to your address book when she tells you what it is. But if she connects through an ISP, she'll probably be assigned a different IP address every time she connects, so she'll have to send you an email or instant message to tell you every time she goes online.

➤ The most popular VON programs use email addresses or unique ID numbers. To use NetMeeting or Windows Messenger, for instance, you sign up for a free Microsoft Hotmail account, and use your Hotmail address to identify yourself. Other users of one of these programs can add your Hotmail address to their contacts list, and the program will show who's online and available (as shown in the screenshot on the following page). Click a name to send an invitation to talk.

The last method is the most reliable, not least because you do at least know that the person you're trying to talk to is online and using a compatible program before you start.

H.323

H.323 is one of the Internet's open standards, designed to make Internet telephony easier and more reliable. If your program and your friend's program are both H.323 compliant, you can make voice calls to each other even though you're not using identical programs. Voice is all you get, though: any other features such as text chat, file transfer or multi-user conferencing, won't be available.

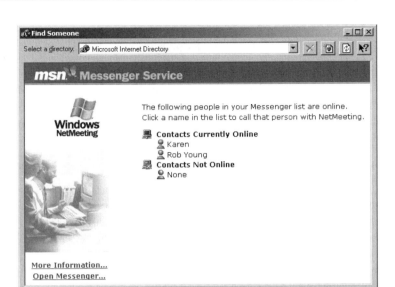

In NetMeeting and Windows Messenger, choose the Directory option to see which of your contacts are online.

The Bells And Whistles

These products offer more than just voice connections. You might want to look for some of the following features in an Internet phone system.

➤ **An answering machine.** Some products have built-in answering machines. If someone tries to contact you while you are not there, your 'answering machine' takes a message. Of course, this works only if your computer is online. Although it's very useful for people with permanent network connections, it's not nearly as useful for people who dial into a service provider.

➤ **Type while you talk capability.** This can be a very handy feature. You can send text messages at the same time you are talking. You can send small memos or copy parts of an email message you're discussing. If you are working on a project with the other person, you may find it convenient to send to-do lists or schedules back and forth. Authors working together can send materials to each other, programmers can send bits of the code they are discussing, and so on. The following figure shows one system in which you can write as you talk.

➤ **Image transmission.** Related to the business card feature and to the white board feature (discussed in a moment), is the capability to send a picture while you're talking. If you haven't seen Aunt Natasha in Siberia for a while, she can send a picture of the kids while you are chatting.

➤ **Conferencing.** Why speak to just one person, when you can talk to a whole crowd? Some of these programs let you set up conferences, so a whole bunch of you can gab at once.

➤ **Group Web-surfing.** Only a few programs have this odd feature. The people connected via the program (in some cases a whole bunch of people) can go on group Web-surfs together. When one person clicks a Web link, the other participants' Web browsers update to show the new page.

➤ **Web-page indicator.** You can automatically add an icon to your Web page showing whether you are online and able to accept calls.

➤ **White Boards.** A white board is one of those big white chalkboard-type things you see in conference rooms. A white board feature functions similarly to the image transmission feature previously mentioned. Instead of typing something, though, you are using a sort of doodle pad thing. You can sketch something and it's transmitted to the person at the other end. You can even use this to send graphic files and you can open the file in the white board so the person at the other end can see it.

➤ **Connecting voice to your Web page.** You can put links in your Web pages that, when clicked, open the user's Voice program so he can talk with you. This is for *real* geeks who rarely leave their computers. (You *do* have Web pages, don't you? See Chapter 8 to find out how to create them.)

Unfortunately, it's not a perfect world, so not all voice programs have all these neat features. You'll just have to find the feature that's most important to you and go with the program that has that feature.

Chat window lets you type messages while you talk.

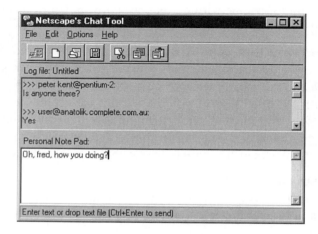

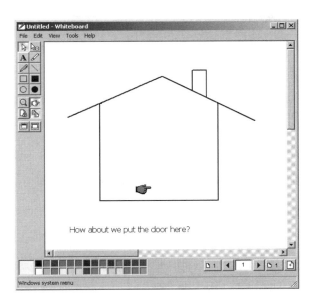

A white board feature lets you send a picture while talking.

Internet-to-Phone Connections

One of the most intriguing uses of this technology is the ability to connect to a computer across the Internet and route onto the local phone service. So, you might connect across the Internet from New York to Sydney and be connected to the Australian phone system – which means you can make international calls at Australian domestic rates. A number of these services are already available because the VON software companies, wanting to make their products as useful as possible, have provided them. The most popular is Net2Phone (**http://www.net2phone.com**), which is available as a stand-alone program, and also provides the PC-to-phone services for Video VoxPhone, MSN Messenger and Windows Messenger.

The problem is, at least from the point of view of the VON software companies, that since VON first appeared on the Internet, real-world phone rates have dropped. And if you can make an ordinary, good-quality phone call for not much more than a poor-quality VON call, that's what you're going to do. In some cases, VON services will be worthwhile; if you need to spend a lot of time on the phone to a country that is in a very expensive call area, you might want to look into using one of these VON services. Otherwise I suspect you'll do what most people have done – ignore VON.

MSN Messenger uses the Net2Phone service to provide PC-to-phone calls.

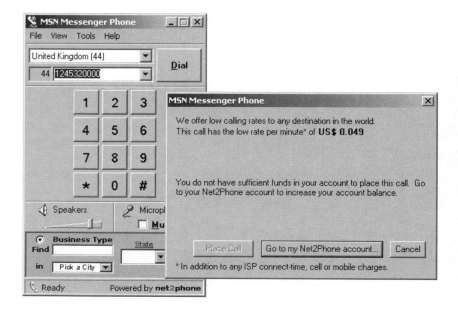

Internet Call Waiting

There's another interesting voice-related Internet service, something called *Internet Call Waiting*. If you use one phone line for both Internet connections and your telephone, an Internet Call Waiting service can let you know when someone is calling you.

Here's how it works. You find an Internet Call Waiting service, such as British Telecom's NetChat service at **http://www.btnetchat.com**, or an independent service like Internet Alert Call Manager from **http://www.otherlandtoys.co.uk**. If you're online when a call comes in, the service will alert you, either by displaying a message on your computer screen or (if the service has its own hardware) on the screen of the service's own gadget. The message should tell you who's calling, usually by displaying their name and/or phone number, and you can choose whether to take or ignore the call. Using BT's NetChat, you don't even have to disconnect from the Internet; as long as you have a soundcard, speakers and microphone, you can answer the call via a PC-to-phone connection.

Video And Other Weird Stuff

The next step is to add video to the 'phone' conversations. The phone companies have been talking about a true video phone for 40 years, but it took the Internet to bring it about. Video has already been added to some of these VON products. For instance, Microsoft NetMeeting, Windows Messenger and Video VoxPhone Gold all include a video window that can display either outgoing video (if you like to watch yourself talk!) or incoming video.

Mind you, this step is a much bigger one than putting voice on the Internet. Voice is fairly simple. There is not too much data involved in transmitting sounds, relatively speaking. The problem with video, though, is bandwidth. The term *bandwidth* refers to the amount of information that can be transmitted across a connection. A 56,000bps connection has greater bandwidth than does a 28,800bps connection, for instance. Video images contain a lot of information, and you want the information right away. After all, video only makes sense if it's in motion. So a number of compromises have to be made. The images are small, are low-resolution, and have few individual images each second. Thus, video transmitted across the Internet can often be blurry and shaky. Unless you really need it, you may find that the novelty soon wears off.

Personally, I don't think video on the Internet will catch on for a few more years – not until very high-speed connections are cheap and easily available. You also need a fast computer, of course. For now, video is limited to companies with network connections. However, that hasn't stopped a variety of companies from selling video software for use on the Internet. (And guess what's the real growth area for video on the Internet? Live sex shows and cybersex, of course!)

These products are generally thought of as video-conferencing products, but the principle is the same: real time communications across the Internet between two or more people. Go back to the Voice on the Net site (**http://www.von.com/**), and you'll find information about this, too.

The best-known product is Cu-SeeMe ('see you, see me,' get it? Yeah, yeah). This product is so well known in the computer business that it's becoming a generic term, in the same way that *Hoover* is a generic term for vacuum cleaners. You can see a demo of this product at work at **http://www.cuseeme.com/**.

Other telecommunications systems will be added to the Internet soon. How about getting your faxes and voice mail connected to your email system? If you live in the United Kingdom but do business in the United States, you can have a phone line set up in New York. Your customers can call and leave voice mail for you or can fax you at that number, and your messages can then be compressed and attached to an email message that is sent to you! You can have a number in London, Paris or Los Angeles, or you can have a US toll-free number. You'll even get the graphics in your faxes sent to you. Visit Trinité Communications (**http://www.trinite.co.uk**) for more information about this. And keep your eyes open for other weird and wonderful telecommunications/ Internet hybrid services.

The Least You Need To Know

➤ You can connect to other users and actually talk on the Internet at a fraction of the cost of long-distance or international calls.

➤ New Internet-to-phone system servers are being set up, which will enable you to connect across the world on the Internet, and then call someone using another country's domestic phone system.

➤ The phone software is plentiful and often cheap or even free. Check out the Web site **http://www.von.com/** for sources.

➤ Most companies have set up servers to which you can connect and find someone to talk to; test the system before you make the rest of your family use it.

➤ Some companies now provide Internet-to-Phone connections, allowing you to make calls across the Internet and connect to a real phone.

➤ Many useful features are available in some products. You can send text or pictures while you talk, talk to a group of people, or even go on group Web trips.

➤ Video phones are available, but they require fast connections to the Internet to work well.

Chapter 14

What On Earth Are All Those File Types?

In This Chapter

➤ About the directory (folder) system

➤ Picking a download directory

➤ File extensions and file types

➤ File types you'll run into

➤ What are compressed files?

➤ Working with compressed and archive files

➤ Avoiding viruses

It's possible to work with a computer for years without really understanding directories and file types. I know people who simply save files from their word processor (the only program they ever use) 'on the disk'. *Where on the disk?* Well ... you know ... on the hard disk. *Yes, but where? Which directory?* Well ... you know ... where the program saves the files.

You can get away with this lack of knowledge if you use only one program and don't use it too much. But if you plan to spend any time on the Internet and plan to make the most of your time there, you'll need to understand a bit more about files and directories. You'll come across a plethora of file types and it helps if you understand what you are looking at.

About Download Directories

I don't want to spend a lot of time explaining what a directory is. This is very basic computing stuff and if you don't understand it, you should probably read an introduction to computing (such as *The Complete Idiot's Guide to PCs*, by Joe Kraynak). However, I'll quickly explain it and that may be enough.

You can think of a directory as an area on your hard disk that stores computer files. You might think of it as a file folder in a filing cabinet. The hard disk is the filing cabinet, holding dozens, maybe hundreds, of folders (directories). In some graphical user interfaces, such as Windows 95 and the Macintosh, directories are called *folders*. (But I've been using the term *directory* too long to give it up now.)

If you look inside a filing cabinet and open a file folder, what do you find? Documents – those are the individual files. And you may also find another folder within the first folder. That's what we call a subdirectory. So, directories can contain files and other directories and those directories can contain more files and more directories (more subdirectories) and so on. Thus you have what is known as the directory tree. (The following figure shows what this 'tree' looks like.) The point of this system is to help you organize your files. It's not uncommon for today's computers to have thousands of files, tens of thousands even. If you don't organize this lot logically, you'll end up with a mess that will make the Gordian Knot look simple.

Directories Are *Not* Areas Of The Hard Disk!

Before you email me saying that a directory is *not* an area on your hard disk, let me say *I know that!* It just *appears* to be an area on your hard disk. Actually, computer files are spread across the disk in an apparently illogical and disorganized manner – a piece of a file here, a piece there. The directory system is simply a visual way to organize the files, to make the hard disk easier to use.

The disk says, 'I have a directory here that contains these files'. But that's a lie, really, as the files are actually scattered willy-nilly all over the place. But it doesn't matter. It's rather like a child who *swears* that he has tidied up his room, that his socks are in the dresser and his shoes are in the closet. They're not, of course; everything's scattered over the floor. But you really don't want to look inside because it will just upset you. So you accept it and think in terms of where things *should be* within the room, without wanting to see the truth.

Folders, within folders, within folders make up the directory tree, shown here in the Norton File Manager program.

A *download directory* is a directory into which you download a file. For instance, let's say that you are using your Web browser to download a shareware program from one of the libraries listed in Appendix C. Where is that file saved? By definition, it's downloaded into the download directory. However, no directory is called the download directory; the download directory is whichever directory you say to put the file in.

The directory chosen by the browser as the download directory is not always the best place to put the file. In many cases it's a lousy choice. Internet Explorer, for instance, wants to place downloaded files on the Windows *desktop*. (In Windows, the desktop is actually a special subdirectory of the WINDOWS directory; anything placed inside that directory will appear on the desktop – the area of your computer screen that is visible when all the programs have been closed.) That's often a bad place to put it; if you download a lot of things, your desktop will soon be as cluttered as my office. (And believe me, that's not pleasant.) Of course you can always move the file to another directory later, but in that case, why not put it where you want it in the first place?

Also, many of the files that you will download are archive files; these are sort of file containers. Although an archive file is a single file, it has other files within it, perhaps hundreds of them. When you extract those files from inside, they are generally placed in the same directory. After you extract those files, you no longer have one easily recognized file on your desktop (or in whichever download directory the program chose). You now have a dozen or more new files there. Do this with several download files and you'll soon become confused; which file came from which archive?

Pick A Download Directory Sensibly

When you download files from the Web, FTP, Gopher, your online service, or wherever, think sensibly about where you place the downloaded file. Many users create a special directory called DOWNLOAD. Some programs even do this automatically: WS_FTP, for instance, creates a DOWNLOAD directory to be used as the default location for down-loaded files. You can place all the files you download directly into that directory. Later you can decide what you want to do with the files.

I prefer to go one step further. When I download a file, I think about where I'll eventually want the file. For instance, if it's a document file related to a book I'm working on, I save it directly into one of the directories I've created to hold the book. If it's a program file, I'll have to create a directory to hold the program at some point, so why not create a directory for the program right now and download the file directly into that directory? (Depending on which operating system and program you are using, you may be able to create the directory while you are telling the program where to save the file; or you may have to use some kind of file-management program to create the directory and *then* save the file.)

Learn about directories. Make sure you understand how to find your way around the directory tree (or folder system as it's known in some operating systems). And make sure you save files in the right places, in such a manner that you can find them when you need them.

A Cornucopia Of File Formats

Many computer users don't understand the concept of file formats because they never really see any files. They open their word processors, do some work, and then save the file. They may notice that when they give the file a name, the program adds a few letters such as .DOC or .WPD at the end, but they don't think much about it. If you're going to be playing on the Net, though, you need to understand just a little about file formats because you'll have to pick and choose the ones you want.

Hidden File Extensions

Windows 95 and later operating systems hide the file extensions from you. I think this is particularly stupid, but then, Microsoft didn't ask me before deciding to do this. To see file extensions, open Windows Explorer and select **Tools**, **Folder Options** (or **View**, **Options** in some older Windows versions). Then, under the **View** tab, clear the check box labelled **Hide file extensions for known file types**.

All computer files have one thing in common. They all save information in the form of zeros and ones. The difference between a file created by one word processor and another, or between a file created by a word processor and one created by a graphics program, is in what those zeros and ones actually *mean*. Just as two languages can use the same basic sounds and string them together to create different words, different programs use the zeros and ones to mean different things. One program uses zeros and ones to create words, another to create sounds, another to create pictures, and so on.

The File Extension

How, then, can a computer program identify one file from another? Well, they can often look for a familiar sequence of zeros and ones at the beginning of a file; if they find it, they know they've got the right file. But there's also something called *file extensions* that identifies files and it has the added advantage of being visible to mere mortals. An extension is a piece of text at the end of a file name, preceded by a dot, that is used to identify the file type. For example, look at this sample file name:

THISDOC.TXT

The extension is the .TXT bit. This means the file is a plain text file; any program that can read what is known as ASCII text can open this file and read it.

Different Extensions, Same Format

Some files are identified by two or more different file extensions. For instance, the .JPEG extension was used on UNIX computers to identify a form of graphics file commonly used on the Web. But because Windows 3.1 and DOS can't display four-character extensions, the file is often seen with the .JPG extension; different extension, but exactly the same file format. You'll also find .HTM and .HTML files, .TXT and .TEXT files, and .AIF and .AIFF files (sound files).

215

Now, in most operating systems (including DOS and Windows), file extensions are typically three characters long, in some cases four. And normally each file has only one file extension. Some operating systems, such as UNIX and Windows 98, for example, allow multiple extensions and extensions with more than three characters such as THISDOC.NEWONE.TEXT. However, this sort of thing is becoming rare on the Internet these days and you'll generally only run into simple three- and four-character extensions.

Macintosh files, by the way, don't require a file extension; rather, an identifier is built into the file, visible to the computer but not to the operator. However, note that Macintosh files stored on the Internet often do have an extension – .hqx or .sea, for instance. This extension is to make them readily identifiable as Macintosh files by human beings. (I find it amusing that the Mac's programmers, for all the talk of making their computers easy to use, didn't realize how important file extensions are to mere humans.)

You might be thinking that there are probably three or four file formats you need to know about. No, not quite. Try four or five dozen. The following table gives a list to keep you going.

File Formats You Should Know

File Format	Type of File It Identifies
.ARC	A PKARC file (a DOS compression file).
.AU, .AIF, .AIFF, .AIFC, .SND	Sound files often used on Macintosh systems; Netscape and Internet Explorer can play these sounds.
.AVI	Video for Windows.
.ASP	Active Server Page, a page containing special scripts run by a Web server immediately before the page is sent to your browser to be displayed.
.BMP, .PCX,	Common bitmap graphics formats.
.CSV	Comma Delimited Data file, a file containing information that can be imported into a database or spreadsheet program.
.DOC	Microsoft Word files, from Word for the Macintosh, Word for Windows, and Windows WordPad.
.EPS	A PostScript image.
.EXE	A program file or a self-extracting archive file.
.FLC, .FLI, .AAS	Autodesk Animator files.
.GIF, .PNG	These are graphics files. They share one thing in common: they are the formats used for graphics images on the Web.
.gzip and .gz	A UNIX compressed file.
.HLP	Windows Help files.
.HTM, .HTML	The basic Web-document format.
.hqx	A BinHex file, a format often used to archive Macintosh files. Programs such as StuffIt Expander can open these.
.JPG, .JPEG, .JPE, .JFIF, .PJPEG, .PJP	JPEG graphics files that most Web browsers can display. A few more variations of the JPEG format that Netscape can display.
.MID, .RMI	MIDI (Musical Instrument Digital Interface) sounds.

.MMM	Microsoft Multimedia Movie Player files.
.MOV .QT	The QuickTime video format.
.MP2	An MPEG audio format.
.mp3	A music format that has the music business terrified. It's close to CD quality, yet only takes up around 1MB for each minute of sound. MP3 files can also include images (CD cover art, for instance), lyrics, artist's bio, and so on.
.MPEG, .MPG, .MPE, .M1V	The MPEG (Motion Pictures Expert Group) video formats.
.PDF	The Portable Document Format, an Adobe Acrobat hypertext file. This format is a very popular means of distributing electronic documents.
.PHP	Like .ASP, a file containing scripts that are run by a Web server before it delivers the page to your browser. Although PHP used to mean Personal Home Page, it's now become a recursive acronym for PHP Hypertext Pre-processor.
.pit	The Macintosh Packit archive format.
.PS	A PostScript document.
.RAM, .RA	RealAudio. This is a sound format that plays while it's being transmitted. Click a link to a RealAudio file and it begins playing within a few seconds (you don't have to wait until the entire file is transferred).
.RTF	Rich Text Format, word processing files that work in a variety of Windows word processors.
.sea	A Macintosh self-extracting archive.
.SGML	A document format.
.shar	A UNIX shell archive file.
.sit	The Macintosh StuffIt archive format.
.tar	A UNIX tar archive file.
.TIF, .TIFF	A common graphics format.
.TSP	TrueSpeech, a sound format similar to RealAudio, though of a higher quality.
.ttf	Windows TrueType font files.
.TXT, .TEXT	A text file. These are displayed in the browser window.
.WAV	The standard Windows wave file sound format.
.WRI	Windows Write word processing files.
.WRL	A VRML (Virtual Reality Modeling Language) 3-D object.
.XBM	Another graphics file that can be displayed by Web browsers.
.XDM	The StreamWorks webTV and webRadio format. This is similar to RealAudio, but it allows the real-time playing of video in addition to sound.
.Z	A UNIX compressed file.
.z	A UNIX packed file.
.ZIP	A PKZIP archive file (a DOS and Windows compression file).
.zoo	A zoo210 archive format available on various systems.

Is that all? By no means! Netscape currently claims that it has over 160 plug-ins. Although many of those duplicate the functions of other plug-ins, including the same file types, this number still represents a lot of different file formats. There are all sorts of file formats out there; to be honest though, you'll only run across a few of them. You may never even run across a few of the ones I included in the table; for instance, the .ARC format, which used to be very common, is quite rare now.

File Compression Basics

Check This Out...

Is It Possible?

This is similar to Dr Who's Tardis, which has much more space inside than would be allowed within a box of that size according to normal physics. And no, I don't plan to explain how it's done. Suffice it to say that, thanks to a little magic and nifty computing tricks, these programs make files smaller.

As you can see from the preceding table, a number of these file formats are archive or compressed formats. These are files containing other files within them. You can use a special program to extract those files; or, in the case of a 'self-extracting archive', the file can automatically extract the file.

Why do people bother to put files inside archive files? Or even, in some cases, a single file within an archive file? Two reasons. First, the programs that create these files compress the files being placed inside. So the single file is much smaller than the combined size of all the files inside.

You can reduce files down to as little as 2% of their normal size, depending on the type of file and the program you use (though 40% to 75% is probably a more normal range). Bitmap graphics, for instance, often compress to a very small size, while program files and Windows Help files can't be compressed so far. If you want to transfer a file across the Internet, it's a lot quicker to transfer a compressed file than an uncompressed file.

The other reason to use these systems is that you can place files inside another file as a sort of packaging or container. If a shareware program has, say, 20 different files that it needs in order to run, it's better to 'wrap' all these into one file than to expect people to transfer all 20 files one at a time.

Which Format?

Most compressed DOS and Windows files are in .ZIP format, a format often created by a program called PKZIP (though as the file format is not owned by anyone, other programs create .ZIP files, too, such as the hugely popular WinZip). There are other programs, though; you may also see .ARJ (created by a program called ARJ) and .LZH (created by LHARC) now and again, but probably not very often. PKZIP won the compression war.

Archive Versus Compressed

What's the difference between an archive file and a compressed file? Well, they're often the same thing and people (including me) tend to use the terms interchangeably. Originally, however, an archive file was a file that stored lots of other files: it archived them. An archive file doesn't have to be a compressed file, it's just a convenient place to put files that you are not using. A compressed file must, of course, be compressed. These days, archive files *are* usually compressed files and compressed files are often used for archiving files. So there's not a lot of difference between the two any more.

In the UNIX world, .Z and .tar files are common archive formats. And on the Macintosh, you'll find .sit (StuffIt) and .pit (Packit) compressed formats, as well as .hqx (BinHex) archive files. This table gives you a quick rundown of the compressed formats you'll see.

Common Compressed File Formats

Extension	Program That Compressed It
.arc	DOS, PKARC (an older method, predating PKZIP).
.exe	A DOS or Windows self-extracting archive.
.gz	Usually a UNIX gzip-compressed file (although there are versions of gzip for other operating systems, they're rarely used).
.hqx	Macintosh BinHex.
.pit	Macintosh Packit.
.sea	A Macintosh self-extracting archive.
.shar	UNIX shell archive.
.sit	Macintosh StuffIt.
.tar	UNIX tar.
.Z	UNIX compress.
.z	UNIX pack.
.ZIP	WinZip, PKZIP and others.
.zoo	zoo210 (available on various systems).

It goes without saying (but I'll say it anyway, just in case) that if you see a file with an extension that is common on an operating system other than yours, it may contain files that won't be any good on your system. Macintosh and UNIX software won't run on Windows, for instance. However, that's not always true. The file may contain text files, for instance, which can be read on any system. So there are cross-platform utilities; for example, Macintosh utilities can uncompress archive files that are not common in the Macintosh world, and some ZIP utilities running in Windows can extract files from .gz and .tar files. For instance, some versions of StuffIt Expander, a Macintosh utility, can open ZIP files, and WinZip, a Windows program, can open .gz and .tar files.

Those Self-Extracting Archives

Check This Out...

In The Meantime ...

How can you download and extract one of these programs before you have a program that will extract an archive file? Don't worry, the programmers thought of that! These utilities are generally stored in self-extracting format, so you can download them and automatically extract them by running them.

Finally, there's something called self-extracting archives. Various programs, such as WinZip, PKZIP, and ARJ, can create files that can be executed (run) to extract the archived files automatically. This is very useful for sending a compressed file to someone when you're not sure if he has the program to decompress the file (or would know how to use it). For instance, WinZip can create a file with an .EXE extension; you can run such a file directly from the DOS prompt just by typing its name and pressing Enter, or by double-clicking the file in the Windows Explorer file-management program. When you do so, all of the compressed files pop out. In the Macintosh world .sea – Self Extracting Archive – files do the same thing. Double-click a .sea file and the contents are automatically extracted.

If you find a file in two formats, .ZIP and .EXE for instance, you may want to take the .EXE format. The .EXE files are not much larger than the .ZIP files and you don't need to worry about finding a program to extract the files. In such a case, you must have a program that can read the .ZIP file and extract the archived files from within.

You may already have such a program. Some Windows file-management programs, for instance, can work with .ZIP files. Otherwise you'll need a program that can extract from the compressed format. See Appendix C for information about file libraries where you can download freeware and shareware that will do the job.

Your Computer Can Get Sick, Too

Downloading all these computer files can lead to problems: computer viruses. File viruses hide out in program files and copy themselves to other program files when someone runs that program. Viruses and other malevolent computer bugs are real and they do real damage. Now and then you'll hear of service providers having to close down temporarily after their systems become infected.

Unfortunately, security on the Internet is lax. The major online services have strict regulations about virus checks. Members generally cannot post directly to public areas, for instance; they post to an area in which the file can be checked for viruses before it's available to the public. But on the Internet, it's up to each system administrator (and there are thousands of them) to keep his own system clean. If just one administrator does a bad job, a virus can get through and be carried by FTP, the Web, or email all over the world. The large shareware archives are probably quite careful, but there are tens of thousands of places to download software on the Internet, and some of those are probably a little careless.

Viruses Under The Microscope

The term virus has become a 'catch-all' for a variety of different digital organisms, such as

➤ **Bacteria**, which reproduce and do no direct damage except using up disk space and memory.

➤ **Rabbits**, which get their name because they reproduce very quickly.

➤ **Trojan horses**, which are viruses embedded in otherwise-useful programs.

➤ **Bombs**, which are programs that just sit and wait for a particular date or event (at which time they wreak destruction); these are often left deep inside programs by disgruntled employees.

➤ **Worms**, which are programs that copy themselves from one computer to another, independent of other executable files, and 'clog' the computers by taking over memory and disk space.

However, having said all that, I've also got to say that the virus threat is also overstated – probably by companies selling antivirus software. We've reached a stage where almost any confusing computer problem is blamed on computer viruses and technical support lines are using it as an excuse not to talk with people. 'Your computer can't read your hard disk? You've been downloading files from the Internet? You must have a virus!'

Most computer users have never been 'hit' by a computer virus. Many who think they have probably haven't; a lot of problems are blamed on viruses these days. So don't get overly worried about it. Take some sensible precautions and you'll be okay.

Tips For Safe Computing

If you are just working with basic ASCII text email and perhaps ftping documents, you're okay. The problem of viruses arises when you transfer programs – including self-extracting archive files – or files that contain mini 'programs'. (For instance, many word processing files can now contain macros, special little programs that may run when you open the file.)

Rule Of Thumb

Here's a rule of thumb to figure out if a file is dangerous. 'If it does something, it can carry a virus; if it has things done to it, it's safe.' Only files that can actually carry out actions (such as script files, program files, and word processing files from the fancy word processors that have built-in macro systems) can pose a threat. If a file can't do anything – it just sits waiting until a program displays or plays it – it's safe. Pictures and sounds, for instance, may offend you personally, but they won't do your computer any harm. (Can self-extracting archives carry viruses? Absolutely. They're programs, and they run – you don't know that they're self-extracting archives until they've extracted, after all.)

If you do plan to transfer programs, perhaps the best advice is to get a good antivirus program. They're available for all computer types. Each time you transmit an executable file, use your antivirus program to check it. Also, make sure you keep good backups of your data. Although backups can also become infected with viruses, if a virus hits, at least you can reload your backup data and use an antivirus program to clean the files (some backup programs check for viruses while backing up).

The Least You Need To Know

➤ Don't transfer files to your computer without thinking about *where* on your hard disk they should be. Create a download directory in a sensible place.

➤ Files are identified by their file extension, typically a three-character (sometimes four-character) 'code' preceded by a dot.

➤ Compressed and archive files are files containing other files within. They provide a convenient way to distribute files across the Internet.

➤ Self-extracting archives are files that don't require a special utility to extract the files from within. Just 'run' the file and the files within are extracted.

➤ Viruses are real, but the threat is exaggerated. Use an antivirus program and then relax.

➤ The virus rule of thumb is this: 'If it does something, it can carry a virus; if it has things done to it, it's safe'.

Chapter 15

Asccessing The Internet With Cool New Devices

In This Chapter

➤ Why other Internet-connection devices are needed

➤ Web-enabled cell phones

➤ Handheld computers, telephones, and TVs

➤ Email devices and Internet computers

➤ Receiving email on your pager

➤ Telephones, printers, and faxes

➤ Connecting elephants and other pets

The growth of the Internet is slowing because so many people who had computer hardware and computer *wetware* (a geek term for brainpower) are already on the Internet. For more people to get onto the Internet, two things must happen:

➤ More people need to begin using computers, so those computers can be connected to the Internet.

➤ Internet capabilities must be built into other devices, so people can connect to the Internet even if they don't have a computer.

Of course, the question is: Why would anyone want to connect to the Internet if he didn't have a computer? The answer is: He probably wouldn't. So, don't expect a huge rush of non-computer-literate people trying to get onto the Internet. There are plenty of people who don't care about the Internet, so however easy it becomes to access the Internet, they won't.

Nonetheless, things will change. Email, for instance, will become pervasive, and eventually even people without Internet access will feel the pressure to use email. A number of Internet services will become so useful that non-users will envy users. For instance, the Internet provides so many ways to get information when planning a trip, it's hard to beat. You can look up businesses in Internet Yellow Pages around the world and even print out maps and directions to those businesses (check to see that the hotel really is 'just a short walk to the beach'). Need to meet someone at a local restaurant? Using the Web, you can get step-by-step directions from your hotel to the restaurant, along with a map. You can see photographs of hotels, check airline schedules and prices, view information about the local climate and bar scene, and so much more. (In the next part of the book, 'Getting Things Done', we'll look at exactly *where* you can find these things.)

Eventually, even non-computer-owning non-Internet users will want these services. Some will buy computers. Others will use some other kind of Internet device. This chapter takes a quick look at alternatives to computers for accessing the Internet.

Before we start, Kent's First Law of Internet Connectivity:

If it *can* be connected, it *will* be connected.

What sorts of things can be connected to the Internet (and therefore *will* be connected to the Internet)? There are basically two types of devices: devices used to access information over the Internet and devices used to feed information to the Internet (some devices do both). Here are a few of the wonderful things that are already hooked up to the Internet or will be soon:

➤ Televisions

➤ Pagers

➤ Telephones

➤ Cars

➤ CD Players

➤ Printers and fax machines

➤ Pets

➤ Parking meters

➤ Police scanners

➤ Your house

226

➤ Clothing

➤ Hot tubs

➤ Ant farms

➤ Elephants

If you want to see a huge sampling of the weird and wonderful things already connected, visit this Yahoo! page: **http://dir.yahoo.com/Computers_and_ Internet/Internet/Devices_Connected_to_the_Internet.** You'll find categories for Audio Equipment, Coffee Machines, Clocks, Calculators, Pagers, Robots, Soda Machines, and more.

So, let's take a look at a variety of interesting ways to access the Internet, and finish with a few odd examples of data being fed into the Internet.

Cell Phone Access

If you think your ear is stuck to your cell phone a little too much, move it around to the front of your face and *look* at it. If you've got one of the new Internet-enabled phones, you'll be able to get online to...

➤ Get your email

➤ View news, stock quotes, weather, and more

➤ Find information about restaurants, and get directions

➤ Buy music or travel and theatre tickets online

➤ Use instant messaging (see Chapter 12)

➤ Get stock quotes

These phones have what are known as *microbrowsers*, simple Web browsers that display text but not graphics. These devices are not intended for accessing normal Web pages, but are designed to get to information that has been specially formatted for them. There's something called HDML – Handheld Device Markup Language – that is derived from HTML and intended for creating Web pages that can be used by microbrowser-enabled phones.

There are many Web-enabled cell phones around; most companies make them, in fact. Note, though, that you'll pay extra to use the Web through a cell phone.

WAP Pages

Want to see an example of a WAP-enabled page? (WAP means Wireless Application Protocol, the system used by wireless devices to access the Internet.) Go to **http://www.lionwap.org/good** and click the icons in the WAP column.

Intercast PC/TV

TV and the Web are slowly being joined, through *intercast PC/TV*. That's the merging of Web pages into TV signals. There's a lot of empty space in a TV signal, and it's possible to transmit extra information, information that the TV doesn't need. For instance, closed captions for the deaf are transmitted in this way, as is the information used in our teletext systems.

So, a TV show can carry a Web page that is related to the show. A cookery show, for instance, could carry a Web page containing recipes. If you like what they're cooking, change to the Web page, read the recipe, and print it out on the printer connected to the TV.

Of course, right now there are very few intercast shows, and intercast TVs are not available, but they soon will be. Already you can get a taste of the combined TV/Web experience via digital TV services such as Sky Active (**http://www.sky.com**) which offers online shopping, email and games.

Handhelds

So-called *handheld* computers, or *PDAs* (*Personal Digital Assistants*), are gaining in popularity as businesspeople grow tired of lugging around laptops. If all you need while travelling is basic computing capabilities, handhelds might be enough. Some of these machines even have modems, email programs, and, yes, Web browsers.

What can you do with these things? Well, you can get to your email, downloading messages from multiple POP accounts if you want. You can view Web pages – as with a cell phone's microbrowser, PDAs work with Web pages designed specifically for them. You can bookmark Web sites, buy products, trade stocks, and save information from Web sites directly into PDA applications.

Handheld Email Devices

There are a number of handheld email devices coming onto the market, the most popular of which will probably be the Blackberry (**http://www.blackberry.com/uk**). These resemble large pagers, with lots of buttons. They can send and receive email messages, and come in various configurations. They can work with Microsoft Outlook, with the Microsoft Exchange email server, or with a provided Internet email account; and the AOL version even works with AOL Instant Messenger (see Chapter 12). They have a built-in personal organizer, too, for contacts, appointments and tasks.

These might seem like a good idea – I certainly like the idea of being able to check my email at any time by pulling a little box out of my pocket and pressing one or two buttons. However, many people will be deterred by the price. They start at around £439, and the monthly fees are around £39 a month.

Mail Devices

A number of devices, intended for email and little else, are turning up on the market. They are very easy to install; plug them into a phone line and follow a simple configuration program, and you're up and running.

For instance, there's the Amstrad e-m@iler Plus (**http://www.amstrad.com**). This product costs £100, plus 12p per dialup call in addition to your normal telephone charges. To look at, it has a lot in common with a telephone (and, in fact, it is a combined telephone/answering machine, among other things) but it has a small pop-up monochrome screen, and a little slide-out keyboard. You can use the e-m@iler Plus to send and receive email (including voice-message attachments), send SMS messages to mobile phones, or view some Web sites (though the quality of the built-in browser leaves Web browsing restricted to the less complex, low-on-graphics type of site).

So who would use the e-m@iler Plus? It's clearly targeted at older users, probably the parents and grandparents of active Internet users who want to get them onto the Internet. It's certainly not the cheapest way of going about it, but it should be simpler and a somewhat less frightening prospect than getting to grips with a PC (although Amstrad warns that you have 'no chance of operating this unit' without reading the manual first).

Pagers

Do you have an alphanumeric pager? Did you know you can receive email on it? A number of services will receive your email, and then forward it to your pager number. Some services even allow someone to enter a message into a Web page, and then click a button to send that message to a pager.

Some pager companies can set you up with an email address, so you can receive your messages. But even if your pager company doesn't do this, you can always get an account with a paging-service company, which might have better features than the pager company. For instance, you might be able to exceed the message limit. If your pager accepts, say, only 100 characters, you can use a service that will break your email messages into several pages, so you can exceed the limit. A service might also allow you to set filters to send some messages to the pager, but forward all others (for instance, pages from your spouse get sent to the pager and pages from your boss get forwarded to your email account, or vice versa depending on your relationships).

Some services will also send news, weather, or stock reports at predetermined times and can retrieve email from your normal email account so you don't need a special email account just for your pager. If you'd like to track down these services, go to a search engine and search for **pager email**.

Refrigerators

Yep, that's right, you'll soon be able to buy a fridge that's Internet connectable. Why? The fridge should be able to keep an eye on food quantities, and order more from your grocer across the Internet. It might also be able to connect to recipe databases, and, er, handle online banking. Whether it can determine the age and digestibility of various things that have been sitting in the back of your fridge for a while before it reorders, I'm not sure. The Electrolux Screenfridge was supposed to be in production already, but Electrolux is now saying that it doesn't know when it will release it. If this is what your home is missing, you can look out for details at **http://www.electrolux.co.uk**.

Printers And Faxes

Need to send a fax to the corporate office in Kuala Lumpur? Why not send it over the Internet? If both offices have fax machines connected to the Internet, the fax can go over the Net for free. If the office in Kuala Lumpur has a printer connected to the Internet, your computer can send a file directly to the printer; the printer is, in effect, an Internet fax machine. Such devices will probably become commonplace not too long from now.

Cash Registers

Many fast-food store cash registers are already connected to the Internet. These *Point of Sale* (*POS*) terminals are mostly based on Windows PCs these days, so it's pretty easy to connect them. But why bother? Well, it allows a restaurant owner to sit at home and view the day's takings, across the Internet, in all his restaurants. With an optional video camera, it also allows him to look in on the store and check up on the kids running it – be sure they're wearing their hats the right way around, and so on.

It's a Wired, Wired, Wired World

Imagine a world in which everything that can be connected is connected. We're going to see all sorts of things connected to the Internet over the next few years. For instance, you probably know that Bill Gates has wired his house – it's what's sometimes called an *intelligent* house. (Bill Gates might not be scared by the thought of Microsoft software controlling his living space, but it would scare the hell out of me.) I don't know whether his house is connected to the Internet, but there's no reason it couldn't be. And that's reason enough to think that eventually many houses will be connected to the Internet.

If you go on a vacation and forget to turn down the heat, don't worry; just connect to your house's heating interface on the Web, and set the heat to whatever you want. Want to check your phone messages? Get them over the Net. After houses are connected to the Internet, of course, new devices will be created – or old devices used in a new way – to provide reasons to connect over the Internet. For instance, you'll be able to view a snapshot of everyone who's rung your doorbell while you've been away, or view a picture of the front garden to see whether the kid next door kept his promise and mowed the lawn.

Some weird connections to the Internet are closer than you might think. Have you heard that parking meters will be networked soon? Networking meters provide all sorts of benefits (in general, not to the parkers, of course, but to the cities that own the meters). For instance, traffic wardens will be able to see exactly which meters are just about to run out of money and rush to get there before the person who parked the car. If you network something, you can connect that network to the Internet. So, some people have been suggesting that cities might connect their parking-meter networks to the Internet, so parkers could feed the meters through a Web page. Of course, there are disadvantages to this, because it makes meter feeding way too easy and might cut down on meter availability, but I wouldn't be surprised if some cities try it.

How about elephants? Sound ridiculous? I've heard about a dairy research farm that considered networking its cows, and it's not so far from cows to elephants. Imagine a research project tracking the movement of Indian elephants. Many such projects already use radio trackers. It's not such a leap of imagination to consider connecting the radio signals to the Web, so people all over the world could watch the movement of the elephants. (It might not be a good idea in areas rife with ivory poachers, of course.) You heard it here first; elephants will be connected to the Internet.

In fact, we're not so far off. Check out Elephant.net, the Malaysian Elephant Tracking Project: **http://boh.com.my/pl/pubdoc/2121**. They use Java maps to show the movement of the elephants they're tracking. It's not real-time – that is, you're not seeing the signal directly from the elephant – but it could be one day.

Now we come to Kent's Second Law of Internet Connectivity:

The degree of usefulness is no predictor of connectivity.

In other words, just because something is useful doesn't mean it will be connected before something that isn't useful. Remember this: some of the first non-computer devices connected to the Internet were drink machines. That's right, some bright computer-science undergraduates figured out that if they connected the department's drink machines to the Internet, they could view information about the machines over the Internet; no more arriving at the machine to discover that one's favourite drink was out of stock! Not too long after drink machines came hot tubs (as if anyone really cares about the temperature of a hot tub in someone's home on the other side of the world). So, no matter how ridiculous or seemingly pointless the connection, it will be made! All sorts of useless stuff will be connected – and is connected – to the Internet. Luckily, plenty of useful stuff will be connected, too.

The Least You Need to Know

➤ Pretty much *everything* that's electronic can be connected to the Internet. If something's not electronic, an electronic device can be added. So elephants will soon be connected to the Net.

➤ Many cell phones contain microbrowsers for Web access.

➤ You can now get your email through handheld devices (such as Blackberry), digital TV, or desktop email devices.

➤ It's very easy to send email and other information, such as news and weather, to a pager.

➤ Telephones, printers, and faxes will soon be connected to the Internet. Fridges, too.

Part 3
Getting Things Done

Now that you've learned how to use the Internet's services, it's time to learn some important general information about working on the Net. This place is so huge, you might have trouble finding what you need. And you'll also need to learn how to stay safe on the Internet. You've heard about the problems that go along with using credit cards on the Internet, about kids finding pornography, and so on.

In addition to covering all of those issues, I'll answer all sorts of questions I've heard from Internet users, from how to keep your email address when you switch service providers to the truth about Internet addiction. Also, in this part, I'll point you towards dozens of the hottest Web sites around, where you can do anything from reading a magazine to buying the Moon, and from finding a job to sending a digital postcard.

Finding Stuff On The Internet

Your connection is humming along sweetly, your software is installed, you know how to use it and you're surfing the Internet. And almost immediately you'll hit a predicament: this thing is huge! How on earth can you find what you're looking for?

As you probably guessed, the Internet is one jump ahead of you on that score: there's no shortage of tools to point you towards Web sites, email addresses, businesses and people. Choosing the best tool to use will depend largely on the type of information you want to find, but don't panic – these tools are ridiculously easy to use and you'll probably use several of them regularly. And, yet again, all you need is your trusty browser.

Finding A Search Site

Anything you can find on the World Wide Web you can find a link to at one of the Web's search sites. Although finding a search site on the Web is easy (especially as I'm about to tell you where the most popular ones are!), picking the one that's going to give the best results is never an exact science. Essentially there are two types of site available: **search engines** and **directories**.

> ➤ **Search engines** are indexes of World Wide Web sites, usually built automatically by a program called a spider, a robot, a worm, or something equally appetising (the AltaVista search engine uses a program it endearingly calls Scooter). These programs scour the Web constantly, and return with information about a page's location, title and contents, which is then added to an index. To search for a certain type of information, just type in keywords and the search engine will display a list of sites containing those words.

> ➤ **Directories** are hand-built lists of pages sorted into categories. Although you can search directories using a keyword search, it's often as easy to click on a category, and then click your way through the ever-more-specific subcategories until you find the subject you're interested in.

Search engines have the benefit of being about as up-to-date in their indexes as it's possible to be, as a result of their automation. The downside is that if you search for **pancake recipe** in a search engine, the resulting list of pages won't all necessarily contain recipes for pancakes – some might just be pages in which the words 'pancake' and 'recipe' coincidentally both happen to appear. However, the robot-programs used by the search engines all vary in the ways they gather their information, so you'll quite likely get results using one engine that you didn't get using another.

Directories don't have this problem because they list the subject of a page rather than the words it contains, but you won't always find the newest sites this way – sites tend to be listed in directories when their authors submit them for inclusion.

Here's a short list of popular search engines and directories to get you started. When you arrive at one of these, it's worth adding it to Internet Explorer's Favorites menu so that you can get back again whenever you need to without a lot of typing.

Search Site	Web Site URL
AltaVista	http://www.altavista.digital.com
Dogpile	http://www.dogpile.com
Excite	http://www.excite.com
Google	http://www.google.com
HotBot	http://www.hotbot.com
Lycos UK	http://www.lycos.co.uk
SearchUK	http://www.searchuk.com
UK Plus	http://www.ukplus.co.uk
Yahoo! UK & Ireland	http://www.yahoo.co.uk

Using A Search Engine

For this example I'll pick **Excite**, but most search engines work in exactly the same way, and look much the same too. Indeed, directories such as **Yahoo!** and **Infoseek** can be used like this if you like the simplicity of keyword searches.

There's One For The Kids Too

The Internet is fairly teeming with Web sites for children, and Yahoo! has a sister site called **Yahooligans** at **http://www.yahooligans. com** dedicated to these sites alone. The format is the same as Yahoo's main site, but all the links lead to pages for, or by, kids, along with some useful advice and information for their parents.

When you arrive at Excite you'll see a page like the one shown in the next screenshot. For the simplest sort of search, type a single word into the text box, and click on **Search**. If you want to search for something that can't be encapsulated in a single word it's worth reading the instructions – you'll probably see a link on the page marked Help or Search Tips or something similar – but there are a few tricks you can use that most search engines will understand (and those that don't will generally just ignore them).

Type a keyword into the search engine's text box and click Search.

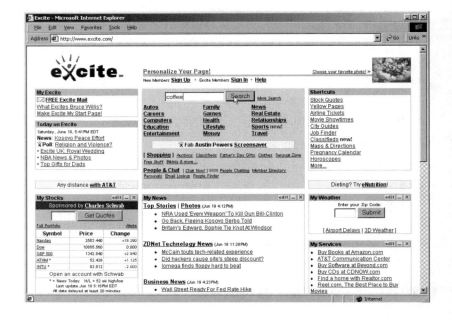

➤ If you enter several keywords, type them in descending order of importance. For example, if you wanted to find pictures of dolphins, type **dolphin pictures**. The list will then present good links to dolphin sites before the rather more general links to sites just containing pictures.

➤ Use capital letters only if you expect to *find* capital letters. Searching for **PARIS** may find very little, but searching for **Paris** should find a lot. If you don't mind whether the word is found capitalized or not, use lower case only (**paris**).

➤ To find a particular phrase, enclose it in 'quote marks'. For example, a search for **"hot dog"** would find only pages containing this phrase and ignore pages that just contained one word or the other.

➤ Prefix a word with a + sign if it must be included, and with a – sign if it must be excluded. For example, to find out more about tourism in Paris, you might search for **paris+tourism**. Similarly you could enter **printer inkjet –laser** if you wanted to find pages about printers, preferably including inkjet printers, but definitely not mentioning laser printers.

After entering the text you want to search for and clicking the **Search** button, your browser will send the information off to the engine, and within a few seconds you should see a new page like the one pictured below listing the sites that matched your search criteria. I used the keyword **coffee**, and Excite has found 297,031 different pages. It's worth remembering that when some search engines say they've found pages *about coffee*, they've really found pages that contain the word 'coffee' somewhere within the page's text. Many of these pages may be *about* something entirely different.

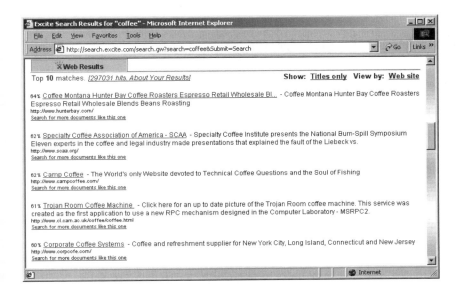

A search for 'coffee' finds more than enough results to keep me up all night.

Of course, you won't find all 297,031 pages listed here. Instead you'll see links to the ten most relevant pages, with a few words quoted from the beginning of each. At the bottom of the page you'll find a button that will lead you to the next ten on the list, and so on. In true Web style, these are all hypertext links – click the link to open any page that sounds promising. If the page fails to live up to that promise, use your browser's **Back** button to return to the search results and try a different one.

Save Your Search For Later

When the search results appear, you can add this page to Internet Explorer's Favorites menu. Not only is the URL of the search site stored, but also the keywords you entered for the search. It's a handy option to remember if you don't have time to visit all the pages found in the search straight away.

239

Most search engines give the pages a score for relevancy, and these are worth keeping an eye on. In many cases, a page scoring below about 70 per cent is unlikely to give much information. If you can't find what you want using one search engine, always try another – because their methods are different, their results can vary dramatically.

Searching The Web Directories

Top of the league of Web directories is Yahoo!, which now has a 'UK & Ireland' site at **http://www.yahoo.co.uk**. When you first arrive at the Yahoo! site, you'll see a search-engine style text-box into which you can type keywords if you prefer to search that way. However, you'll also see a collection of hypertext links below that, and these are the key to the directory system. Starting from a choice of broad categories on this page, you can dig more deeply into the system to find links to more specific information.

To take an example, click on the **computers and internet** link. On the next page, you'll see the list of subcategories, which includes **graphics**, **hardware**, **multimedia**, **training**, and many more computer- or Internet-related subjects. Click on the **multimedia** link, and you'll see another list of multimedia-related categories, shown in the following screenshot. Below this list of categories, you'll see another list: these are links to multimedia-related sites rather than more Yahoo! categories. To find out more about multimedia generally, you might click one of these

Choose a more specific Yahoo! category from the upper list, or a direct link to a Web site from the lower.

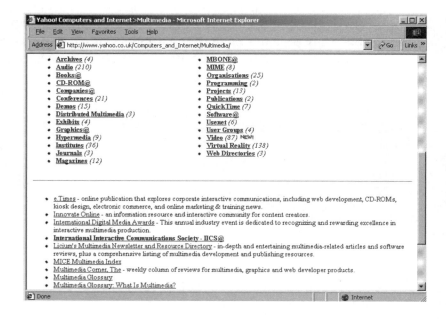

to visit that site; to find out more about a specific area of multimedia such as sound, video or virtual reality, you'd click that category in the upper list.

The layout is pretty easy to follow when you've browsed around for a few minutes, but Yahoo! has simplified it further by using bold and plain text to help you identify where you're going. Bold text means that this is a link to another Yahoo! category; plain text indicates that it's a link to a page elsewhere on the Web that contains the sort of information you've been searching for. Beside most of the bold category-links, you'll also see a number in brackets, such as **Pictures (448)**. This number tells you how many links you'll find in that category.

Why The '@' Symbol?

The '@' symbol indicates a cross reference to a different main category. For example, click on **companies@** and you'll be moving from the **computers and internet** heading to the **business and economy** heading. You'll find links to multimedia companies here, but other categories will be more related to business matters than to computing.

Which Search Site Is Best?

So should you use a search engine or a directory? And which one should you choose? There really isn't a 'best site', of course, though you'll probably come across a few candidates for the 'worst search site' title on your travels. Most users try a few search sites in their early days on the Web, settle on one or two they like best and stick with them. Here are quick introductions to four popular but very different sites, all well worth a look.

AltaVista UK

AltaVista has long been one of the 'heavyweight' US-based search engines, and now has a UK site at **http://uk.altavista.com**. Two option buttons let you choose whether to search in the UK or worldwide, and a drop-down list lets you find pages in particular languages. Using the tabbed links above the search box, you can run searches for images, video clips or audio files, and (in common with most search engines) you can switch to Advanced Search mode to refine your search query with more specific options. One useful (or, sometimes, amusing) feature is that if you come across a page in a foreign language among your search results, you can click the Translate link and AltaVista will have a brave stab at translating it for you.

Google

As other search engines have grown ever more cluttered and complicated, Google has taken the search engine back to basics: you want to search, you want to find. As a result, when you arrive at Google (**http://www.google.com**) you won't find much more than a text box to type your query into and a Google Search button to begin searching. But this simplicity hides a very fast and powerful engine indeed: every search result presents a link to a Yahoo!-style directory structure where you can find similar pages, and gives you an idea of the size of the page found. Best of all, if the page no longer exists at its original location, Google may have its own cached copy of it which you can reach by clicking the Cached link.

Google: refreshingly simple, deceptively powerful.

Yahoo! UK & Ireland

Yahoo! was the site that invented the whole Web-searching concept, and it's still a well-loved and widely-used workhorse. Its UK and Ireland site at **http://www.yahoo.co.uk** has all the variety, speed and reliability of its US-based counterpart, but it also lets you choose between searching the entire Web or just the UK and Ireland sections of it. Even if you choose to search the whole Web, any UK or Irish sites found will be placed at the top of the list and indicated by flags to grab your attention. You'll also see a sunglasses icon beside sites that the folk at Yahoo! thought were especially 'cool'. The layout is plain and functional, to the point of being dull, and site descriptions range from short to non-existent, but its power is hard to beat. Be warned though: both Yahoo! and its kids' counterpart at **http://www.yahooligans.com** can be addictive! If you start exploring those categories, rather than running a quick keyword search and going away again, it's easy to lose track of the time you've spent online!

242

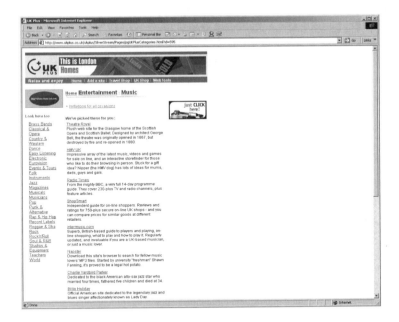

UK Plus: a smart and straightforward starting-point for finding UK sites.

UK Plus

Like Yahoo!, UK Plus at **http://www.ukplus.co.uk** uses a directory format in which you pick a category from its front page and dig deeper into the subcategories until you reach the subject you're looking for. Apart from being a much more attractive site than Yahoo!, there are a couple of more important differences. First, only UK sites and sites of particular interest to UK users are listed, and second, every site is accompanied by a useful, honest description written by the UK Plus staff. Although the UK Plus directory is tiny by Yahoo! standards, it's probably the best and simplest place to start looking when nothing but a UK site will do.

Keep It Friendly

One problem with search engines is that they can provide links to all manner of sites you weren't expecting. For instance, a perfectly innocent search for a well-known actress or pop star could produce a large number of undesirable links (and possibly with higher rankings than the type of site you *were* expecting). So most search engines now offer some form of 'family-friendly' search which filters out links the average user would find offensive. There's no agreed-upon name for the feature, but look out for options named Parental Controls, Family Filter, or something similar on the front page of the site, or a link that allows you to set Options or Preferences. In many cases, safe searching is switched on by default.

Easy Web Searching With Internet Explorer

To reach a search site quickly in Internet Explorer, click the **Search** button on the toolbar (a globe icon with a magnifying glass). A frame will appear at the left of Explorer's window, similar to the Favorites and History list panels, displaying a mini version of a search engine. Explorer chooses the search engine for you, but you can choose a different one by clicking the **New** or **Customize** buttons. Type in your query, click the obvious button and the results will appear in the same frame with the usual **Next 10** button at the bottom.

Instant Searching

Instead of clicking the **Search** button and waiting for the search page to load, Internet Explorer offers a quicker method. In the address bar, type the word(s) you want to search for then press **Enter**. If a matching Web site can be found, Explorer will open it; if not, your words will be passed to the search engine and the search frame will appear to display the results.

Internet Explorer's search panel keeps your results visible as you work your way through the most promising links.

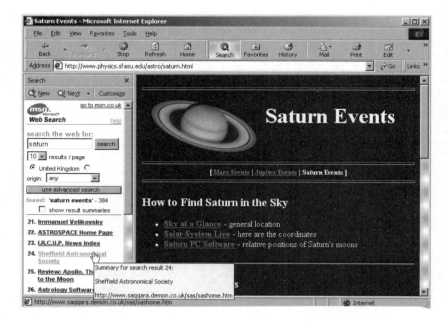

The great benefit of this method of searching is that you can click any entry in the list to open it in the main part of the window without losing track of the search results. For a brief description of each site found, hold your mouse-pointer over the link for a moment as shown in the screenshot above (or, in the case of Excite, click the tiny button beside a link to show or hide its description).

Finding People On The Net

Finding people on the Internet is a bit of a black art – after all, there are in excess of 40 million users, and few would bother to 'register' their details even if there were an established directory. In addition, of course, if you move your access account to a different online service or ISP, your email address will change too (more on that in Chapter 18). So it's all a bit hit and miss, but let's look at a few possibilities.

Flick Through The White Pages

In the UK, the term Yellow Pages is synonymous with finding businesses. White pages is a type of directory listing *people* (what we usually just call a phone book), and the Internet has a few 'white pages' directories that may turn up trumps. Some of these rely on people actually submitting their details voluntarily; others take the more crafty approach of searching the newsgroups and adding the email addresses of anyone posting an article. Searching white pages is just like using any other search engine, usually requiring you to enter the user's first and last names and click on a Search button.

> ➤ **BT Directory Enquires.** Visit **http://www.bt.com** and click the Directory Enquiries link at the top-right of the page for the familiar UK service online. You can also use 192.com at **http://www.192.com/peoplesearch.cfm**.

> ➤ **Yahoo! People Search** at **http://people.yahoo.com** (or **http://ukie.people. yahoo.com** to find folk in the UK and Ireland). This is the biggest and most popular 'people locator' in the States, which searches the Internet for email addresses and accepts individual submissions. Details found here may include a user's hobbies, postal address and phone number, but most entries are from the USA.

> ➤ **Infospace at http://www.infospace.com** (click the **Email** link in the **White Pages** section). Choose the appropriate country (but ignore the State/Province box unless you're searching for someone in the US or Canada) and enter any other details you can, such as name and city. Infospace also has a handy Phone Numbers lookup, reached by scrolling to the bottom of the page, which can often provide a postal address and other details.

If you're prepared to wait a little while for a result, you might be lucky at MIT (Massachusetts Institute of Technology), which regularly scans Usenet archives to extract names and email addresses. Send an email message to **mail-server@rtfm.mit.edu**, with the text **send usenet-addresses/*name*** as the body of the message (remembering not to add your email signature on the end). Provided that the person you're trying to trace has posted a message to a newsgroup in the past, you should receive a reply containing the email address. (It's worth remembering that this will work only if the person has posted an article to Usenet using their own name; some users frequent the type of newsgroup in which it's common to post under an alias.)

Can I Find The Email Addresses Of Famous People?

If they've ever posted an article to a newsgroup you may be lucky, although you may get a list of dozens of Hugh Grants or Jennifer Anistons. One site to try that keeps a handy list is called simply Celebrity Email Addresses. Although there are no guarantees of accuracy, if you want to email Shania Twain, Brad Pitt or Madonna (among others) head for **http://celebrityemail.hollywood.com** or **http://www.addresses.site2go.com**, and see if you can get a famous penpal!

Back To The Search Engines

Some of the popular search engines mentioned earlier have 'people-finder' options too. Both Excite and AltaVista have an easy-to-find People Finder link near the top of their home pages. Dogpile has a White Pages link, and Yahoo! and Lycos have a People Search link.

Yellow Pages – Searching For Businesses

So far we've been looking at fairly general searches – you want a particular type of information and you don't mind where it is or who put it there, and consequently the results can be hit and miss. Searching for a specific business or service is different; either you find it or you don't. But businesses want to be found, to the extent that they'll pay to be listed in specialized 'yellow pages' directories, so these searches will almost always yield results. Two of the most useful for finding UK businesses are Yell.com (a lot like an online version of the Yellow Pages we all know and love), and Scoot.

Yell.com, the ideal place to find contact details of UK companies.

* New website design online from early November 2002.

Yell.com at **http://www.yell.com** is an ideal place to begin a search for a UK company or business. Type in one or more of the following boxes: 'I am looking for' (such as garden centres) or 'a company called' (such as Trees Garden Centre) 'located in' (such as Nottingham) and click the **Search** button to view relevant results. The results show relevant company information, plus links to the company's Web site, if it has one, and local area maps to help you find your way on the ground.

Check This Out...

Guesswork Is Good

If you can't trace the URL of a company's Web site, try typing a few guesses into your browser's address bar. Most companies use their own name as their domain name, so if you're looking for a company called Dodgy Goods plc, try **www. dodgygoods.com or www.dodgygoods.co.uk.** If you look at the company URLs given throughout this book, you'll see how likely this is to get a result.

The Scoot site, at **http://www.scoot.co.uk**, works in a slightly different way to Yell.com. Although you can click the **Company Name** link to find a specific company, Scoot specializes in locating a particular *type* of business in your chosen area. This is a great way to search if, for example, you need a plumber and you're currently too damp to care which plumber it is.

If you haven't found the company yet, it's either American or it doesn't want to be found! To search for US companies, head off to Excite at **http://www.excite.com** and click the **Yellow Pages** link at the bottom of the page. Enter a company name and category description, together with location details if known, and click the search button. If the category you chose doesn't match an Excite category, you'll be given a list of similar categories to choose from. You can also try **http://www.companiesonline.com**, a new addition to the Lycos search engine family. If you're looking for financial or performance-related information about a company, visit Infoseek and select **Company Profiles** from the drop-down list to search through almost 50,000 US companies. Finally, of course, there's the good old workhorse, Yahoo!. Visit **http://uk.dir.yahoo.com/ business_and_economy/ directories/companies** and you'll be presented with a list of over 100 categories. The sites you'll find in Yahoo's categories cover the UK and Ireland as well as America and elsewhere.

Searching The Newsgroups

There's more value to searching Usenet newsgroups than there appears at first. For example, with so many thousands of groups to choose from, a quick search for the keywords that sum up your favourite topic might help you determine the most suitable newsgroup to subscribe to. Or perhaps you need an answer to a technical question quickly – it's almost certainly been answered in a newsgroup article.

One of the best places to search for newsgroups and articles is Google Groups (well known as Deja News until its recent takeover by the Google search engine folk) at **http://groups.google.com**. The simplest way to find newsgroups is to delve into the directory structure of group names, for example by clicking the **Alt** link. On the next page, a drop-down list box gives you access to alphabetical lists of group names in the alt hierarchy. Click on the name of your chosen group to browse through its threads (or search them) using your browser.

Stick To What You Know

If you search Google Groups for newsgroups, you can click any group name you find and browse through the threads and articles in the group. But although it's possible, it's not the easiest way to navigate a newsgroup – you'll find it simpler to run your newsreader program and read the articles from the chosen group with that instead.

If you're looking for individual articles rather than groups, you can use the text box to search for them using keywords. Alternatively, click the Advanced Groups Search link and enter more specific details about the information you want to find. The search results list ten articles at a time, with the usual links at the end of the page to fetch the next ten, and include authors' details and the names of the groups in which the articles were found. As usual, click any link to read the article.

Just Tell Me In English

The latest thing in search engines is natural-language searching. The problem with most search engines is that they're not particularly friendly. They expect you to ask a question in just the right way. But hang on a minute; haven't we all seen *Star Trek* and *2001: A Space Odyssey*? Aren't we supposed to talk to these stupid computers in plain English?

In theory, a natural-language search engine enables you to ask a question in plain English: Where can I find pictures of rabbits?, for instance, or How do I find cheap airline tickets? In practice ... well, they work pretty well although, as with most computer programs, far from perfectly. The best known of these systems is Ask Jeeves (**http://www.ask.com/**). This system responds with a number of things: first, it asks a number of questions, and if one of the questions is close to your question and you click on the **Ask** button next to it, you'll probably find the information you want. It also provides links to pages that it found through several other search systems – WebCrawler, Infoseek, Excite, Yahoo!, and AltaVista. When asked **'Where can I find pictures of rabbits?'**, it responded with *'Where can I see pictures of rabbits?'*, *'Where can I find a concise encyclopedia article on rabbits?,'* *'Where can I find information about rabbits as pets?'*, *'How can I determine the sex of my rabbit?'*, and *'Where can I search an online database of images?'* All pretty good matches. Use common words (such as *picture* and *rabbit*) and there's a good chance you'll get some useful information.

The Least You Need To Know

➤ A search engine is a program that searches for a word or phrase you enter.

➤ A directory is a categorized listing of Web links. Choose a category, then a subcategory, then another subcategory, and so on until you find what you want.

➤ There is no single directory of Internet users, so the easiest way to find someone's email address is to ask them.

➤ Directories like Yell or Scoot can help you find almost any business, company or service in the UK. Some search engines, such as Infoseek and Excite, can help you track down company info in the USA and other countries.

249

➤ Services such as Google Groups let you search for newsgroups covering a particular topic, or even just single newsgroup messages.

➤ Natural-language searches allow you to ask a plain-English question … and you'll often get a good answer, too.

Staying Safe On The Internet

There are many dangers on the Internet … most of them imagined or exaggerated. We're led to believe that our children will become corrupted or kidnapped, our credit cards will be stolen and we'll be arrested for copyright infringement.

Well, okay, some of these dangers are real. But remember, you're sitting in front of a computer at the end of a long cable. Just how dangerous can that be? If you use a little common sense, it doesn't have to be very dangerous at all.

Will Your Kids Be Safe On The Net?

The Internet has its fair share of sex and smut, just as it has motoring, cookery, sports, films and so on. I'm not going to pretend that your kids *can't* come into contact with explicit images and language, but there are two important points to note. First, you're no more likely to stumble upon pornography while looking for a sports site than you are to stumble upon film reviews or recipes. If you want to find that sort of content, you have to go looking for it. Second, most of the sexually explicit sites on the World Wide Web are *private* – to get inside you need a credit card. Nevertheless, there *are* dangers on the Net and, given unrestricted freedom, your kids may come into contact with unsuitable material.

Check This Out...

What Sort Of Material Could My Kids Find?

On the Web, the front pages of those private sites are accessible to all. Some contain images and language designed to titillate and to part you from some cash. The Web's search engines are another risk – enter the wrong keywords (or the *right* keywords, depending on your viewpoint) and you'll be presented with direct links to explicit sites accompanied by colourful descriptions.

However, these are not good reasons to deny children access to the Internet. Quite simply, the Internet is a fact of life that isn't going to go away and will feature more strongly in our children's lives than it does in ours. More and more schools are recognizing this and promoting use of the Internet in homework and class projects. The wealth of Web sites created by and for children is a great indicator of their active participation in the growth of the Net. Rather than depriving children of this incredible resource, agree a few ground rules at the outset: when they can surf, why they should never give out their address, school name, or telephone number, what sort of sites they can visit, and what to do if they receive messages that make them uncomfortable. For some excellent practical advice on this subject, I recommend all parents visit Yahooligans at **http://www.yahooligans.com/docs/safety**.

If you're ever concerned about the Web sites your children might be visiting, remember that you can open Internet Explorer's History panel to see a list of all recently accessed pages, as explained in Chapter 4.

Finally, there are two Internet services that are definitely *not* suitable places for children to visit unsupervised: newsgroups and IRC chat channels. Many access providers refuse to carry certain newsgroups, such as the **alt.sex** and **alt.binaries.pictures** hierarchies, but articles in some quite innocent newsgroups may contain views or language you wouldn't want your kids to read. The same goes for IRC. As I mentioned in Chapter 12, many chat channels are sexual in nature and often in name too. But the type of people trying to make contact with children through IRC won't limit themselves to those channels. I'd simply suggest that if you have kids in the house, you don't have an IRC program installed on your computer.

Is *Any* Type Of Chat Safe For Kids?

Online services' general chat rooms are *moderated* (controlled by a representative of the service) to keep things friendly – I especially recommend AOL in that department. If you access the Net through an Internet service provider, give your children a copy of Surf Monkey (**http://www.surfmonkey.com**), a free 'Rocketship' Web browser that has moderated cartoon chat rooms.

Get A Little Extra Help

If all this seems a bit too much to handle on your own, don't worry! There are many software programs around that can take over some of the supervision for you. For example, if you use an online service, you'll probably find that it offers some way of filtering out areas you don't want your kids to get to. America Online has had such tools for a long time.

You'll also soon find blocking tools built into most Web browsers. Internet Explorer already has blocking tools. To use them, choose **Tools, Internet Options, Content** and click the **Enable** button. You'll find an area in which you can turn a filtering system on and off. This system is based on the Recreational Software Advisory Council's ratings (although you can add other systems when they become available), and you can turn it on and off using a password. You can set it up to completely block certain sites or to allow access with a password (just in case you don't practice what you preach!). The following figure shows a site that's blocked except for password entry.

Don't Lock Yourself Out!

You'll need to use this password whenever you want to alter Internet Explorer's security settings, or view restricted sites yourself, so don't forget it!

With Internet Explorer's Ratings turned on, your kids can't get in – but you can.

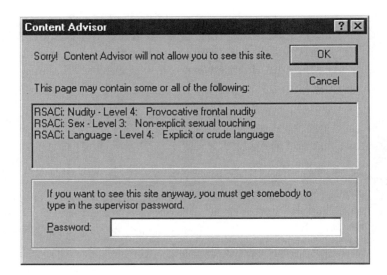

Although Internet Explorer's ratings system is reasonably good, it gives no control over other Internet services such as newsgroups, chat, and email, and you may find that your kids are barred from many quite acceptable Web sites simply because they have no official RSACi rating. However, in Internet Explorer 5 and 6, you can add these 'safe' sites to the **Approved Sites** list.

Don't Take These Tools For Granted

Ratings systems and 'babysitter' programs are useful tools, but a curious or technology-minded child might still find ways to override them. It isn't easy, but these are the same kids that remind *us* how to set the video-recorder!

To balance maximum access with maximum security, you need a program that can identify the actual *content* about to be viewed, rather than the name of the page or site. There are many such programs available, but here's a shortlist of the most respected:

➤ **Net Nanny** from **http://www.netnanny.com**

➤ **CYBERsitter** from **http://www.cybersitter.com**

➤ **SurfWatch** from **http://www.surfwatch.com**

➤ **Cyber Patrol** from **http://www.cyberpatrol.com**

Some of these programs can also prevent personal information such as addresses and credit card numbers from being sent via email or in a chat room, and mask any words or phrases received that are regarded as inappropriate

Your Private Email Turned Up In *The Times*

The words *email* and *private* don't go together well. I'm not saying that the world and his dog are going to read every message you send, but email *can* get you into trouble (and people have got into very deep water from using email where a phone call or a quiet chat would have been wiser). If you're concerned about who could read it, don't write it.

The most obvious problem is that your 'private' messages can be easily forwarded or redirected, or the recipient might simply fail to delete an incriminating message after reading it. But apart from existing on your computer and the recipient's computer, however briefly, the message also spends time on your access provider's mail server and that of the recipient's access provider. Will the message really be deleted from both? And what if the administrator of one of these systems decides to run a backup while your message is waiting to be delivered? If you really must use email to exchange sensitive messages, you might want to consider using encryption to scramble them (see Chapter 3).

If you don't have an email program with built-in encryption you can find an add-on system. A good way to start is to search for the word **encryption** at any of the Web's search sites. There's a problem with these systems, though. Right now they're complicated to use. PGP (the most popular system, and short for Pretty Good Privacy) can be very complicated indeed. If you want to use it, I suggest that you get one of the 'front-end' programs that make it easier, such as WinPGP. In addition, because few people use encryption anyway, if you want to use it you'll have to arrange with the recipient that that's what you're going to do. Remember, also, that even if you encrypt your messages, they're not completely secure: you're still trusting the recipient not to pass on the *decrypted* message to someone else!

255

Digital Signatures

You can also use public-key encryption systems to digitally sign documents. When you encrypt a message with the private key, it can be decrypted only with your public key. After all, your public key is public. But if it can be decrypted with your public key, it must have come from your private key. Therefore, it must have come from you.

Prince Charming Is A Toad!

I'm not sure why I should have to explain this, but I'll remind you that when you meet someone online, you *don't* know who that person is! There's something about electronic communications that allows people to quickly feel as if they know the person with whom they are communicating ... but they don't!

There are two problems here. First, cyberspace is not the real world. People communicate in a different way online. As another author told me recently, 'I know people who seem to be real jerks online, but who are really nice people offline. And I've met people who seemed to be great online, but were complete jerks offline'.

Profiles

If you are a member of an online service, be careful about what you put in your profile. Most services allow you to list information about yourself – information that is available to other members. Omit your address, phone number, and any other identifying information!

Then there's the misrepresentation problem. Some people simply lie. A man who claims to be single may be married. A woman who claims to look like Michelle Pfeiffer may actually look like Roseanne. A '35-year-old movie executive who graduated from Harvard' may actually be a 21-year-old unemployed graduate of Podunk Bartending School. It's easy to lie online when nobody can see you. Couple that with a natural tendency to feel like you know the people you meet online, and you have trouble.

Not everyone lies online though. As my friend Phyllis Phlegar wrote in *Love Online* (Addison Wesley), 'Even though some individuals choose to be deceptive, many others see the online world as the ultimate place in which to be totally honest, because they feel safe enough to do so'. (Phyllis actually met her husband online.) But she also recognizes the dangers: 'As long as the person or people you are talking to can't trace you, free-flowing communication between strangers is very safe'. But if you're not careful and you give out information that can be used to trace you, Prince Charming may turn out to be the Black Prince. And if you do choose to meet someone 'live' after meeting them online, be cautious.

She's A He, And I'm Embarrassed!

Chapter 12 covers chat systems, which make for a great place to meet people. For many, they're a great place to meet people of the opposite sex (or of whatever sex you are interested in meeting). But you should know that sometimes people are not of the sex that they claim to be. I don't pretend to understand this, but some people evidently get a kick out of masquerading as a member of the opposite sex. Usually men masquerade as women, which could be construed as the ultimate compliment to womanhood or could simply be blamed on the perversity of men. Either way, there's a lot of it around, as the saying goes. (I recently heard chat systems described as being full of '14-year-old boys chatting with other 14-year-old boys claiming to be 21-year-old women'. True, it's an exaggeration, but it illustrates the point well.)

If you hook up with someone online, bear in mind that she (or he) may not be quite who he (or she) says (s)he is.

Internet Stalkers

Internet stalkers are for real. People have been murdered, raped, and seriously assaulted by people they've met online. But remember, they can't get to you unless you provide them with the information to reach you. Getting into trouble is unlikely, but it can happen, so use some common sense. Avoid giving out addresses, places of work or school, phone numbers, and so on. If you really have to meet someone you've run into online, don't go alone and always meet in a public place.

I Was 'Researching' At *Playboy* Online And Now I'm Unemployed

This title is more than a joke. Some people really have been fired for viewing 'inappropriate' Web sites during work hours. Of course, you can avoid such problems by staying away from the sites in the first place. But, if you really *have* to go there, practise safe surfing by clearing the cache when you finish! (We discussed the cache in Chapter 5.)

It's Bugged!

You should know that with some new, special software programs, your boss can spy on your Internet activities whether you clear the cache and history list or not! So maybe you'd better just get back to work.

When you visit a site, a copy of the Web page is saved on your hard disk in case you want to view it again at a later time. In effect, this creates a history of where you've been. And speaking of history, some browsers (such as Internet Explorer) have excellent multisession history lists – which will also list every Web page you've seen!

To cover your tracks, clear the cache to remove the offending pages. Then clear the history list (either clear it completely, or remove just the offending entries).

I'm Not Using *My* Credit Card On The Net!

Another popular myth about the Internet is that credit card transactions are risky because your card number can be stolen. To put this in perspective, consider how you use your credit or debit card in the 'real world'. How many people get to see your card number during a normal week? How much time does your card spend out of your view when you use it? Do you always ask for the carbon paper after signing for a credit card purchase? The truth is, card numbers are *easy* to steal. It takes a lot more effort and technical know-how to steal numbers on the Internet and a single card number isn't valuable enough to warrant the exertion.

Making the computer-hacker's job more difficult in this department, modern browsers can now encrypt the data they send and most of the Web sites at which you can use your credit card run on secure servers that have their own built-in encryption. So when you visit one of these secure sites, enter your card number and click the button to send it, your number will appear as meaningless gibberish to anyone managing to hack into the system. In fact, credit card companies actually regard online transactions as being the *safest* kind.

Is This A Secure Site?

In Internet Explorer, look for a little padlock symbol in the lower right corner of the browser. In Netscape's lower left corner you'll see a similar padlock which will be 'locked' at secure sites and 'unlocked' at the rest. You'll also notice that the http:// prefix in the address bar changes to https://. More and more shopping sites are becoming secure all the time, and those that aren't usually offer alternative payment methods, but even an *insecure* site presents a smaller risk than a restaurant or petrol station transaction. Skip back to Chapter 6 for more about secure sites and how to recognize them.

I 'Borrowed' A Picture And Now They're Suing Me!

As you've seen throughout this book, grabbing things from the Internet is as easy as stealing from a baby – but there's none of the guilt. It's so easy and so guilt free that many Internet users have come to believe in a sort of 'finder's keepers' copyright morality. If it's there and if you can take it, you can use it.

The law says otherwise, though. Here's a quick summary of copyright law: if you created it, it belongs to you (or to your boss if he paid you to create it). You can put it anywhere you want, but unless you actually sign a contract giving away rights to it, you still own the copyright. You don't have to register copyright, either.

Copyright law is quite complicated, however and this summary misses many essential details. The important thing to understand is that it *doesn't* belong to you if you didn't create it! Unless something has been placed on the Internet with a notice explicitly stating that you can take and use it, you can take it for personal use but you can't use it publicly. You can't steal pictures to use at your Web site, for instance. (And even if there is a notice stating that the item is in the public domain, it may not be. After all, how do you know that the person giving it away really created it?)

Can I Take It For Personal Use?

In most cases, you probably can. When you connect to a Web site, all the things that are transferred to your computer end up in the cache anyway. However, some enthusiastic copyright lawyers claim that the use of a cache is in itself illegal – that even storing images and text on your hard drive goes against copyright law.

Copyright law even extends to newsgroups and mailing lists. You can't just steal someone's poetry, story, ruminations, or whatever from a message and distribute it in any way you want. It doesn't belong to you. And of course, if you are concerned that your work will be taken from a newsgroup or mailing list and distributed, don't put it there!

I Downloaded A File And Now My Computer's Queasy

Yes, you know what I'm talking about: computer viruses. These are nasty little programs that get loose in your computer and do things they shouldn't, like wipe your hard drive or destroy the directory information that allows your computer to find files on the drive.

First, my role as contrarian dictates that I inform you that much of the fuss about viruses is exaggerated – greatly exaggerated. When something goes wrong with a computer, a virus usually gets the blame. An example of how the virus threat is exaggerated is the famous Good Times virus. This virus never actually existed; it was a myth from the start. The story was that an email message containing a virus was being passed around the Internet. The story was obviously wrong because a plain email message without a file attached cannot contain a virus.

Only files that 'do things' can contain viruses. That includes program files, as well as document files created by programs that have macro languages. For instance, a variety of Word for Windows macro viruses have appeared in the last couple of years or so (what took them so long?). If a file can do nothing by itself – if it has to have another program to do something to it – it can't carry a virus. A plain text file (including text messages) can't do anything, and .GIF or .JPG image files cannot cause harm. (I'm just waiting for the next big hoax: someone will start a rumour that there's an image file used at many Web sites that contains a virus and that all you have to do is load the page with the image to infect your computer …)

Yes, viruses do exist. Yes, you should protect yourself. There are many good antivirus programs around, so if you plan to download software from the Web (not just images and documents from applications other than advanced word processors), you should get one. On the other hand, viruses are not worth losing sleep over.

The Least You Need To Know

➤ Yes, there's sex on the Internet, but not as much as the press claims. Get a filtering and blocking program if you want to keep the kids away.

➤ Email can easily be stolen or forwarded. Don't write anything that you could be embarrassed by later.

➤ People on the Internet sometimes lie (just like in the real world). They may not be who they say they are (or even the sex they claim to be).

➤ Your boss can find out what Web sites you are visiting, so watch out!

➤ Credit card transactions made on the Internet are safer than those made in the real world.

➤ You don't own what you find on the Internet; it's copyright-protected.

➤ Viruses are relatively few and far between; but it's a good idea to protect yourself with an antivirus program.

Chapter 18

FAQ – Internet Questions And Answers

In this chapter you'll find answers to some questions you may have and a few problems you may run into – everything from the meaning of certain terms to solutions for certain problems.

Why Is The Web So Slow Today?

There could be several answers to this one. To start with, it may be to do with the *time* you connect. The Internet is at its quietest (and therefore its speediest) while the USA is sleeping, and at varying degrees of 'busy' at all other times. Although it isn't a cheap time to connect, you'll normally get a faster response by going online in the morning than the evening. If you're having trouble with just one particular site, you can sometimes get things moving by clicking the link again, or, if the page started to download and then stopped, clicking the **Stop** button on the toolbar followed by the **Reload** or **Refresh** button. But if everything seems unreasonably slow, try logging off and then logging back on again – this often seems to result in a faster connection.

Why Can't I Open This URL?

When you click a link to a Web page, type in a URL, or even select an entry on your Favorites list, you may see a page like the screenshot below (or a similar page containing more text and headed 'The page cannot be displayed'). Not what you were expecting at all. So what went wrong?

It's a 404! The page has been moved, removed, or renamed.

The page in the screenshot above is referring to an HTTP 404 error: the page you're trying to open can't be found by the server. In other words, either you've made a mistake in typing the URL or the page has been moved, deleted, or renamed. There are several things you can do to try to locate the page:

➤ Try changing the file extension from .htm to .html (or vice versa).

➤ Try replacing uppercase letters in the URL with lowercase letters.

➤ Try deleting sections from the end of the URL (deleting back to the previous slash each time) and pressing **Enter** until you do find a document on that site – it may contain a link to the (now retitled) page you were looking for.

If you see a page headed 'The page cannot be displayed', with the more useful note 'Cannot find server' in the title bar, things may be more serious. After ruling out a spelling mistake, either the Web server is too busy to reply at the moment, it's not running, or the domain name you entered is no longer used by any server on the Net. Try pressing **Refresh** a few times to see if the situation changes after a few minutes, but if you can't get in when you try hours or days later, you've got to face the fact that this is an ex-Web site.

My Connection Crashed During A Download. Have I Lost The File?

A lot depends upon the server from which you're downloading the file, but you may be lucky. Restart your connection and your browser may pick up the download from where it was interrupted. If it doesn't, or the 'Downloading File' dialog box is no longer on the screen, click the same link to the file as if you were starting the download again from scratch. Your browser may find the matching incomplete file in its cache directory and just grab the missing portion. For a little more certainty, a handy little utility called GetRight from **http://www.headlightsw.com** can manage your downloads for you and complete partial downloads. (Remember – you can minimize the chances of being disconnected by turning off Call Waiting!)

If I Leave My Service Provider, Will I Lose My Email Address?

Yes you will, and it can be a real pain. If you use email a lot, it's worth hanging onto that first account for a while as you pass out your *new* email address to everyone and give things a chance to settle down. But there are a couple of things you can do to ensure that your email address will *never* change.

The first of these is quick, simple and free. You can set up a Web-based email account with a service like Hotmail (**http://www.hotmail.com**) or Yahoo! (**http://mail.yahoo.co.uk**). As you access this account by visiting a Web site to read and write messages, it isn't tied to your current service provider, so the address need never change. It has the extra benefit that you can pick up your email on the move, using Internet-connected computers in cybercafés, libraries and hotels.

A more expensive, but flashier, way to go is to register your own domain name (such as *myname.co.uk* or *myname.com*). Visit **http://www.123-reg.co.uk** or **http://www.netnames.co.uk** to see if your chosen domain is available. If it is, shop around for a good deal by searching for **domain registration** at a UK search engine. It's possible to get your hands on a .co.uk domain for as little as £3 for the first two years. Many registration companies will throw in redirection for free: when somebody types your new domain into their browser they'll be taken straight to your Web site, wherever it is; if they send a message to your new email address it'll be passed to your current address. If you switch to a different ISP, just contact the registration company to change the redirection details.

I Suppose My Web Site URL Will Change Too?

If you took advantage of your service provider's generous allocation of free Web space to create your own site, you'll find that this generosity comes to a sudden halt if you cancel your account with them. You still have all the files that make up your site on your own hard disk, of course, so you can recreate this site quickly and easily by uploading them to your new service provider's computer. The problem is that your site's URL will change and your regular visitors won't know where to find it.

There are several options here, all of which should be treated as preventions rather than cures. One is to buy your own domain name, as mentioned above, which you can then carry with you from one provider to another. Many domain-name registration companies provide Web forwarding free, and have a handy online control panel you can use to type in the new URL of your site if you have to move it elsewhere. The second is to take advantage of free Web space offers from companies such as GeoCities (**http://www.geocities.com**) and FortuneCity (**http://www.fortunecity.com**) instead of using the space provided by your service provider. A third option is to visit **http://www.v3.com**, a site that provides a free Web forwarding service in much the same way that Bigfoot provides email forwarding. You can choose a catchy URL such as **http://surf.to/MySite**, and everyone visiting this URL will be redirected to your Web site. Whenever you change your ISP or your site URL, you can return to the V3.com site and update your redirection details. If you don't like the 'surf.to' part, you can choose others such as **welcome.to**, **travel.to** or **start.at**.

How Can I Stop All This Junk Email Arriving?

Although there's no sure-fire solution, it helps to know a bit about *why* you're getting junk email. Your email address can be picked up and added to a list by a number of methods:

➤ You post messages on newsgroups, discussion forums and mailing lists.

➤ You enter it at Web sites which ask for an email address to log on: many Web sites collect email addresses for the sole purpose of building (and perhaps selling) address lists.

➤ Your address appears on your own Web site.

➤ You subscribed to a mailing list operated by a company (perhaps for technical support or software upgrade notifications) which shares or sells its list of addresses.

➤ You follow the removal instructions contained in some junk email messages: sometimes this works; often, though, it just serves to confirm that your email address is active and you received the message, laying you open to more of the same.

➤ You use a large, popular ISP: almost any pronounceable series of letters followed by **@aol.com** (to take an obvious example) will arrive at an active email address, so a 'junk factory' could churn out thousands of guessed addresses a minute with a pretty good success rate.

It's a sad fact of life that once you've started getting junk mail at an email address, it's not going to stop. The best way to prevent it starting, of course, is to keep your email address as private as you can, using your account only to email friends, family and colleagues. Set up a second account (such as a Web-based account, mentioned above) and enter that address when required for Web site access and mailing list subscriptions. If you post messages to newsgroups, edit the settings used by your newsgroup software so that the email address it uses contains dummy characters. For instance, if your address is **MyName@myisp.net**, change it to **MyJunkProofName@myisp.net**. You can add a note to the messages you post telling readers to remove the 'JunkProof' if they want to reply by email. The software used by the junk factories will pull out this non-existent address – it's not sophisticated enough to read the note you add to the message.

Want To Know More About Junk Email?

Stop Junk Email is an excellent site offering clear, practical advice, a wealth of useful information to help you avoid becoming a victim, and examples to help you fight back. Point your browser at **http://www.jcrdesign.com/junkemail.html**. Another useful site is SpamCop at **http://www.spamcop.net**.

If you're already plagued by junk, the best you can do is to avoid seeing it. Many email programs and services have facilities to delete junk email from your mailbox without downloading it (or to download it to a particular Junk folder you create in your email program so that you can check it really *is* junk before deleting it). Outlook Express calls this feature Message Rules, Eudora and other programs call it Filters, but they all work in the same way: you define a rule or filter that specifies a sender's name, an email address, or text that usually appears in the Subject line, and choose what action should be taken when messages matching those criteria are received. (If you follow my suggestion of setting up a second email address, you can create a filter that puts all mail sent to that address straight into your Junk folder, or deletes it immediately.) In Outlook Express and the Web-based Hotmail, you can also choose to 'block' particular senders so that their mail goes straight into your Deleted Items folder. However, Web-based email accounts and accounts with online services such as AOL offer poor filtering options (as well as attracting the largest quantities of junk mail) – you're better off using an ISP that provides a POP3 mail account.

Can I Be Anonymous On The Net?

There may be many non-criminal reasons why you'd want to surf the Internet in anonymity and it isn't difficult to do. The best way to hide your identity completely is to take out an account with an ISP or online service using an account name (or *username*) that's nothing like your own. The only way someone could learn your true identity would be to persuade your access provider to disclose it.

If you want to send untraceable email messages and newsgroup articles, you can use an **anonymous remailer**. By following the instructions, you send your message to the remailer which will remove your personal details and send it on to its final

Visit Bigfoot and take a large step towards ridding yourself of junk email.

destination. Any replies will come back to you via the remailer, but the sender won't know who you are. Although the job they do seems simple, remailers can be tricky to use – they all need their own brand of special commands. You can find out more about the remailers and their instructions at **http://www.stack.nl/~galactus/remailers**, and you'll find another useful site at **http://anonymous.to**. If you find it all a bit baffling, a program called Private Idaho (from **http://www.eskimo.com/~joelm/pi.html**) may be able to simplify things.

Anonymity *Not* Guaranteed!

Anonymous remailers are viewed with (understandable) suspicion by the police and other law-enforcement agencies. Faced with the threat of prosecution, as many have been, the remailer's administrator may elect to surrender his records.

Could Someone Be Forging My Email?

Yes, they could. It doesn't happen often, but it does happen. It's easy to do, too. Every time you send an email message, your name and email address are attached to its header. When the recipient retrieves his email, these details are displayed so that it is obvious who the message is from. But how does your email program know what details to enter? When you installed your email software and filled in those little boxes on its options page, you told it! So, of course, if you go back to that options page and enter something different, those are the details that will go out with your email.

So it's entirely possible that someone could attach *your* name and email address to a message they send from their computer and it would be difficult (although not impossible) to trace it back to them. Actually, it's a wonder that email forgery hasn't become a major pastime on the Net, because there's nothing you can do to prevent it happening other than to be careful what you say in chat rooms and newsgroups and avoid flame wars (which I'll discuss in a moment). You could digitally sign all your messages, as discussed in Chapter 3, although that might be overkill.

Can I Sign Up With More Than One Service Provider?

Yes you can, and in these days of free access there's little reason not to. Most service providers simply install a new icon in your Dial-Up Networking or Network Connections folder (located inside the Windows Control Panel), add a new email account to Outlook Express and a new dial-up connection to Internet Explorer. You won't end up with multiple copies of Internet Explorer on your system, and (as long as it's a free account you're adding) there's no need to bother uninstalling or cancelling anything if you find you never use a particular account.

Why Would I Want More Than One ISP?

A common reason is that access providers' services tend to vary in quality over time as their membership increases; some ISPs are busier than others at different times of day. If you're unable to connect to the Net using a particular ISP, or the connection is slow, you can hang up and dial in using a different ISP account.

I do have a few words of caution, though. First, some service provider accounts don't co-exist happily on a system that has an online service such as AOL or CompuServe installed. Second, every time you add a new account to your computer, it will be set as your default account – the account that's dialled whenever you want Internet access, and the primary email account. You can switch defaults easily, though: go to the **Tools, Internet Options, Connections** tab in Internet Explorer, and **Tools, Accounts, Mail** in Outlook Express. (Most ISPs assume you're using Outlook Express for email; if you're not, you'll have to add the new account to your email program yourself.)

Which Of These Sites Should I Download From?

A major conundrum when you're about to download a large file, is that some Web sites are just *too helpful!* You arrive at the download page and they offer you a dozen different links to the same file. Which one should you choose? Here's a couple of rules worth following. First, discount any links pointing to FTP sites if you can – your browser often takes longer to connect to them and downloads tend to be slower and less reliable. Second, choose the HTTP link that's geographically closest to you, ideally marked as a UK or European site.

Of course, there's no guarantee that you've found the best link using this method. And even if you *have* got a fast link, you'll still be sitting there wondering if a different one might have been quicker still! For times like this, there's a nifty little utility called Dipstick, from **http://www.klever.net/kin/dipstick.html**, that's worth keeping handy. Drag the links into Dipstick's window and it will test the speed of each and then give you a button to click to begin downloading from the site that gave the fastest response.

Are .com And .net Interchangeable?

What's the difference between .com, .net, and .org? Often not much, except that .com is often assumed. These are known as TLDs, Top Level Domains. A .com domain is supposed to be a commercial domain; a .net domain is in some way Internet-related (Internet service providers often have .net domains), and a .org domain is supposed to be some kind of organization, such as a charity or professional body. But partly because browsers were set up to work with .com as the default (type any word into your browser's address bar and press **Enter** and your browser will try to go to *thatword*.com), .com has become the domain to get. So even if a service provider has a .net domain, it probably has a .com domain too. (Both **http://www.demon.net** and **http://www.demon.com** will take you to Demon Internet's Web site, for example.)

That's not to say you can interchange .com and .net, or .org for that matter. If you're given a URL containing a .net domain, you need to use .net because .com might not work (or it might take you to an entirely unconnected Web site). However, more and more companies are registering matching domain names – .com, .net and .org. The registration companies are encouraging this, perhaps as a way to make more money. It certainly negates the purpose of having different TLDs.

Things are finally beginning to change, though. After years of rumours and discussions, many more TLDs are arriving: .info, .biz and .name have recently been added; .eu should be with us soon; and .aero, .coop, .museum and .pro are just around the corner. The days of .com dominance are coming to an end.

What's A Flame?

I've heard it said that the Internet will lead to world peace. As people use the Net to communicate with others around the world, a new era of understanding will come to pass … blah, blah, blah … .

The same was said about telegraph and the television, but so far there hasn't been much of a peace spin-off from those technologies! But what makes me sure that the Internet will not lead to world peace is the prevalence of flame wars in mailing lists and newsgroups.

A *flame* is a message that is intended as an assault on another person, an *ad hominem* attack. Such messages are common and lead to flame wars, as the victim responds and others get in on the act. In some discussion groups, flame wars are almost the purpose of the group. You'll find that the Internet is no haven of peace and goodwill – and I haven't even mentioned the obnoxious behaviour of many in chat rooms.

Just One More Question …

You're going to come away from this book with lots of questions because the Internet is big, there are many different ways to connect to it, and there's a huge amount of strange stuff out there. I hope this book has helped you start, but I know you'll have many more questions.

Once you are on your own, what do you do? Try these suggestions:

➤ **Get the FAQs.** FAQ means 'frequently asked questions' and it refers to a document with questions and answers about a particular subject. Many newsgroups and mailing lists have FAQs explaining how to use them, for example. Look for these FAQs and read them!

➤ **Continue your reading.** I've written about a dozen Internet books and really need to sell them, so you can continue buying and reading them. Well, okay, there are other writers putting out Internet books too (you may have noticed a few). Seriously, though, to become a real cybergeek, you'll need to learn much more. So check out a few of the books that are out there.

➤ **Read the documentation.** There are literally thousands of Internet programs and each is a little different. Make sure you read all the documentation that comes with your programs so you know how to get the best out of them.

➤ **Ask your service provider!** I've said it before and I'll say it again: if your service provider won't help you, get another service provider! The Internet is too complicated to travel around without help. Now and again you'll have to ask your service provider's staff for information. Don't be scared to ask – and don't be scared to find another provider if the one you're with won't or can't answer your questions.

The Least You Need To Know

➤ You can safeguard your email address at Bigfoot, or be flashy and buy your own personal domain name as long as you know that someone will host it for you.

➤ When faced with a choice of download sites for a file, choose the one that's geographically closest to you.

➤ You may have a fast modem, but if the Internet itself is busy, things will still move slowly.

➤ You can be anonymous on the Internet – if you are careful.

➤ If your service provider won't answer your questions, you need a different service provider!

Chapter 19

Making Money On The Internet

In This Chapter

➤ Ways to make money on the Internet

➤ Is the Internet for every business?

➤ How much will using the Internet for business cost?

➤ Bringing people to your Web site

➤ Using email as a marketing tool

Want to make money on the Internet? That used to be easy. First, start a business selling some kind of Internet service or software. Run it for a few months on a shoestring, and then go public. It didn't appear to matter what the intrinsic value of the company was – as long as it had the word 'Internet' attached to it somehow, you'd get rich.

Finally, the Internet-investment hype is dying out. During 2000 and 2001 the bottom dropped out of the 'dotcom' investment market. Internet companies were dropping like flies, and they still are. The Internet bubble has burst. Some dotcoms are even going out of business before their launch parties, in a matter of weeks rather than months or years. Two years ago, Amazon.com was worth over $22 billion. Today, as I write this, Amazon's total market capitalization – the value of all its stock based on the current stock price – is just $6.1 billion.

Andy Grove, the chairman of Intel, said a few years ago, 'It remains to be seen whether the Internet companies that have essentially infinite access to capital will be able to grow up to be self-sufficient institutions and adjust to a future when money won't be free'. Translation 1: These companies might not be worth what people are paying for them. Translation 2: When the investment money runs out, these companies might be in trouble. Well, it's finally happened, and a huge proportion of these companies are on the way out of business, or already history.

There's Another Way

But there *are* companies making money on the Internet, and doing *very* well. Not so long ago, the only people making money on the Internet were people selling Internet services: software companies, service providers, hardware manufacturers, and so on. It seemed that almost nobody was making money on the Internet unless they were selling goods or services to people who wanted to make money on the Internet, sort of like an author making lots of money by selling get-rich-quick schemes to people who'd never get rich. In fact, the high failure rate of Internet businesses was a joke among Internet insiders. A few years ago, when I told an executive at a major Internet software company that I wanted to write a book about companies that have figured out how to make money on the Internet, he said, 'Is anyone making money? I mean, we are, but is anyone else?'

These days it's easy to find companies that are succeeding. Many companies, including small one-person businesses, are taking orders online or using the Internet to successfully promote their business. I've spoken with a small publishing company selling £3000 worth of books at their Web site each month, a small gaming-software publisher that finds a 'significant' proportion of its new customers on the Web, and a two-man business selling toys online – and selling lots of them. *I* make money on the Internet, too. I sell enough books at my Web site (**http://www.topfloor.com/**) to make far more than just pin money! I also know of a new business that started a mailing list discussion group. This business doesn't sell anything online, but the owner told me the mailing list became such a great promotional tool that it was the single most important factor in the business's growth and success.

I do a lot of radio interviews, and the most common question I hear is, 'Can you really make money on the Internet?'. My response is, 'Yes, but you probably won't'. Yes, because *many* people are doing it. You probably won't, because most people aren't doing it right. To point you in the right direction, this chapter will give you a few guidelines for using the Internet as a business tool.

Do You Have A Product?

A lot of people have rushed into business on the Internet with the idea that as long as they have something – anything – to sell, they can make money. The Internet is paved with gold, so it's just a matter of kneeling down and digging it up. Many people who've never run a business before see the Internet as such a great opportunity that they'd better get in fast. Never mind that they don't know the first thing about selling, or filling orders, or managing a business. They want to get in, and they want to get in now.

But Internet users are not stupid – at least, no more stupid than anyone else. If you're selling garbage, you'll have a hard sell. The first step in going into business on the Internet is the same as going into business in real life: you've got to have a product or service people want to buy.

Can A Web Site Help Every Business?

There's so much hype on the Internet (remove the hype and it would collapse within hours) that many people now believe that every business should have, must have, a Web site. But in many cases a Web site won't do a lot of good. Don't expect a sudden rush of sales just because you have a couple of Web pages.

Take, for instance, the case of a small local plumbing business. Will setting up a Web site be worth the time and hassle (and believe me, it can take a lot of both), not to mention money (it doesn't have to take much money, though)? Probably not. Few people will search the Web looking for a plumbing company; they're more likely to look in the Yellow Pages (and even if they do look online, they'll probably use the online Yellow Page systems, such as Yell.com or Scoot mentioned in Chapter 16, which won't take them to a company's Web site). Spending a lot of money on a Web site probably won't be cost-effective.

However, maybe a plumbing company *can* use a Web site. Let's say this company sells plumbing supplies and perhaps even has a plumbing supply catalogue that it sends to independent plumbers. In this case, it makes sense for the company to have a Web site. The company's market may be nationwide, and the Web can become one more channel for reaching customers.

There's another very low-cost way that a Web site might help a small company. As radio-show host Tom King has suggested, a Web site can be used as what he called an 'electronic business card' for businesses that are out and about providing services. The plumbing company could put its URL on the sides of the vans, in large letters: **http://UnplugQuick.com/**, or whatever. In effect, the vans become links to a little catalog of the company's services on the Web.

Some people will remember the URL they've seen on the side of the truck and may go to the site rather than look in the Yellow Pages. Such a business card site isn't intended to attract visitors or do much more than provide a way for someone who's seen the URL to find the company's phone number, mailing address, information about services, perhaps a map showing where to find the company and so on. Most people who see the URL won't visit the site, but a small Web site can be so cheap that it can still be affordable and worth using to catch the few who will. That's one of the nice things about the Web – you can experiment at a very low cost.

273

How Cheap?

Web sites can be very affordable, especially if you're willing to do the work yourself. Here's a quick breakdown of costs for a very basic 'business-card' Web site:

Domain name registration	£50 for two years
Web site hosting	£50 to £500 per year
Good HTML authoring program	£25 to £75, or perhaps free
Your time	???

Let's have a quick look at these items.

Domain Name Registration

To do any business Web site properly, you need your own domain name. That's the first part of a Web site. For instance, I have the domain name **poorrichard.com,** so my Web-site domain is **http://PoorRichard.com/ or http://www.PoorRichard.com/**.

Your own domain name sounds better, more professional, and it's generally shorter and easier for your visitors to remember. If you move the Web site from one host to another, you can keep the domain name. It's also easier to get your own domain name registered on Yahoo!, the most important search system on the Web (it has a bias against Web sites that are subdomains of other domain names, such as **http://www. bigbiz.com/PoorRichard**).

Registering a .co.uk domain name can cost as little as £3 for the first two years if you shop around, with .com/.net/.info/.biz names available for around £20 for the same period (you can register these for more than two years at the outset if you want to). At the time of writing, one of the cheapest and most flexible domain registrations companies is 123-Reg (**http://www.123-reg.co.uk**), but there's a lot of competition in this area so you may still find a better price elsewhere. So the cost of your domain name should be between about 12p and 85p a month.

Web Site Hosting

We discussed Web hosting in Chapter 8, 'Setting Up Your Own Web Site'. You can host a simple Web site for free if your ISP or online service includes Web space with its subscription: when you register your domain name, you can use the domain-registration company's Web forwarding options to point your snappy domain name to your less-than-snappy web space URL. You won't have a lot of flexibility if you use free space, though – you may not be able to get the additional services you need, and some ISPs don't allow commercial sites to be run from free space.

The company you use to register your domain name can probably offer hosting services, or you can find a company that specializes in hosting commercial Web sites. The price you pay will depend on the extra services you need (which can usually be added as you need them) but you can host a basic Web site for around £4.16 a month.

HTML Authoring Program

In Chapter 8, you saw how to create Web pages. You can create a very simple 'business-card' Web site doing the HTML yourself. But you can also buy an HTML-authoring program, or even use shareware or freeware, and create things very quickly that would be quite complicated if you had to learn all the HTML. A good HTML authoring program costs around £25 to £75. That's £1.04 to £3.12 over the first two-year period you'll own your domain name.

You may even be able to get away with paying nothing. If you use Netscape Communicator, for example, you have a program called Netscape Composer. It's not a full-featured authoring program, but it will do all the basics. There are many other free HTML programs around, too.

Your Time

This one's tricky. It depends how you value your time. You'll have to spend some time finding a hosting company and learning how to use the HTML program. How long? Hard to say. You may end up spending five hours looking for a hosting company, perhaps less if you're not very choosy (remember to see my free report, *20 Things to Ask a Web-Hosting Company* at **http://www.poorrichard.com/freeinfo/special_ reports.htm**). Then perhaps another five hours really getting to know your HTML authoring program. Within ten hours, perhaps a lot less, you could have a decent little site up and running.

So what's the total cost? Depending on your choices, around £1.16 to £3.97 a month for the domain and authoring program over the first two years, plus whatever you decide to pay for hosting, which will be somewhere between zero to £40 a month. Not a huge investment. Note, however, that this amount is for a simple business-card type site. The more complicated you get, the more you'll end up paying, although the real cost may be in terms of the time you put into the site.

There's No Such Thing As An Internet Business

There is, however, such a thing as a business that uses the Internet as a business tool. It's important to remember this because, ultimately, if you're in business on the Internet, you're still in business. And that can be lots of hard work. If you're selling products on the Internet, most of the work may be done *off* the Internet, for example.

Creating the products, processing orders (which, for many small businesses, may be done off-line), fulfilling orders, and addressing customer service problems are all issues that you must deal with. It's important to remember that if you're going to set up a business on the Internet, you are still setting up a real business, and you need to understand all the real-world concerns that entails.

Search Engines Are Not Enough

You've probably heard that a Web site is a billboard on the information superhighway. This Internet mantra has been kept alive by the Web design companies that want your business. Guess what? It's not true.

You can see a billboard as you drive by on the road. A Web site just sits there in the darkness of cyberspace, waiting for someone to visit. It's not a matter of 'build it and they will come'. If you don't *bring* visitors to the site somehow, nobody will see it. There are many ways to bring visitors to the site, the most obvious being using search engines. But there are problems with that method.

There are millions of Web sites on the Internet, all vying for business. And there seem to be thousands of businesses claiming that they can put you right at the top of the search engines' lists. These companies create special coding, which will be read by any search engines that look at the Web pages in your site. This coding, known as META tags, is designed to push your Web site to the top of its category at the search engines. Be a little wary of these claims, though.

First, it's going to cost you, perhaps 10p or more for every person who comes to your Web site thanks to a listing created by a search optimization company. But cost may not be too much of a problem, because the company may not send much traffic your way; one company told me that on average it sends around 25 people a day to a Web site using its service – not exactly a flood.

Results from search engine optimization don't work well for a few reasons. First, you can't fool Yahoo!, the single most important search site; entries are added to Yahoo! by real human beings, not a computer program, so they don't care about META tags. As for the other search sites, they're constantly modifying the way they index pages, trying to stop these companies from fooling them into putting Web pages high into their lists. Finally, there's an awful lot of competition; we can't all be at the top of a list.

It's important to get your Web site registered at the major search sites: Yahoo!, Excite, AltaVista, HotBot, Lycos, and so on. Visit each site and find a registration link. The number one tip for good site registrations is to make sure the title tag in the page you are registering is descriptive of the page, including keywords that people are likely to use when looking for pages like yours. But relying on search sites is not enough; you need more ways to bring people to your site.

Why Would Anyone Come To Your Site?

First, consider why anyone would want to come to your site. The billboard idea doesn't work; setting up a Web site and waiting for people to arrive doesn't work. But 'make it useful, let people know about it, and then they'll come' really does. If your site is useful, and you do your best to let people know about it, people will visit.

Think about your Web site. Ask yourself, 'Why would anyone come to my site? If it wasn't *my* site, would I visit?' If you can't answer the first question, and the answer to the second is no, then you've got a problem.

Check This Out...

Don't Be Cool

Remember this basic concept when creating a Web site: *Forget cool – think useful!* Don't get carried away with all the hype about multimedia and 'cool' Web sites, but think carefully about why people would come to your site.

Don't Forget The Real World

If you're already in business, you already have ways to tell people about your Web site: your business cards; the side of your car, van, or truck; your letterhead; your print, radio, and TV ads. Let people know about your Web site and give them a reason to visit. If you're not in business yet, but plan to launch an Internet business, you'll ignore the real world at your peril. Notice that all the large Web businesses advertise in the real world. They do that because they know they can't ignore the real world and focus solely on Internet promotions. (Yahoo!, by the way, doesn't place its own banner ads on the Web, but it does spend a lot of money on TV and print ads. Yahoo! sells banner ads, so they know they don't work.)

Don't forget to use the press, too. If you have a Web site of interest to horse lovers, make sure the horse magazines know about it; if your site is aimed at sailors, send a press release to the sailing magazines, and so on.

Look For Partnerships

Here's something else all the large Internet companies already do. They look for partnerships with other Web sites. For instance, do a search for some kind of music subject at Yahoo!, and you're likely to see a CDnow logo pop up along with the list of Web sites. CDnow paid a lot of money for that partnership, of course, but partnerships can start at a very low level. Ask people to link to your Web site; if someone has a list of links, a directory to useful resources, perhaps your site should be in the directory.

Offer to give away products at someone's Web site. I've done book giveaways to promote new books. Web site owners are often happy to do this, because they feel it adds value to their site. You'll need a form at your Web site (which is a little out of the scope of this chapter, but simple feedback forms are often easy to install, or at least cheap to have installed for you). People who want to win the product can then register their email address with you. You can then use the list to announce the winners and gently plug the product, too. I've used this method to build my Poor Richard's Web Site News newsletter (**http://www.PoorRichard.com/newsltr/**). When people signed up for a free copy of one of my books, I asked if they wanted a free subscription to my newsletter, too – and most did. Look carefully for ways to work with other sites; they're often very powerful ways to bring people to your site.

Use Mailing Lists And Newsgroups (Carefully!)

You can also promote your site in discussion groups, but do so very carefully. Don't go into these groups and simply advertise your site. But if group members would find your site interesting, you can mention that. For instance, a law site may mention articles of interest to writers and publishers in the writing and publishing discussion groups; a horse site may announce schedules of competitions in horse show groups; and so on. The discussion groups provide a great way to reach people, as long as you're careful not to annoy them with obnoxious advertising.

Don't Forget Email

It's easy, with all the hype about the Web, to forget the power of email. But email publishing is very popular and very effective. Even many successful Web sites use email as a promotion. For instance, the CDnow site (**http://www.cdnow.com/**) has a periodic, customizable newsletter that's free for the asking – and hundreds of thousands of people have asked! You can select particular types of music, and CDnow will send you announcements about those genres. This fantastic marketing tool is really low cost, next to nothing when compared to the cost of doing a real-world mailing to that many people.

Your mailing list is unlikely to be that large, at least for a while. But it's still worth building. Consider creating bulletins, newsletters, and product announcements. Don't turn every one into an ad; make sure there's something of value in every message you send out. But don't ignore the value of contacting people via email, either.

Read My Special Reports

I've barely scratched the surface here; there's an awful lot to learn if you want to set up business on the Internet. Visit my site for free reports on the subject, and hey, why not sign up for my free newsletter, too? You can find details at **http://www.PoorRichard.com/**.

The Least You Need To Know

➤ Thousands of people are making money on the Internet; you can too, perhaps, but only if you know the ropes.

➤ Think carefully about if and how a Web site can help your business. Depending on what you're trying to do, you may find the cost doesn't outweigh the benefits.

➤ Web sites can be very cheap. A simple 'business-card' site may cost between £1 and £20 a month.

➤ A Web site is not a billboard. You have to bring people to your site somehow, and that takes work.

➤ Register with the search engines, but don't get hung up about them; you can't rely on them to bring in all your business.

➤ Look for other ways to bring in visitors. Give people a reason to visit your site, and then get the word out about the site every way you can think of.

➤ Don't forget to use email; it's an essential marketing tool.

Chapter 20

The Web – Your Complete Entertainment Guide

In This Chapter

➤ Use electronic TV and radio guides

➤ See the latest films and book theatre tickets online

➤ Find out what's on in towns and cities around the UK

➤ Book hotels, holidays, flights, and car hire

➤ Check travel timetables and traffic conditions

➤ Giggles, games, and gambling online

It's a paper world. It doesn't matter what you want to do, nine times out of ten you have to consult a piece of paper before you can do it. Want to watch TV? Book a holiday? See what's on at your local cinema or theatre? Plan a trip or a day out? If you do any of those things, you've probably got a mountain of guides, catalogues, brochures, and local newspapers, and many of them are probably out of date! So let's go paperless …

Use Online TV And Radio Listings

No more scrabbling around to see which of those 28 Sunday supplements contains the TV listings this week – just hit the Web instead! Visit the BBC's Radio Times guide at **http://www.radiotimes.beeb.com** and use the Television or Film sections to do a quick search of what's on today, or click the Listings Search tab to find out what's on in the next two weeks. You can click any programme title for more information about it, and of course you can save the list to your own disk to read offline by selecting **File, Save As**.

Need Satellite TV Listings?

The Sky TV site at **http://www.sky.com** has a TV Listings link taking you to a page which you can reach directly via **http://www.skynow. co.uk/tvguide/tv_channel.jsp**. Most satellite and digital channels have their own Web sites, of course, such as **www.discovery.com**, **http://www.disney.co.uk/DisneyChannel** and **www.cnn.com**.

You'd expect Auntie Beeb to have her own Web site, and indeed she does. Visit **http://www.bbc.co.uk/a-z** for a massive site covering every aspect of the BBC you could imagine. Many of the most popular TV and radio shows also have their own mini sites here, including *Tomorrow's World*, *Top Gear*, *Blue Peter* and *EastEnders*.

Need a few more TV and radio links?

➤ **http://www.itv.co.uk**. A single searchable site for the entire ITV network with news, programme listings and features.

➤ **http://www.sesameworkshop.org**. This *Sesame Street* site expertly combines fun and education for young children, although a little parental help might be needed.

➤ **http://uk.dir.yahoo.com/regional/countries/united_kingdom/ news_and_media/radio/stations**. Links to over 80 local, hospital and university radio station websites.

➤ **http://www.channel4.com**. A well-designed and stylish site for Channel 4, complete with programme listings and an easy-to-navigate set of buttons. And not to be outdone, you can find Channel 5 at **http://www.channel5.co.uk** (and you won't even need your browser retuned!).

Want To Take In A Film?

The Web can tell you just about everything you want to know about films and cinemas except for the price of the popcorn, and the site to check out is MovieWeb at **http:// movieweb.com/**. Here you'll find an alphabetical list of films going back to 1995 with cast information and plot synopses, pictures and posters, and a lot more. MovieWeb gets previews of new films long before they hit the cinema and you can view these online in QuickTime movie format. And if you're not sure what's worth seeing, the weekly Top 25 box office charts should point you in the right direction.

Once you've chosen the film you'd like to see, it's time to find the local cinema showing it. To do that, head off to Yell.com's Film Finder page at **http://search.yell.com/ search/FilmSearch** and enter your location. Or maybe you were looking for older films to buy on video? If so, get your credit card details ready and visit Amazon at **http://www.amazon.co.uk**. (If you haven't bought anything online before, skip ahead to Chapter 22 to see how it all works.)

If you're a real film addict, it's worth visiting the UK Internet Movie Database at **http://uk.imdb.com/a2z**. This site doesn't go in for previews, unlike MovieWeb, but it's one of the most-visited sites in the UK for the range of information it does cover, from up-to-the-minute news and reviews to lists of Oscar recipients, famous marriages and recent releases.

How About A Night At The Opera?

Well, not necessarily an opera. Perhaps a ballet, an ice show, a pantomime, a kids show, or the latest Andrew Lloyd Webber musical. Make your way to What's On Stage at **http://www.whatsonstage.com** (shown in the next figure) and run a simple search for live entertainment in your area. You can select a single region or the whole of the UK and choose one of 12 categories of stage show if you're looking for something in particular. You can even confine your search to particular dates, or use keywords.

Check This Out...

Finding More Culture

UK Calling (at **http://www.uk-calling.co.uk**) is a very attractive site with extensive listings in eight categories including Classical Music, Art Galleries, Dance, Theatre, and Museums. Or visit the Going Out section of Ananova at **http://www.ananova.com**, choose a category and enter the name of a show, venue or town to find out what's on.

When you've found a show you'd like to see, you can usually book tickets online. Click the **Buy Tickets** link, fill in the form and you should receive email confirmation within three days.

Stage show news, reviews and easy ticket booking at www. whatsonstage.com.

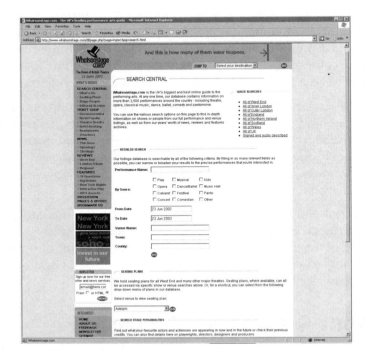

Get Away For The Weekend

If you're going to book to see a show, why not make a weekend of it? To find somewhere to stay, check out Expotel at **http://www.expotel.co.uk**. By clicking the **Search For Hotels** link, you can enter the name of a town anywhere in the world and Expotel will display prices and details of all hotels found. You can also select from a list of forthcoming events and conferences to find accommodation in the right area, and sort out travel tickets and car rental. Click the **Book Now** button to fill in the secure online booking form.

Check This Out...

Capital Letter

If you're looking for accommodation in London, take a visit to **http://www.london-hotels.co.uk**. This free service divides the capital's hotels into three bands – Superior, Tourist and Budget – and claims to offer discounts of 15–25% over travel agents' prices.

If you can't find what you're looking for at Expotel, try the UK Hotel & Guest House Directory at **http://www.s-h-systems.co.uk/shs.html**. This uses handy clickable maps to pinpoint a location (along with ordinary hypertext links for the geographically challenged!) and gives all the important information about each hotel. Booking isn't quite as nifty here: you send an email which is delivered to the hotel as a fax, and they should then get in touch with you to confirm the details.

Where To Go, What To Do

So you've got tickets to a show and booked a hotel, but what will you do with the rest of the weekend? Once again, the Web leaps in to help – try one of these sites:

➤ **Virgin Net Days Out.** Pick the type of activity you're looking for, the place you're going and when, and this handy site at **http://www.virgin.net/daysout** will provide a list of things to do.

➤ **Travel Britain.** A handy UK travel site covering car hire, hotel and rail booking, domestic and international flights, and a small amount of 'what's on' information. If you're looking for places to go in London, particularly, this site should be your first port of call. Head for **http://www.travelbritain.com**.

➤ **World Wide Events.** If you're going a little further afield, visit **http://www.wwevents.com** and find out what's going on in Europe, North America or Australasia while you're there.

And don't forget our old pal Yahoo! Point your browser at **http://uk.dir. yahoo.com/regional/countries/united_kingdom/cities_and_towns** for a list of hundreds of cities, towns, and villages. The entries for a particular town can be a bit of a mixed bag – all types of local information may be listed here, from tourist attractions and restaurants to butchers and council offices. If you're looking for something particular, such as a zoo or theme park, visit Yahoo!'s front page (**http://www. yahoo.co.uk**) and use a keyword search.

Want to Play A Round?

What better way to relax than to hit a little ball very hard and then go looking for it? If you're tired of looking in all the usual places, visit **http://www.golfweb.com/** and try a change of course.

Getting From A To B

Finally, let's sort out those travel arrangements. For this, there's one magical Web site that handles the lot – the UK Online All-In-One page, at **http://www.ukonline. net/travel**. From here, you can access dozens of European and international airlines and airports and check flight information; find the departure and arrival times of trains and National Express coaches; and book seats on planes, trains, and buses. If that isn't enough, you can hire a car from one of four companies (or visit Hertz at **http://www.hertz.com**), check the latest news on motorways, London traffic and the tube, or look at the World Ski Report.

A tiny slice of UK Online's incredible resource for travellers.

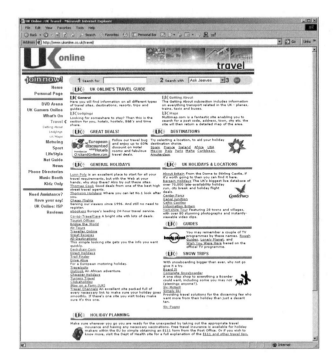

Book Your Holiday On The Web

If you want to journey further afield, the Internet has to be the ideal place to start. With a few clicks you can book flights and accommodation, read city guides, swot up on culture and currency, and check local events. You might even find a few photos that don't have painted blue skies! Here's a tiny taste of some of the best sites:

➤ **American Express Travel** at **http://travel.americanexpress.com**. A great travel resource for buying flights, finding last-minute offers, organizing insurance and travellers cheques, tracking flights, checking weather reports, and learning more about your chosen destination before you go.

➤ **World Travel Guide** at **http://www.wtg-online.com/navigate/world.asp**. Find out anything you want to know about every country, region, city and airport in the world before you visit.

➤ **Thomas Cook** at **http://www.thomascook.co.uk**. A mine of useful information including currency conversion, special offers, and links to other sites.

➤ **Eurostar** at **http://www.eurostar.com**. Fare and timetable information for passenger services through the Channel Tunnel, as well as online reservations.

➤ **Internet Travel Services** at **http://www.itsnet.co.uk**. Links to sites offering information about every aspect of travel you could imagine, including Health, Self-catering, Insurance, Ferries, Cycling Holidays, Travel Agents … the list is almost endless.

To find general *What's On?* information in the major cities of the world, a couple of useful starting points are Excite Travel (**http://travel.excite.com**) and Time Out magazine (**http://www.timeout.com**).

Let's Talk Travel

Usenet is a useful source of travel information and real-life experiences. Check out the **alt.travel** and **rec.travel.marketplace** newsgroups and take a look at the rest of the **rec.travel** hierarchy.

Amuse the Kids (And Yourself!) Online

Once you've discovered the Web, you've got a whole new world of entertainment at your fingertips. The effort that people put into creating some of these sites is stunning and they do it for no particular reward. There's no 'licence fee' to pay, and you won't get interrupted by advertisements every 15 minutes!

Entertainment Sites For Kids

The best children's sites are the ones that take a little education and add a sugar-coating of fun and interactivity, and the USA is leagues ahead of the UK in this department. In fact, UK kids' sites are thin on the ground and *good* sites are probably still a year or two away. As long as you're not too concerned about the odd bit of weird spelling, point your kids at **http://www.yahooligans.com** for a mass of links to tried and trusted Web pages.

Of course, you may not be convinced that the Internet is a safe or worthwhile place for kids. Prepare to be persuaded! Fire up your browser and visit **http://www. bonus.com**, shown in the following figure. As soon as you arrive, the 'worthwhile' element should be obvious: there are over 500 activities for kids, including games and puzzles, animations, interactive adventures, scientific explorations, and a whole lot more. The entire site is colourful, stylish, and easy to navigate. But apart from the incredible content you'll find here, this site illustrates the sense of responsibility found increasingly on the Web – your kids are locked in and they can't escape! Whenever you visit this site, a second browser window opens automatically, minus

Bonus.com, one of the most absorbing sites on the Web. But give your kids a go too!

toolbars and menus, to display the pages; your children can move around this site to their hearts' content, but the only way to access a different site is to return to the original window and choose a Favorites item or type a URL into the address bar.

Another site that knows how to keep kids entertained, not surprisingly, is Disney at **http://www.disney.co.uk**. Although the content here is clearly tilted towards the latest cinema and video releases, there's no big sell. Instead, you'll find games and activities that tie in cleverly with the films, with plenty of favourite cartoon characters, animated story-books, and a very friendly, 'kids-club' feel. You can also find out more about the various Disney resorts and watch live-camera broadcasts from Main Street.

Spin A Yarn For The Web

Do you have a budding novelist in the family? Point your kids at The Young Writers Club (**http://www.cs.bilkent. edu.tr/~david/ derya/ywc.html**) where they can submit their own stories and read other children's creations online.

The sheer novelty value of surfing the Internet can be enough to keep kids amused for hours at a stretch (if your phone bill can stand it!), and a particular branch of Web-based entertainment also makes a great starting point for learning how the Net works – the online scavenger hunt. Working from a set of clues, the goal is to track down pictures, pages and information on the Internet, like a treasure hunt at a kids' party. In fact, scavenger hunts are popular with adults too (especially the ones that pay cash prizes!) and often lead you to explore areas of the Internet that you'd studiously avoided, such as Gopher or Telnet. Yahoo!'s UK site keeps a list of current scavenger hunts, but its location seems to change periodically, so head off to **http://www.yahoo.co.uk** and enter the keywords 'scavenger hunts' to see where they're keeping it these days.

Play Online Games With Other Web-Surfers

If you like computer games, the Web is exactly what you've been waiting for. Forget Minesweeper and Solitaire – Yahoo! offers 45 different categories of online games at **http://dir.yahoo.com/Recreation/Games/Computer_Games/Internet_ Games/Web_Games**. Some of these are single-user games in which you play against the clock, solve a brain-teaser, or try to beat someone else's highest score; others are multi-user games in which you play against anyone else that happens to be visiting the same site at the same time.

If you're stuck for somewhere to start, here are a few suggestions:

➤ **Gamesville** at **http://www.gamesville.com**. This Lycos site proudly announces that it's been wasting your time since 1996, and it's obviously keen to go on doing so. There's poker, bingo, blackjack, pop quizzes, and links to many more types of games (including kids' games, puzzles and Pokemon games).

➤ **Casino Royale** at **http://www.funscape.com**. If you like a gamble, visit this site and play poker, blackjack, roulette, slot machines, and more. It really *is* a gamble, though – you can win real money, you can lose real money, and you'll have to pay a few dollars of real money to open an account before you start!

➤ **Tucows** at **http://tucows.mirror.ac.uk**. Tucows is an excellent source of Internet software, and the Games link at the top of this page will point you towards dozens of online games including shoot-'em-ups, board games, casinos, and trivia quizzes.

Maybe you don't need to go hunting for games on the Web at all, though. Recent editions of Windows (including Windows XP) include a range of Internet games you can reach from your own Start menu, including Backgammon, Hearts and Reversi. These games automatically connect you to a suitable player somewhere in the world, or you can visit the MSN Gaming Zone (**http://zone.msn.com**) to choose your own opponent or pick from bundles of other games.

Gags And Giggles Galore

The World Wide Web has a seemingly endless store of joke pages, cartoons, comic strips and comedy sites. For instance, go to **http://www.davecovcomedy.com/ comedysites.htm** and you'll find links to dozens of mini sites dedicated to classic British TV comedies. If you're a fan of sci-fi fantasy writer Terry Pratchett, you can find a page of hilarious quotes at **http://www.us.lspace.org**. For reams and reams of jokes and humour links, try The Comedy Corner at **http://www.geocities.com/ Eureka/2531** or the British Comedy Library at **http://start.at/britcomlib**.

If you're a cartoon fan, your first stop should be CartoonStock at **http://www. cartoonstock.com**. Although the main aim of the site is to promote cartoon artists and sell their work, you'll find thousands of cartoons online in the Daily Cartoons and Artist Samples sections, and more still if you click the Search link and pick a category. For a taste of 'real life' humour from around the world, try Dumb Warnings at **http://www.dumbwarnings.com**, a collection of the silly warning labels included on product packaging (such as Nytol Sleep Aid's warning, 'May cause drowsiness', or the vital instructions on packs of American Airlines peanuts, 'Open packet, eat nuts'). While you're there, follow the links to Dumb Laws, Dumb Facts and Dumb Criminal Acts for more of the same.

Whatever flavour of humour you prefer, you'll find another generous helping on Usenet. A couple of self-explanatory newsgroups are **alt.binaries.pictures. cartoons** and **rec.arts.comics.strips**, and there are many more lurking in the **rec.humor**, **alt.humor** and **alt.jokes** hierarchies.

Online News And Current Affairs

Everybody in the world wants news of one sort or another. And, of course, there's plenty of it – it's being made all the time! But where traditional newspapers can print no more than two or three editions per day, Internet news services can be updated hour-by-hour, or even minute-by-minute. In this chapter you'll find some of the best sources of UK and world news and learn how to build your own tailor-made news service.

Read Your Newspaper On The Web

Unexpectedly, it's the broadsheets that have made it to the Internet first and they've made a surprisingly good job of combining content, style, and usability. If you find the paper versions of *The Times* and *The Daily Telegraph* a bit stuffy, their online versions are going to come as a revelation.

Not that the broadsheets are alone on the Net, by any means, but let's take *The Times* as an example. Go to **http://www.timesonline.co.uk**, and as soon as you arrive at the site's front page you'll see clear links to the major sections of the paper (Britain, World, Business, Sports, and so on), plus summaries of the major stories in several categories with hypertext links to the related articles if you'd like more detail. In true newspaper style, you'll also find links to classified ads, crosswords, cartoons, and puzzles.

At any online newspaper, just click a headline to read the complete article.

So, it's all there and it's easy to navigate. But what makes it better than an ordinary paper version? In a word – storage! *The Times* and all the other online newspapers are building ever-expanding databases of news articles. With a quick keyword search, you can retrace the path of a news story you missed, track down articles on a particular subject, or find out what made headline news on any particular day. And, of course, it's a lot easier to save and store useful articles on your own hard disk for future reference than it is to keep a stack of newspaper clippings!

Information Swapping

Although access is usually free, when you first visit many online newspapers and magazines, you'll have to fill in one of those infamous registration forms, giving your name and address and a few other details. Provided you're honest, this provides useful marketing information for the publishers, which they regard as a fair exchange for the information they're giving *you*.

So where can you find your favourite paper online? Perhaps it's one of these:

Newspaper	Web Site URL
The Daily Telegraph	http://www.telegraph.co.uk
The Mirror	http://www.mirror.co.uk
The Sun	http://www.the-sun.co.uk
The Guardian	http://www.guardian.co.uk
The Sunday People	http://www.people.co.uk
The Independent	http://www.independent.co.uk

Let's Talk About The Weather

The weather is officially the most popular topic of conversation in the UK. Probably because we have so much of it. And the Internet has a solution to that centuries-old problem, *What can you do when there's no-one around to listen?* Just start up your newsreader and head for **alt.talk.weather** or **uk.sci.weather**.

To become a real authority on the subject, though, you need to know what the weather's going to do next. One option is to consult the online newspapers mentioned above, but here's a better one: head for **http://weather.yahoo.com/ regional/UKXX.html**. On this page you'll find a hypertext list of almost every town in the UK – click on the appropriate town to see a five-day local weather forecast. (You might want to add the forecast page to your Bookmarks or Favorites menu or create a shortcut to it on your desktop for quick access.)

For more detailed weather information, including shipping forecasts and meteorological data, visit the Met Office site at **http://www.metoffice.com/weather/europe/uk/ukforecast.html**.

You Will Meet A Tall Dark Stranger

Yes, the Net has horoscopes too! One of the best known is Jonathan Cainer's Zodiac Forecasts at **http://stars.metawire.com**. Or, for a more humorous approach, visit **http://www.xmission.com/~mustard/cosmo.html**.

Play The Money Markets Online

There's little that *can't* be done on the Internet, but a few things cost money, and share dealing is one of them. Because the sort of information you're looking for is worth money, you'll have to whip out your credit card and cross palms with silver before you can trade. Nevertheless, there's no shortage of companies on the Internet holding their palms out expectantly, and one of the better known is E*TRADE at **https://uk.etrade.com**. Alternatively, nip along to The Share Centre at **http://www.share.co.uk** – this is a good, easy-to-follow site for new investors, offering plenty of straightforward help and explanations of the financial world.

For information on more wide-ranging money matters, the place to be is MoneyExtra (**http://www.moneyextra.com**), shown in the next screenshot. This is a huge and popular site covering every aspect of personal finance you can imagine – homebuying and mortgages, ISAs, unit and investment trusts and company performance, to name but a few. You can read the London closing business report, check the FTSE 100 and 250, view regularly updated world prices and consult the glossary to find out what everyone's talking about. And if MoneyExtra doesn't have the information you're looking for, you'll find links to other financial services and organizations in the UK and abroad.

Money Talks

Usenet has several newsgroups for people wanting to give or receive a little financial advice. A good starting point is **uk.finance**. For more international input, try **misc.invest** and **misc.invest.stocks** and have a look at the **clari.biz.stocks** hierarchy.

MX MoneyExtra, an excellent starting point for all things financial.

Online newspapers such as *The Electronic Telegraph*, mentioned earlier in this chapter, also provide city news and prices just like their disposable counterparts, but if you need in-depth analysis, you can find the major finance publications on the Web too:

➤ *The Financial Times* at **http://www.ft.com**

➤ *The Wall Street Journal* at **http://www.wsj.com**

➤ *The Economist* at **http://www.economist.com**

Create Your Own Custom News Page

You probably buy a newspaper every day and perhaps a weekly or monthly trade journal of some sort. But do you actually read them all from cover to cover? The chances are that you glance at the headlines or the contents page, read the articles that interest you and ignore the rest. Wouldn't it be great if there were one publication you could buy that gave you just the stories that appealed to you and left out everything else? Well there is. In fact there are quite a few and you don't even have to pay for them!

The 'personal page' is a recent arrival to the Web, but more and more online publications are building the option into their sites. If you find a trade journal that covers one of your hobbies or interests, take a look around the site to see if they offer the service, or send them an email to ask if it's in the pipeline.

One of the best non-specialist services is provided by Yahoo!, the Web-search chaps, and it takes only a couple of minutes to set it up. Point your browser at **http://my.yahoo.com** and click the Sign Up Now link. The next step is to fill in a registration form – although this is a free service, Yahoo! needs to assign you a unique username and password to personalize your page. When you come to choose these, make sure you pick something that's easy to remember; it doesn't matter if it's easy for someone else to guess, since there's no security issue at work here.

As soon as you've filled in the registration form you can start building your own page by clicking the buttons in the example news page to edit or remove content, and choose your own custom content by checking boxes in all sorts of categories covering entertainment, news, sports and leisure activities. From now on, whenever you visit the main My Yahoo! page at **http://my.yahoo.com** you'll see your personal page. Your browser should store and send your username and password to save you the bother of entering it every time, but make sure you keep a note of it somewhere, just in case!

All-In-One News And Weather

If you prefer to find your news, weather and sports information all in one place, go to **http://uk.news.yahoo.com** and choose news headlines or summaries in several categories together with UK, Irish and worldwide weather forecasts.

Chart Hits And Bestsellers

Want to take a look at the UK albums and singles charts? The law of averages says you do – Dotmusic, at **http://www.dotmusic.co.uk**, is one of the most successful UK sites on the Web. Along with these charts and other information about the music scene, you'll find the Indie singles and albums charts, dance, R & B and club charts, and the US Airplay chart. While you're there, watch out for the little basket icons – if a CD you want to buy has one of these symbols beside it, you can click to add it to your 'shopping basket' and pay at the checkout when you're ready to leave.

Your bank account isn't running the same risks at the Publishers Weekly Bestseller Lists (**http://www.publishersweekly.com/bestsellersindex.asp**), but you'll find useful lists of the current bestsellers sorted into hardback and paperback, fiction and non-fiction, children's, religious, computer, and audio books. For more general information and reviews, the main Bookwire site makes an ideal starting point – head for the home page at **http://www.publishersweekly.com**.

Politics And Politicians On The Internet

Whether you want to explore 10 Downing Street, delve into government archives, read press releases and speeches, or check electoral and constituency information, the Internet has all the resources you need. But let's start with the obvious – if you're interested in politics, the first place you'll want to go is your own party's Web site, so consult the table below and pay it a visit.

Political Party	Web Site URL
Conservative Party	http://www.conservatives.com
Green Party	http://www.greenparty.org.uk
Labour Party	http://www.labour.org.uk
Liberal Democratic Party	http://www.libdems.org.uk
Plaid Cymru	http://www.plaidcymru.org
Scottish National Party	http://www.snp.org.uk

If you're more interested in the real workings of government, head for the Government Information Office at **http://www.open.gov.uk**. This is a huge site containing links to every department of central and local government, from the Adjudicators Office to the Zoos Forum. If you know which department you want you can simply pick it from an alphabetical listing, but it's often best to type a word or two into the Search box to find what you're looking for. The 'Your Life' section provides details on specific issues (such as moving home, having a baby, and dealing with crime). Another section of the site, reached from **http://www.ukonline. gov.uk/Quickfind/QFLocServ**, offers a mine of local information covering post offices, schools, job centres, health services, and much more.

Until recently, one of the few ways to get a look around 10 Downing Street was to become a politician – rather a high price to pay when one look is probably enough. Thanks to the wonders of the Web, you can tramp around to your heart's content at **http://www.number-10.gov.uk**, and read a selection of speeches, interviews, and press releases while you're there. Or jump on a virtual bus to **http://www. parliament.uk** to tour the House of Commons and the House of Lords, and search through the parliamentary archives.

Check This Out...

An Eye On The Net

You don't have to take politics entirely seriously, of course. For a more satirical view, try *Private Eye* at **http://www.cix.co.uk/ ~private-eye**.

For all the government departments and official bodies on the Web, one of the most useful and informative sites I've come across is actually *unofficial*. UKPOL Magazine (**http://www.ukpol.co.uk**) is a veritable goldmine that includes local and national electoral information, constituency lists and analyses, local government details, and a useful Basic Information section. There are even lists of MPs' personal Web pages and email addresses!

Chapter 22

Stay At Home And Go Cyber-Shopping

In This Chapter

➤ Learn how to buy goods online

➤ Visit shopping centres to find the big High Street names

➤ Buy your groceries on the Web

➤ Online banking, books, loans, wine, and more

➤ Cyber-romance – kisses, cards, and flowers

The Internet connection is starting to look like the Swiss army knife of the 21st century. In earlier chapters you've seen how the Net has tools to replace the telephone, answerphone, radio, TV, newspapers and magazines, fax machine, and a fair bit more. Granted, there's no tool for getting stones out of horses' hooves, but they're probably working on it. And now, with the recent arrival of secure transmission on the Internet, you can use your credit card at thousands of online 'cyberstores' to buy anything from a car to a … well, a Swiss army knife. It's quick, it's easy, and in this chapter I'll show you how to do it and point you towards some of the best stores in cyberspace.

Are These The Stores Of The Future?

So will we be doing all our shopping in cyberspace sometime in the future? Definitely not. Let's face it, shopping is fun! Online stores cover the Web, but they've been slow to really 'take off'. To a certain degree that's because of an imagined concern about the safety of using a credit card online, but it's also because people like their shopping the way it is. To buy an item without speaking to a cashier, or a voice on the end of a phone, is a curiously unsatisfying feeling.

That's bad news for the online stores, but it's good news for humanity. The much-vaunted prophecy that we'll live our entire lives hunched in front of computer screens is obviously nonsense – there are comparatively few purchases you'd want to make without first seeing, touching, and testing the goods. The main use of online shopping is for products like books, computers, videos, and cars – the type of item you don't need to see before buying – and for 'impersonal' goods and services such as travel bookings, insurance, or theatre tickets.

Should I Only Buy From Cyberstores In The UK?

If a store has a good, honest reputation, you could buy from them regardless of where they're situated. If you don't know anything about the company, it's easier to deal with any problems that arise if that company is based in the UK. Otherwise, there's no doubt that a lot of goods are far cheaper in the US than in the UK or Europe, and there's no reason not to buy from America or any other country. Always check the exchange rate so that you know how much you're spending, and look at the cost of packing and delivery. When buying from outside Europe, most goods valued at over £18 are subject to an import duty (imposed by our own Customs & Excise) which you'll have to pay when the goods arrive at your door.

How Do I Buy Stuff Online?

In almost any online store you visit, the routine will be pretty much the same. The layout will vary, of course, just as real stores all look different once you're inside, but most stores use a readily-accepted 'supermarket' metaphor that involves placing items in an electronic shopping cart and then going to the checkout to pay. As an example, follow me through a quick spending spree at Amazon (**http://www.amazon.co.uk**), one of the best-known UK cyberstores for CD, video, books, and DVD.

Step one: choose a product to buy.

From Amazon's front page I chose the link to the Rock Music Chart page, arriving at the page shown in the figure above. Every item has an **Add to Shopping Basket** button beside it, so I click the button beside the CD I want to buy. At the top of the page there's a little basket icon – at any point in my shopping trip I could click that button to go and pay.

Clicking the **Add to Shopping Basket** button takes me to a **Shopping Basket** page which shows all the items I've placed in my 'basket' – just a single CD so far. I could change the quantity of any item by typing a new figure to replace the **1** shown, or remove an item from the basket by clicking the **Delete** button beside it if I've had a change of heart. I haven't, so I take a quick glance at what's in the cart so far and choose what to do next: should I buy more stuff, or **Proceed to Checkout**? Throwing caution

Step two: verify the item and quantity, and decide what to do next.

*Step three: enter
your contact and
delivery details.*

to the wind, I decide to buy more stuff, so I click the **Back** button to return to the music charts page.

A few minutes later I'm back at the **Shopping Basket** page (shown in the figure on the previous page) after clicking the **Add to Shopping Basket** button beside another CD. My cart now boasts two items and I'm ready to pay up and leave, so this time I click the **Proceed to Checkout** button.

From this point on, Amazon keeps me posted on my progress with a set of six icons across the top of the screen (shown in the figure above). As this is my first visit I have

*Step four: enter
your credit card
details and
confirm your
purchase.*

to enter all my contact information – name, address, phone number, and so on. (Notice Internet Explorer's padlock symbol in the lower right corner and the https:// prefix in the address bar, both indicating that these pages are secure – see Chapter 17.)

After one final check on the items in the cart and the total price including VAT and delivery, I arrive at the Pay stage (shown in the figure on the previous page) where I enter my credit card details and choose a password I'll be able to remember on future visits to save retyping all the same details again. In the final step, which commits me to the transaction, all these details are passed to Amazon. I click on **File, Save As** in the browser to save the order-confirmation Web page to my own disk in case I want to refer to it later, and an emailed confirmation of my order arrives a few minutes later. Exhausted, I search for their cafeteria, but they don't seem to have one.

Take A Tour Of The Shopping Centres

Where do you go when you want to find the biggest selection of stores and merchandise quickly and easily? A shopping centre, of course! The theory behind shopping centres or malls in your local town translates perfectly to the Internet – not only are all your favourite stores within easy reach, but while you're there you might be tempted to do a spot of 'window shopping'.

You've probably guessed, from the generic name shopping malls, that most of these are US centres. Elsewhere in cyberspace it make little difference which part of the world you're looking at, but online shopping tends to be different. You may not be at ease working in dollars, for instance, or you may not want to wait so much longer for transatlantic delivery. So, for this section, I'm going to stick to just UK malls and stores.

Actually, these days it's not too difficult to stick to UK malls. Not only are there a lot more of them now than there were a couple of years ago, but the quality and choice has improved dramatically. A good example is the UK Shopping Centre at **http://www.ukshops.co.uk**. Choose a product category from the list of over 100, or pick one of the 15 'city zones' such as Technology, Property or Sports. Among the centre's stores you'll find some of the best-known High Street names, such as Comet, WH Smith, Mothercare and the RAC, along with a bundle of not-so-well-known but nicely varied sites.

Here are some more malls worth a visit:

➤ **Shops On The Net** at **http://www.shopsonthenet.com**. Browse directory-style through 20 categories of shopping site (with useful indicators of the number of links in each category) or search by keyword for a shop or a product.

➤ **British Shopping Links** at **http://www.british-shopping.com**. A deceptively simple site with over 160 categories of store, descriptions of every store listed, and icons to indicate whether secure payment can be made at each site.

303

Search For A Store

Some items are hard to find wherever you go. If you need to find a particular product, such as a cricket bat, try using your favourite search engine, entering something like **cricket+shopping online** (substituting the word **shopping** with **buy** if that doesn't yield results).

Groceries In Cyberspace

When you've been on the Net a short while, you get so used to electronic shopping carts that the idea of pushing one of those wire things around a supermarket loses all its appeal! No problem – head for Tesco at **http://www.tesco.com** to see if you can do your grocery shopping online too. Choose **Groceries from your local Tesco** link and you'll be taken to the Register page where you can find out if the service is available in your area. If it is, follow the registration process (it's free and takes about five minutes), and you'll be able to fill your cart with goodies, pay by credit card, and arrange delivery for a time that suits you.

UK users are now spending a billion pounds a year on online grocery shopping (roughly half the total UK online spend), so this is big business indeed, with many

Tesco's technically-advanced, but easy to use, online supermarket.

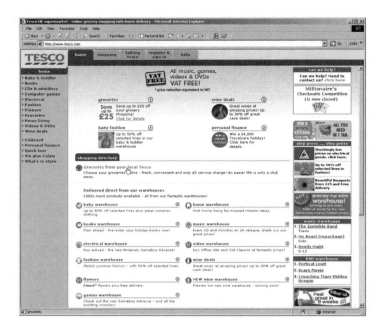

other supermarkets following Tesco's lead. At Sainsbury's (**http://www. sainsburystoyou.co.uk**), enter your postcode to find out whether you're close enough to a participating store. You can also wheel a virtual trolley through the aisles to get a feel for online grocery shopping before you order anything. If you prefer to buy from Iceland (the store, not the country), head for **http://www.iceland.co.uk**, or you can shop at Asda by visiting **http://www.asda.com**.

Have A Wander Down The High Street

Away from the organized aisles of supermarkets and shopping centres, the Internet has thousands of individual shops gamely vying for your attention. So let's grab a carrier-bag and venture out into the fresh air of the global village to see what's about.

How about a new car? CarSource (at **http://www.carsource.co.uk**) offers a free service to private buyers and will happily give you a quote on the model you want. Or, if you're in the market for a used motor, search the database of over 75,000 'previously owned' vehicles. If you can't find what you want, submit your details to CarSource and it'll try to track it down for you. Alternatively, nip into What Car Online (**http://www.whatcar. co.uk**) where you can buy or sell a car, get a valuation, and organize insurance.

Shopping All Over The World

If you can't get what you want from the sites in this chapter, the trusty Yahoo! has a mammoth page of UK shopping sites at **http://uk.shopping.yahoo.com**, or worldwide sites at **http://shopping.yahoo.com**.

Perhaps you need a loan to buy your dream machine. If so, Abbey National (**http:// www.abbeynational.co.uk**) should give you the information you need and you can use its handy loan calculator to work out what it's going to cost. Finally you'll need car insurance, and EasyCover might be able to help you out: visit **http://www. easycover.co.uk**, fill in the details, and EasyCover will submit them to ten major (and not-so-major) insurance companies on your behalf. While you're there you can get quotes for home and travel insurance too. One of the popular insurance companies that doesn't appear on EasyCover's list is Direct Line at **http://www.directline.co.uk**.

Next, a brief stop at Wine Cellar. You can find this wonderful, friendly site at **http://www.winecellar.co.uk**, browse through tempting categories such as Wine, Champagne and Spirits, and top up with soft drinks and cigars. Not content with simply selling, Wine Cellar offers some nice extras. Click the **Magazine** icon, for example, and you'll find a range of interesting recipes with suggested accompanying wines.

The Wine Cellar – so good you can almost smell the feet.

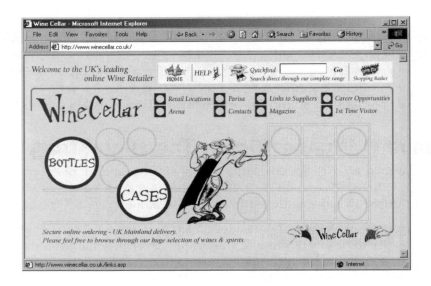

After a nice meal and a crate of Beaujolais, you'd probably want to settle down with a good book. Visit Waterstones at **http://www.waterstones.co.uk** or The Internet Bookshop at **http://www.bookshop.co.uk** and search by title, author, or ISBN. Better still, go to BookBrain at **http://www.bookbrain.co.uk**: BookBrain doesn't sell books itself, it searches over a dozen other bookstores to find the best price on the book you want. On a slightly different tack, try Online Originals (**http://www.onlineoriginals.com**), a site which publishes original works in email and e-book (electronic book) form only. Read synopses and samples on the Web site and if you find something you like, you can pay around £6 to have the complete text sent to you by email.

Classic Literature Online

If your reading tastes include authors like Somerset Maugham, Daniel Defoe, Oscar Wilde, and Arthur Conan Doyle, visit Project Gutenberg at **http://www.promo.net/pg**, which publishes out-of-copyright works in electronic format.

After all this spending, it's probably about time to check your bank balance and settle your credit card bill. No, don't get up – you can do that online too! Many of the UK's biggest banks, including Barclays (**http://www.barclays.co.uk**), Lloyds TSB (**http://www.lloydstsb.com**) and NatWest (**http://www.natwest.co.uk**), offer their account-holders online banking, allowing you to transfer funds, pay bills,

306

and check balances at any hour of the day or night. There are also a couple of banks specifically aimed at Internet users: Cahoot at **http://www.cahoot.com** and egg at **http://www.egg.com**. If you're a Barclaycard holder, register at **http://www. barclaycard.co.uk** and settle your account online using your bank debit card.

It Must Be Love ...

Here's a branch of Internet shopping that romantic males won't be able to resist. Surprise Your Woman (**http://www.surpriseyourwoman.com**) specializes in gifts for the lady in your life, from a single red rose to a 'Microlight flying experience' (perhaps more suited to scareyourwomantobits.com?). The site can also remind you about upcoming anniversaries and birthdays, and suggest the ideal gift based on personality profiles. There's no Surprise Your Man equivalent, but if you want to find unusual gifts for the gadget-mad male, try Big Boys Toys at **http://www.big-boys-toys.net**. To surprise someone in a slightly more economic way, visit **http://www.cyberkisses.com/Kisses** where you can send virtual kisses by email, complete with your choice of background music and poetry.

Virtual cards are all the rage on the Internet as more and more people take to email as an alternative to the post. A couple of free 'all-purpose' card shops are E-greetings at **http://www.egreetings.com,** and Awesome Cyber-Cards at **http://www.marlo.com**. You can also send customized digital postcards with pictures, music, and Web links from **http://www.all-yours.net**.

Online Lunar-cy

Have you ever promised someone the moon? Now you can put your money where your mouth is. Visit the MoonShop at **http://www.moonshop.com**, hand over about £20 to the official Lunar Embassy and you'll receive documentary title to your lunar property and its mineral rights. Getting planning permission for it might be more tricky, of course ...

In the time-honoured traditions of romance, you won't be taken seriously if you don't send flowers. Head for Interflora at **http://www.interflora.co.uk**, browse through the catalogue and place your order online complete with accompanying message.

To finish, let's assume those virtual kisses did the trick and a wedding is imminent. Head along to Wedding Bells at **http://www. weddingbells.com** to find out what's involved. This is a US site, so you might prefer not to buy goods here (you can visit the UK's Wedding Day Guide at **http://www. wedding-day.co.uk** to find bridalwear, cars, cakes, and so on), but the other resources are valuable and free: you'll find an Idea Pool, wedding facts and figures, a selection of toasts for worried speech-makers, gift suggestions, wedding etiquette and style advice, and a whole lot more to virtually guarantee a successful day.

Chapter 23

Research And Work On The Internet

In This Chapter

➤ Use online dictionaries, encyclopaedias, thesauruses, and more

➤ Search for specialist research material at Wired Source

➤ Locate online maps, atlases, and city guides

➤ Find pictures, videos, and information about the entire universe

➤ Online schools, universities, and study tools

➤ How the Internet can help you find a job

Whatever you do in your daily life, the Internet can help. It can provide you with vital reference and research materials; supply information about complementary or competing companies; enable you to work or study from home; and put you in touch with other users working in a similar field. And if your daily life leaves you too much time for aimless surfing, the Internet can even help you find a job!

Look It Up Online

I'm not going to pretend that you'll be using 'lookup' references on the Internet a great deal. In the UK, where few of us have unmetered Internet connections, going online to check the spelling of a word or find a synonym is hardly a quick or economical pastime. More than likely, your word processor has a built-in spellchecker and thesaurus; you may have a CD-ROM-based multimedia encyclopaedia too. But it's a safe bet that the Internet outweighs your book and CD-ROM collections, so here are some of the resources you can call on when you need to.

Encyclopaedias

The words 'online encyclopaedia' sound a bit odd. After all, the Internet itself is the ultimate encyclopaedia, so why would you search its contents for a smaller version? A search engine will provide a greater number and variety of links to information than any encyclopaedia. So the only time you're likely to want an online encyclopaedia is when you need concise, comprehensive information on a subject fast, and as in 'real life', the only contender is the *Encyclopaedia Britannica's* online incarnation at **http://www. eb.com**.

The Britannica site itself is excellent – you'll find an Image Tour, a word game, Random Article features, news and current events articles, Birthday Lookup, and masses more. As for the reason you visited it in the first place, the search facilities are fast and powerful: you can enter a keyword or phrase, or even type a question in standard English. The search engine will then give you the information intelligently – if it believes it's answered your question, it will display the relevant article, or the portion of an article that seems to contain the answer. As with keyword searches, you'll also find more links to related articles to help you dig deeper.

For home and family users Britannica is a subscription service, and not a particularly cheap one at $9.95 per month (roughly £6.70). You can sign up for a rather mean 3-day trial, but you can still use a cut-down version of the service for searching or browsing free of charge.

The other big name in encyclopaedias is Microsoft's CD-ROM-based Encarta, which has recently made the transition from disk to Net. You can use Encarta's online edition for free at **http://encarta.msn.com**.

Kids Encyclopaedia

Kids and teenagers can find a good reference site at **http://www. letsfindout.com**. This encyclopaedia allows keyword searches, browsing through its nine categories, or a trawl through its entire list of entries. Although it's a US site with an obviously US slant, the information is well-presented and might make all the difference to school projects or homework.

Dictionaries

I don't know who has the time or energy to put them there, but dictionaries of all types abound on the Internet. One of the best spelling and definition lookups is Merriam-Webster at **http://www.m-w.com/netdict.htm**. As usual, enter a keyword, and its pronunciation and definition will appear. If you're not sure of the spelling, just get as close as you can – Webster's will suggest some alternatives if it doesn't recognize your word. A great all-rounder is the OneLook Dictionaries site at **http://www. onelook.com**. This handy resource can search through 740 dictionaries simultaneously, or you can restrict your search to a particular area such as medical, computer-related, or religious dictionaries. Both Webster's and OneLook support the use of wildcards, allowing you to find multiple words or hedge your bets on the spelling.

Of course, neither of the above sites can help you much when you receive an email from your Hungarian penpal. For that you need a dual-language dictionary, and Dictionaries On The Web (**http://www.iki.fi/hezu/dict.html**) is the place to find one. This page contains links to a huge number of foreign dictionaries including Russian, Estonian, Czech, Latin, and German, most of which translate to or from English.

The OneLook Dictionaries site has 4,822,971 different words. It makes you feel guilty asking for just one, doesn't it?

If you prefer to start with a less demanding language, here's a couple of oddball sites you might like. The Aussie Slang & Phrase Dictionary (**http://members.tripod.com/~thisthat/slang.html**) is a real 'ripper' worth a 'burl'. BritSpeak is a site that introduces English as a second language for Americans (although it also has an American–English version). It's intended to be tongue-in-cheek, but some of its humour is quite unintentional, though they'll probably call me a 'bounder' for saying so. You can find BritSpeak at **http://pages.prodigy.com/britspeak/main.html**.

Still No Rhyme For 'Orange'

The word 'orange' continues to look an unlikely candidate for your latest love-poem, as confirmed by the Rhyming Dictionary at **http://www.rhymezone.com**. This keyword search lets you choose between perfect and partial rhymes, or homophones (such as there/their/they're).

Thesauruses

The most pristine book in my collection is *Roget's Thesaurus*. To look at it, you'd think I care for it deeply. I don't – I find it very unfriendly (hostile, antagonistic, and, indeed, adverse). Fortunately, Roget's online version, at **http://humanities.uchicago.edu/forms_unrest/ROGET.html**, uses the now-traditional keyword search. Just type in a word and then choose the desired meaning from the resulting list to see its synonyms.

Quotations

'The Internet is a great way to get on the Net'. So sayeth US Senator Bob Dole and it takes a brave man to disagree. Another good way is to say something sufficiently wise, amusing, or obtuse, so that people will include it in their online quotation pages. Everyone from Shakespeare to Stallone has said something quotable and the best place to find it is **http://www.geocities.com/Athens/Forum/1327/quotearc.html**. This page gives an immense hypertext list of words from 'Ability' to 'Zest' – just click a likely word to open a page of related quotes.

Alternatively, visit Bartleby at **http://www.bartleby.com/99** to read quotes by choosing an author from the list, or by running a keyword search. The quotes are limited to classical literature (no Oscar Wildes or George Bernard Shaws here), and the search engine responds best to a single-word entry.

ASCII Art

If you're looking for quotes and one-liners to use as an email signature, hop along to **http://huizen.dds.nl/ ~mwpieter/sigs**. Along with the gags, poems, and opinions, you'll find a huge collection of ASCII art (pictures created using ordinary ASCII characters).

If you're in the market for humorous quotations, try the Random Quotes page at **http://www.tomkoinc.com/random_quote.html**, or the Insulting Sarcasm page at **http://www.corsinet.com/braincandy/getinsulted.html**.

And Lots More Besides ...

Need to find the meaning of some of those acronyms and abbreviations that seem to crop up so often in modern life? Head off to the Acronym Lookup at **http://www. ucc.ie/cgi-bin/acronym**. This simple service consists of just a textbox (nope, no button!). Type in your acronym and press **Enter** to see the results.

Another often-needed reference is a weights and measures converter. For a straightforward list of units and their conversion factors, visit **http://www.soton.ac.uk/~scp93ch/units**. The list is comprehensive and appears on a single page, so you could even save the page to your own hard disk for easy use. But if you'd prefer to avoid the brain-exercise of doing the maths yourself, the Measurement Converter at Convert-me (**http://www.convert-me.com/en**) has the answer. Choose one of the 12 categories (such as Weight, Speed, Pressure, or Area), type a figure in the appropriate box and press the **Tab** key to see the equivalent value instantly displayed for all the other unit types.

Along similar lines, you'll find a useful currency converter at **http://www.xe.com/ucc**. Type an amount into the textbox, select your Convert From and Convert To currencies from the drop-down lists and click the button to see the result based on the latest exchange rates.

The Writer's Bible

Confused by the comma? Perplexed by the apostrophe? You need *The Elements of Style* by Strunk and White. In fact, if you write anything more adventurous than a shopping-list, this captivating little book is a must-have. But don't take my word for it – read it online at **http://www.bartleby.com/people/Strunk-W.html**.

Finally, a little bit of everything on one unusual site: Research-It! at **http://www. itools.com/research-it/**. On this single well-organized page you'll find a choice of dictionaries and thesauruses, a translator (with a range of options such as a verb conjugator and an anagram creator), biographical lookup, biblical lookup, maps, CIA factbook, currency converter, stock quotes, and even more.

The Earth Unearthed

The world is generally accepted to be a pretty big place and most calculations indicate that the universe is bigger still, so the potential for acquiring knowledge is inexhaustible. Whether you're looking for fact, conjecture, or opinion, the Internet can help you find anything from a street-map of Dallas, the best restaurant in Prague, or a video of a lunar eclipse, to several answers to the mystery of crop-circles.

Discover The World

There's no single, comprehensive site for maps and atlases, so if you want something particular you may have to be prepared for a bit of traipsing around, but here's a good place to start: Multimap.com at (you guessed it) **http://www.multimap.com**. This well-designed site offers street maps of the UK, including even the tiniest of towns, with a little local information to accompany them, aerial photos, a London tube map, and slightly-less-detailed maps of Europe and the World. You can type a town or country name or a postcode to run a keyword search, or (more enjoyably) click your way through the interactive maps to home in on the area you want. Click the **Printer Friendly** button to switch to a format you can print out for reference.

Another useful map site is Streetmap.com at **http://www.streetmap.com**, which includes links to a number of other map sites alongside its own maps. Although the USA is disproportionately well served, you'll also find maps of cities elsewhere in the world, atlases and historical maps, plus a few links to interactive and virtual-reality maps.

For historical maps, check out the Bodleian Library Map Room at **http://www.bodley. ox.ac.uk/guides/maps/mapcase.htm**. You can also visit the Ordnance Survey online at two sites: **http://www.ordnancesurvey.co.uk** is the official government site, while **http://www.mapzone.co.uk** is an animated educational site aimed at children which includes an Action Zone, Info Zone, Competition Zone, and plenty of imaginative map-related fun.

Flying Colours

Looking for flags of the world? Visit **http://www.fotw.net/flags** and search for a flag by clicking interactive maps or entering keywords. The flags can be downloaded as GIF image files and each is accompanied by a page of fascinating historical background.

Zooming out for a global view, there's a mass of information available. If you need to check up on a time zone in a hurry, head along to **http://tycho.usno.navy.mil/tzones.html**, a US Navy site, and click the initial letter of the country you're interested in. For a slower, but stylishly interactive, way of reaching similar information, the WorldTime site at **http://www.worldtime.com** will keep you clicking around in fascination for ages as you zoom in and out and switch between night and day.

Change The World

There are a number of pressure groups and organizations dedicated to educating and improving the world and you'll find many of them online. If you know the name of a particular organization or society, try entering it into your favourite search engine; if you don't, enter descriptive keywords such as **wildlife protection**. Here are a few organizations you might want to visit:

Organization	Web Site URL
Amnesty International	http://www.amnesty.org.uk
OneWorld.net	http://www.oneworld.net
Friends Of The Earth	http://www.foe.co.uk
Greenpeace International	http://www.greenpeace.org
Save The Children	http://www.oneworld.org/scf

The Universe ... And Beyond!

If you need information about the rest of our solar system, the obvious starting point is NASA. In fact, the primary NASA site at **http://www.nasa.gov** is so immense it's hard to believe you'll ever need *another* site! Alongside image and film/video galleries, there are sound files, details of new and current missions, information about the types of technology involved, the history of space travel and the NASA organization itself.

If you want to find undiluted Shuttle information, go to **http://spaceflight.nasa.gov**. This is an in-depth, but friendly, NASA site about Shuttle and Space Station life, with videos of the spacecraft taken from both inside and out, latest news about the Shuttle programme and a wealth of fascinating information you won't find anywhere else.

To boldly go where no man has gone before, head for the Royal Greenwich Observatory at **http://www.ast.cam.ac.uk**. The site itself is uninspiring, but its links can lead you to pictures from the Hubble Space Telescope and many more observatories around the world (some of which provide live camera feeds to the Web from their telescopes).

Visit NASA, and you'll probably never be seen again!

A popular topic of discussion on the Internet, as elsewhere, concerns the existence of little green men (and women, presumably) from outer space, and many Web sites and newsgroups have sprung up to present, discuss, and dispute the evidence for UFOs. The best of these is Mystical Universe at **http://mysticaluniverse.com**, which also covers crop circles, ancient civilizations, paranormal phenomena and many more mysteries and unanswered questions. Confirmed UFO addicts will want to check out these sites too:

➤ Bufora, the British UFO Research Association, at **http://www.bufora.org.uk**

➤ UFO Magazine at **http://www.ufomag.co.uk**

➤ Alien-UK at **http://www.cwd.co.uk/alien-uk**

➤ SETI Institute at **http://www.seti-inst.edu**

Usenet, as usual, can put you in touch with other people around the world interested in the known and unknown universe. Take a look at the **sci.space** and **sci.astro** hierarchies, or drop in at **alt.sci.planetary**. You'll also find an **alt.paranormal** hierarchy and there's a scattering of UFO-related groups that you can track down by filtering the list with **ufo**.

Education On The Internet

Education is at an interesting stage in its online development. Although universities and colleges were among the first sites to appear on the Net, online classes are still few and far between. The technology is there: conferencing programs like NetMeeting (see page 206) can link students to classes using video and sound; course-work can be sent back and forth by email; reference materials can be downloaded by FTP or read from the World Wide Web.

One of the few UK organizations that can provide courses over the Internet, although currently only a few, is the Open University. Their site, at **http://www.open.ac.uk**, explains how the system works, and they'll even provide you with the software you need (you'll have to find your own computer, though!). There are details of all the available courses here, and you can apply for a place on a course by email.

Schools On The Web

Learning Alive (at **http://www.learningalive.co.uk**) is a site dedicated to UK schools on the Internet, with national curriculum information, a noticeboard, and a penpals page. You'll also find a list of email addresses and Web page links for thousands of schools nationwide.

The tradition for universities and colleges to have a presence on the Internet hasn't abated, and you can track them all down easily from the clickable maps at **http://scitsc.wlv.ac.uk/ukinfo/uk.map.html**. This page shows universities, and two links at the top of the page open similar maps for UK colleges and research establishments – click on any location and you'll be whisked straight to its Web page. The links to research venues, especially, are many and varied, including museums, libraries and observatories, and make excellent resources for your own online research. The university sites have an extra value you might not think of straight away – many of them include a fund of local information such as bus and train timetables, maps, and places of interest.

Useful Web sites have been slow to appear for GCSE, SAT and 'A'-level students, but they're here at last. Among the best is the BBC's Schools Online site at **http://www.bbc.co.uk/education/schools/revision**, shown in the next screenshot. Along with areas for parents, and primary and secondary school children, you can choose from a range of subjects in the drop-down lists according to the grade you're studying. If you get stuck, the 'Ask a Teacher' service may be able to provide an answer.

The BBC's Schools Online site provides an excellent resource for students of all ages.

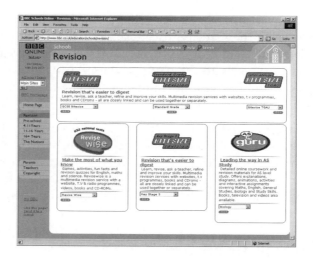

Here are a few more education and revision sites worth a look:

➤ **Schoolsnet** at **http://www.schoolsnet.co.uk** provides GCSE revision lessons in a number of popular subjects, along with discussion boards, information for teachers, and a textbook shop.

➤ **GCSE Answers** at **http://www.gcse.com** covers GCSE Mathematics, Physics, French, English, and English Literature, with downloadable revision notes and plenty of exam tips and techniques.

➤ **a-levels.co.uk** at (you guessed it) **http://www.a-levels.co.uk** has a vast collection of links for students of Biology, Maths, Chemistry, French, Psychology, and other subjects, with more on the way.

Find A Job Online

We all get involved in the employment market at some time in our lives and it's usually a frustrating, hit and miss ordeal. Although the Internet can't give you any firm guarantees, it *can* give you access to resources that your 'unwired' competitors don't have, and it puts all these right on your computer desktop to take some of the drudgery out of job-searching and self-promotion.

If you're looking for (or offering) full or part-time work, two UK sites are head and shoulders above the rest, between them offering many thousands of vacancies. PeopleBank, at **http://www.peoplebank.com**, gives its services free to jobseekers. Just fill in the online registration form and you can then submit your CV or browse through the database of job vacancies. JobSearch UK (**http://www.jobsearch.co.uk**) offers a free mailing list of vacancies, and (like Workthing at **http://www. workthing.com**) allows searching by keyword or job category and submission of your CV to their database.

If there's a particular company you'd like to work for, it's worth visiting its Web site. Many companies list their job vacancies online (although it sometimes takes a bit of clicking around to find the right page) and you can usually submit an application and CV by email. If you don't know the company's Web address, use your favourite search engine to search for the company name, or try **www.*company-name*.co.uk** or **www.*company-name*.com**.

If you want to be even more enterprising, why not publish your CV on the World Wide Web for all to see? If your line of work involves something that can be demonstrated on a computer, such as graphic design, journalism, or music, you could even include examples on your Web site. Most service providers and online services provide free Web space, along with information and tools to help you design and build your site.

Jobs By Mail

It doesn't get much easier than having job vacancies delivered automatically to your mailbox does it? Head for **http://paml. net/subjects/employment.html** and look for a promising mailing list. Clicking the list name will give you details about subscribing to the list.

Newsgroups provide valuable methods of 'meeting' potential employers, employees, collaborators, and customers. If you filter your newsgroup list with the word **job** you'll see a number of useful groups, including **alt.jobs**, **alt.jobs.overseas**, and an entire **uk.jobs** hierarchy that includes **uk.jobs.offered** and **uk.jobs.wanted**. It's well worth looking for newsgroups catering for your particular profession or vocation too: sometimes the only way to learn of a job opportunity is to be on 'speaking terms' with the type of people who can point you in the right direction.

Chapter 24

Pursue Your Hobbies And Interests

In This Chapter

➤ Read online versions of leisure and specialist magazines

➤ Find other Internet users who share your hobbies

➤ Find out where to seek advice and support on the Net

➤ Find friendship (or even love!) in cyberspace

➤ Follow your favourite sports, teams, and players online

➤ See the sights of the world without leaving home

However solitary a pursuit your hobby is, it probably isn't something you like to follow *completely* alone. Whether you like gardening, fishing, stamp collecting, or origami, part of the enjoyment is being able to talk about it with other enthusiasts, share knowledge and skills, and just chat. The Internet can help in this department, but far from just being a place to air your origami anecdotes, it can teach you more about your hobby, give you advice and support on a range of issues and help you to organize your own clubs and societies.

Read Your Favourite Magazines Online

The chances are good (and getting better all the time) that your favourite magazine has an online edition in the form of a Web site. If so, the URL will probably be listed somewhere in the magazine itself, but it's worth visiting a search engine and typing its name into a keyword search. If that doesn't work, it's a racing certainty that there's an online magazine *somewhere* that fits the bill, so try a search in the form **magazine** *your hobby*.

Pros And Cons Of Online Magazines

Online versions of magazines are usually free, but you pay a price of sorts. Often the online version will be 'published' a week or two later than the paper version and it may not be a complete copy. In their favour, though, you can save a small fortune if you normally buy several magazines every month, *and* you can store interesting articles on disk rather than snipping out pages!

To point you in the right direction, two of the UK's biggest magazine publishers have sites containing all their magazines in online form. Head along to MAG.net (home of VNU Publications) at **http://www.vnu.co.uk**, or FutureNet (Future Publishing's site) at **http://www.futurenet.co.uk,** and fill in the registration forms to get free access to dozens of major magazines. But, in case that's not enough, here's a few more:

Magazine	Web Site URL
Cosmopolitan	http://www.cosmomag.com
Esquire	http://www.esquire.com
Exchange and Mart	http://www.exchangeandmart.co.uk
Gourmet World	http://www.gourmetworld.co.uk
Q Magazine	http://www.q4music.com
Reader's Digest	http://www.readersdigest.co.uk
Empire	http://www.empireonline.co.uk
Hello!	http://www.hello-magazine.co.uk

Still not found the magazine you're looking for? Yahoo! lists a full 43 categories of magazine at **http://uk.dir.yahoo.com/regional/countries/united_kingdom/ news_and_media/magazines**.

Get In Touch With Other Enthusiasts

The most obvious way to make contact with others that share your hobby is through Usenet. The **rec.** and **talk.** hierarchies cover a vast number of interests between them, but if yours isn't there, use your newsreader's filter option to find it – if a group like **alt.macdonalds.ketchup** can exist, there must be something there for you!

A better method still might be to subscribe to a related mailing list. Mailing lists greatly outnumber newsgroups, but there's no sure-fire way to find out what's available. You'll find a good selection of lists at the Publicly Accessible Mailing Lists site (**http://www. paml.net**), but a more reliable method, paradoxically, might be to join a newsgroup and find out which mailing lists the other subscribers belong to.

Check This Out...

Share It On The Web

The majority of Web sites are created by personal users like you and me who want to share their interests, so why not join them? As well as being a satisfying achievement, it adds another opportunity for meeting people (as long as you include your email address).

There are bound to be sites on the World Wide Web relating to your hobby, and a keyword search in your favourite search engine should find them. It's a safe bet that anyone creating a Web site on a particular topic is an enthusiast, so why not check the site for an email address and get in touch?

Support And Advice At Your Fingertips

The Internet is the ideal place to find advice and support groups for any issue imaginable. In some cases, the Net is the *only* way you could ever access these services – if they exist in the 'real world' at all, they may be based on a different continent! If you know the name of an established organization or group, you might be able to find it on the Web using a search engine. Otherwise, use a descriptive keyword search such as **advice legal** or **support disability**. Here's a brief taste of some of the help available:

➤ Law Lounge is a complete one-stop free legal advice centre that can also point you to UK solicitors and barristers, law schools, and a range of other services. Visit **http://www.lawlounge.com**.

➤ For consumer advice, go to **http://www.oft.gov.uk/Consumer/ default.htm** at the Office of Fair Trading. The site contains useful information about your rights when shopping, as well as online shopping, unfair terms in contracts, and how to get help.

➤ If you're looking for some straightforward health tips, head for CyberDiet at **http://www.cyberdiet.com**. Despite its name, the site covers all aspects of healthy living and provides copious tips.

Let CyberDiet tell you if you've exceeded your daily cheeseburger ration.

Passively reading a Web page may give you the information you need, but in some cases you'll want to draw on the experiences of others. In one recent case, after being told that nothing could be done for her child, a mother appealed for help in a support newsgroup and learned of a potentially life-saving operation in South America. There are many such newsgroups available – either filter your list with the word **support**, or take a look at the extensive **alt.support** hierarchy.

Share Your Interests With A Penpal

This is really one for the kids – after all, grown-ups have Usenet largely to themselves, don't they? There's quite a range of sites that can put you in touch with an email penpal and you can find a good selection of them at **http://uk.dir.yahoo.com/ social_science/communications/writing/correspondence/pen_pals/childre n**. Two of the best, though, are KeyPals at **http://www.teaching.com/keypals** and KidNews.com at **http://www.kidnews.com/penpals.html**. KeyPals has the benefit of being secure, making it a good choice for young children. It's also searchable, so once you've registered you can look for your perfect penpal based on age, location, and interests.

How Do My Kids Know That Their Penpals Really Are Kids?

They don't, necessarily, so a little parental involvement would be wise in the early stages. However, if an adult was up to no good, he'd be more likely to initiate contact himself than to register at a penpal site and wait for kids to contact him. A little extra caution is advisable when your kids receive unsolicited email.

KidNews.com is a lot more free and easy than KeyPals, requiring no registration and offering no protective measures (although email addresses are never posted without parent or teacher permission). Penpal seekers are sorted into 'archives', with the most recent in the latest archive. Pick someone who sounds interesting and click the email link to get in touch.

For a wider choice of penpals and some casual online chat into the bargain, take a look at the newsgroups. By far the most popular is **soc.penpals**, but you'll also find plenty of movement going on in **alt.kids-talk.penpals** and **alt.teens.penpals**.

Try Some Real Computer Dating!

No, I'm not suggesting you should take your Pentium out to dinner. By *real* computer dating, I mean that you can finally use your own computer to search a database of people waiting anxiously to meet you. Visit Dateline at **http://www.dateline.uk.com** and give the service a trial run by checking off the attributes your perfect partner should possess and then searching the database.

Before you can even think of meeting anyone, however, you'll have to register with the service and part with some cash. After you've spent a little time on the Net, the idea of actually *paying* for a service starts to seem like an unnecessary extravagance –

why not just search a little harder for a free service instead? In the dating game, unfortunately, there's very little option: although free dating services do exist, most seem to have databases of about five people, all of whom live in a different hemisphere from you.

Keep Up With Your Favourite Sport

Whatever your sport, you'll find it on the Net in abundance – team Web sites, sporting facts and figures, fan pages, fantasy games, and much more. The search engines are your key to finding these sites, as usual, by entering the name of your sport, team, or player. Here's a mixed bag of links to get you started:

Sports Site	Web Site URL
Adidas Webzine	http://www.adidas.com
Athletics Statistics Page	http://users.rcn.com/bricklan/athletic/athletic.html
Formula 1	http://f1.racing-live.com
GolfWeb Europe	http://www.golfweb.com
SoccerNet	http://soccernet.com
Paralympic Games	http://www.paralympic.org
Rugby Leaguer	http://www.rugbyleaguer.co.uk
Tennis	http://www.tennis.com

If you're a football fan, don't waste your time tracking down separate sites at the search engines, head straight for Planet Football at **http://www.soccercity.com** instead. Here you'll find soccer news from all over the world, links to team and fan sites, statistics, league tables, you name it! For tennis fans, the place to be is **http://www. wimbledon.com**. During the Wimbledon championships this site is truly 'live', with up-to-the-minute news and scores, plus live camera views of Centre Court during play. For the rest of the year, it still promises to be one of the most comprehensive tennis sites in the UK.

For almost any sports fan, the Sporting Life's online edition (**http://www. sporting-life.com**) is a good candidate for your Bookmarks or Favorites menu, covering Soccer, Rugby, Racing, Golf, Cricket, and more, together with the latest sports news and a messages centre.

The Sporting Life *site should be a regular port of call for all sports fans.*

Track Down Your Favourite Celebrity

Everyone wants to know what their favourite film star, band, or singer is up to, and you'll find at least one Web site devoted to every celebrity you've ever heard of (and quite a few that you haven't). Visits to some of these sites can turn up biographies, interviews, photos, film clips and the latest reviews and news. You can use a search engine to track down these pages by entering the celebrity's name, but it's helpful to know how your chosen engine works before you do so. If it allows you to, enclose the name in quote marks (such as **"Jennifer Aniston"**) so that you'll only see pages in which both names appear. Alternatively, prefix each name with a plus sign (**+Jennifer +Aniston**).

If all that seems a little complicated, start by visiting Yahoo! You'll find a massive list of links to movie-star pages at **http://uk.dir.yahoo.com/entertainment/actors_ and_actresses**, and a similar list of musical artists at **http://uk.dir.yahoo.com/ entertainment/music/artists**. Both lists are so long that they've been grouped into separate alphabetical pages: click an initial letter at the top of the page corresponding to the name of the band or the surname of the celebrity you're looking for. Most fan pages contain links to other fan pages, so when you've found your way to one you'll probably have easy access to the best sites around.

The Sounds Of The Stars

If you're looking for interviews with the stars, visit Yahoo! Music at **http://www.broadcast.com/music/interviews** armed with your Windows Media Player or RealAudio player. There are also video chats, concerts and music channels that you can reach by removing the **/interviews** directory from the URL above.

For news and chat, celebrities have a similar level of coverage in the newsgroups as well. There are large **alt.fan** and **alt.music** hierarchies with groups dedicated to specific artists such as **alt.music.paul-simon** and **alt.fan.vic-reeves**, plus more general groups like **alt.music.midi** and **alt.music.bluegrass**.

Take A Cyber-Sightseeing Tour

One interest that most of us share is an ambition to 'see the world' – that vague term that encompasses natural and architectural wonders, famous works of art and the ruins of ancient kingdoms. The trouble is, unless you're extremely wealthy and have no pressing engagements for the next few years, it's a difficult ambition to realize.

Fortunately, the sights that we'd happily travel for days to see are just a few clicks away on the Internet and can usually be found with a keyword search. Many of these Web sites include background information too, but if you need a little more depth you might be able to find a 'travelogue' site created by someone who's actually visited that country – try a search for **travelogue** *country*. To save you a little searching time, here's a few of the sights you're probably itching to see:

Sight	Web Site Address
Golden Gate Bridge	http://www.goldengate.org
Grand Canyon	http://www.kaibab.org
Great Barrier Reef	http://www.greatbarrierreef.com
Leaning Tower of Pisa	http://ww2.webcomp.com/virtuale/us/pisa/opera.htm
Le Louvre	http://www.louvre.fr/louvrea.htm
Mount Rushmore	http://mountrushmore.areaparks.com
Niagara Falls	http://www.niagarafallslive.com
Seven Wonders of the Ancient World	http://ce.eng.usf.edu/pharos/wonders
Yellowstone National Park	http://www.yellowstone-natl-park.com

Part 4
Resources

You'll find reference information in this part of the book. I'll tell you where to find the software you need, which might include programs to help you on your travels around the Internet, games, print drivers, and unlimited other things. I'll also give you some background information about picking a service provider, in case you don't have Internet access yet or you want to find a new ISP. And there's a glossary of Internet terms and a quick look at the Internet tools built into Windows 98, Millennium Edition and XP.

Speak Like A Geek: The Complete Archive

ActiveX A multimedia-authoring system for the World Wide Web from Microsoft.

ADSL Asynchronous Digital Subscriber Line, a very fast digital line provided by the phone company if you're very lucky. By the time this book is in the bookstores, ADSL should be available to about 90% of the UK.

alias A name that is substituted for a more complicated name, usually in an email program. For example, you can use a simple alias (pkent) instead of a more complicated mailing address (**pkent@topfloor.com**) for a mailing list.

America Online (AOL) A popular online information service and generous donator of CD-ROMs to just about every North American and British household.

anchor A techie word for an *HTML* tag used as a link from one document to another.

anonymous FTP A system by which members of the Internet 'public' can access files at certain *FTP* sites without needing a login name; they simply log in as anonymous.

Archie An index system that helps you find files in more than 1000 *FTP* sites.

archive file A file that contains other files (usually compressed files). It is used to store files that are not used often or files that may be downloaded from a file library by Internet users.

ARPANET The Advanced Research Projects Agency (of the US Department of Defense) computer network, which was the forerunner of the Internet.

article A message in an Internet newsgroup.

ASCII American Standard Code for Information Interchange, a standard system used by computers to recognize text. An ASCII text file can contain the letters of the alphabet, the punctuation characters, and a few special characters. The nice thing about ASCII is that it's recognized by thousands of programs and many different types of computers.

B2B A geek business term meaning Business-to-Business; a mode of operation in which a business sells products or services to other businesses.

B2C A geek business term meaning Business-to-Consumer; a mode of operation in which a business sells products or services directly to consumers.

backbone A network through which other networks connect.

bandwidth Widely used to mean the amount of information that can be sent through a particular communications channel.

baud rate A measurement of how quickly a modem transfers data. Although, strictly speaking, this is not the same as bps (*bits per second*), the two terms are often used interchangeably.

BBS See *bulletin board system*.

beta test A program test based on the premise, 'This program is virtually finished, but because we need a little help smoothing out the rough edges, we'll give it to a few more people'.

BITNET The 'Because It's Time' network (really!). A large network connected to the Internet. Before the Internet became affordable to learning institutions, BITNET was the network of choice for communicating.

bits per second (bps) A measure of the speed of data transmission; the number of bits of data that can be transmitted each second.

bookmark A URL that has been saved in some way so that you can quickly and easily return to a particular Web document.

bounce The action of an email message being returned because of some kind of error.

bps See *bits per second*.

broadband An Internet connection that allows higher transfer speeds than the humble *modem* can manage, making it possible to view content that would otherwise be too large to download in a reasonable time (such as *streaming* music and video). Common broadband connection methods are *ADSL* and cable.

browser, Web A program that lets you read *HTML* documents and navigate the Web.

BTW An abbreviation for 'by the way', it's commonly used in email and newsgroup messages.

bug A malfunction in a computer program. Internet software seems to have led the software business to new levels of bug inclusion.

bug-like feature When a programmer or technical support person, talking about the stupid way in which a program handles a particular procedure, says, 'That's not a bug, that's the way we designed it' – that's a bug-like feature. This term may have been coined by the *Mosaic* programmers at *NCSA*, who understood that just because you designed something one way, it doesn't mean you *should have* designed it that way.

bulletin board system (BBS) A computer system to which other computers can connect so their users can read and leave messages or retrieve and leave files.

cable modem A device that connects a network card in your computer to a cable-TV line to provide Internet access. Some of these systems are very fast, at a very good price – probably the best value in Internet connectivity you can find. If you can get one of these (it's not available in all areas) you should do it!

cache A place where a browser stores Web documents that have been retrieved. The cache may be on the hard disk, in memory, or a combination of the two. Documents you 'return to' are retrieved from the cache, which saves transmission time.

CDF Channel Data Format, a system used to prepare information for *Webcasting*.

CERN The European Particle Physics Laboratory in Switzerland, the original home of the World Wide Web.

chat A system in which people can communicate by typing messages. Unlike email messages, chat messages are sent and received as you type (like a real chat – only without the voice). The most popular Internet chat system is Internet Relay Chat. There are a number of Web-site based chat systems, too. The best and most popular of all the chat systems, however, are on the online services. See also *talk*.

CIX The Commercial Internet Exchange, an organization of commercial Internet service providers.

client A program or computer that is 'serviced' by another program or computer (the *server*). For instance, a Web client – that is, a Web *browser* – requests Web pages from a Web server.

compressed files Computer files that have been reduced in size by a compression program. Such programs are available for all computer systems (for example, PKZIP in DOS and Windows, tar and compress in UNIX, and StuffIt and PackIt for the Macintosh). Sometimes known as *archive* files, although the terms are not really synonymous; an archive file is not necessarily compressed (although many are).

CompuServe A large online information service, recently bought by AOL.

cracker Someone who tries to enter a computer system without permission. This is the correct term, although the term *hacker* is often mistakenly used in its place.

CSLIP (Compressed SLIP) See *Serial Line Internet Protocol (SLIP)*.

cyberspace The area in which computer users travel when navigating a network or the Internet.

DARPANET The Defense Advanced Research Projects Agency network, which was created by combining *ARPANET* and *MILNET*. The forerunner of the Internet.

DDN The Defense Data Network is a US military network that is part of the Internet. *MILNET* is part of the DDN.

dedicated line A telephone line that is leased from the telephone company and is used for one purpose only. On the Internet, dedicated lines connect organizations to service providers' computers, providing dedicated service.

dedicated service See *permanent connection*.

dial-in direct connection An Internet connection that you access by dialing into a computer through a telephone line. Once connected, your computer acts as if it were an Internet host. You can run *client* software (such as Web *browsers* and *FTP* programs). This type of service is often called *SLIP*, *CSLIP*, or *PPP*. Compare to *dial-in terminal connection*.

dial-in service A networking service that you can use by dialing into a computer through a telephone line.

dial-in terminal connection An Internet connection that you can access by dialing into a computer through a telephone line. Once connected, your computer acts as if it were a terminal connected to the service provider's computer. This type of service is often called *interactive* or *dial-up*. Compare to *dial-in direct connection*.

dial-up service A common Internet term for a *dial-in terminal connection*.

direct connection See *permanent connection*.

DNS See *Domain Name System*.

domain name A name given to a host computer on the Internet.

Domain Name System (DNS) A system by which one Internet host can find another so it can send email, connect *FTP* sessions, and so on. The hierarchical system of Internet host domain names (**domainname.domainname.domainname**) uses the Domain Name System. The DNS, in effect, translates words into numbers that the Internet's computers can understand. For instance, if you use the domain name **poorrichard.com**, DNS translates it into 207.33.11.236.

dot address An informal term used for an *IP address*, which is in the form *n.n.n.n*, where each *n* is a number. For instance, 192.17.3.3.

download The process of transferring information from one computer to another. You download a file from another computer to yours. See also *upload*.

DSL Digital Subscriber Line (see also *ADSL*), a very fast digital line provided by the phone company if you're very lucky.

EARN The European network associated with BITNET.

EFF See *Electronic Frontier Foundation*.

EFLA Extended Four-Letter Acronym. Acronyms are essential to the well-being of the Internet. See *TLA*.

Electronic Frontier Foundation (EFF) An organization interested in social, legal, and political issues related to the use of computers. The EFF is particularly interested in fighting government restrictions on the use of computer technology.

email Short for electronic mail, the system that lets people send and receive messages with their computers. The system might be on a large network (such as the Internet), on a bulletin board or online service (such as CompuServe), or over a company's own office network.

emoticon The techie name for small symbols created using typed characters, such as *smileys* :)

encryption The modification of data so that unauthorized recipients cannot use or understand it. See also *public-key encryption*.

etext Electronic text, a book or other document in electronic form, often simple ASCII text.

Ethernet A protocol, or standard, by which computers may be connected to one another to exchange information and messages.

FAQ (Frequently Asked Questions) A document containing a list of common questions and corresponding answers. You'll often find FAQs at *Web sites*, in *newsgroups*, and at *FTP* and *Gopher* sites.

Favorites The term used by Internet Explorer for its *bookmark* list.

Fidonet An important network that is also connected to the Internet. Well known in geek circles.

file transfer The copying of files from one computer to another over a network or telephone line. See *File Transfer Protocol*.

File Transfer Protocol A *protocol* defining how files transfer from one computer to another; generally abbreviated as *FTP*. FTP programs transfer files across the Internet. You can also use FTP as a verb to describe the procedure of using FTP, as in, 'FTP to **ftp.demon.co.uk**', or 'I FTPed to their system and grabbed the file'.

Finger A program used to find information about a user on a host computer. Often used in the early days of the Internet boom, this system has now been largely forgotten.

flame An abusive newsgroup or mailing list message. Things you can do to earn a flame are to ask dumb questions, offend people, not read the FAQ, or simply get on the wrong side of someone with an attitude. When these things get out of control, a flame war erupts. Sometimes also used to refer to an abusive email message.

335

flamer Someone who wrote a flame.

Flash A popular animation format used in Web sites, created by Macromedia.

form A *Web* form is a sort of interactive document. The document can contain fields into which readers can type information. This information may be used as part of a survey, to purchase an item, to search a database, and so on.

forms support A Web *browser* that has forms support can work with a Web *form*. Not all browsers can use forms (more recent ones can, though).

forum The term used by CompuServe for its individual bulletin boards or discussion groups (similar to Internet *newsgroups*).

frames Some Web pages are split into different frames (or panes); in effect, these frames create two or more independent subwindows within the main browser window.

freeware Software provided free by its creator. (It's not the same as *public domain software*, for which the author retains copyright.) See also *shareware*.

FTP See *File Transfer Protocol*.

gateway A system by which two incompatible networks or applications can communicate with each other.

geek Someone who knows a lot about computers, but very little about communicating with his fellow man – and, perhaps more importantly, with his fellow woman. (Vice versa if the geek happens to be a woman, although the majority of geeks are men.) Geeks spend more time in front of their computers than talking with real people. The term 'geek' may have started as a derogatory term, but many geeks are proud of their geekness – and many have become very rich because of it. As Dave Barry (who got rich before becoming a computer geek) once said, 'I'm a happy geek in cyberspace, where nobody can see my haircut'.

Gopher A system using Gopher *clients* and *servers* to provide a menu system for navigating the Internet. Most Web browsers can act as Gopher clients. Gopher was started at the University of Minnesota, which has a gopher as its mascot.

Gopherspace Anywhere and everywhere you can get to using *Gopher* is known as Gopherspace.

GUI (Graphical User Interface) Pronounced *goo-ey*, this is a program that provides a user with onscreen tools such as menus, buttons, dialog boxes, a mouse pointer, and so on.

hacker Someone who enjoys spending most of his life with his head stuck inside a computer, either literally or metaphorically. See also *geek* and *cracker*.

helper See *viewer*.

336

history list A list of Web documents that you've seen in the current session (some browsers' history lists also show documents from previous sessions). You can return to a document by selecting it in the history list.

home page 1. The Web document your browser displays when you start the program or when you use the browser's Home command. 2. A sort of main page at a Web site. (Personally, I don't like this second definition, but there's not much I can do about it.)

host A computer connected directly to the Internet. A service provider's computer is a host, as are computers with permanent connections. Computers with *dial-in terminal connections* are not; they are terminals connected to the service provider's host. Computers with *dial-in direct connections* can be thought of as 'sort of' hosts: They act like hosts while connected.

host address See *IP address*.

hostname The name given to a *host*. Computers connected to the Internet really have *host numbers*, but hostnames are easier to remember and work with. A hostname provides a simpler way to address a host than using a number.

host number See *IP address*.

hotlist A list of URLs of Web documents you want to save for future use. You can return to a particular document by selecting its *bookmark* from the hotlist.

HTML (Hypertext Markup Language) The basic coding system used to create Web documents.

HTTP (Hypertext Transfer Protocol) The data-transmission *protocol* used to transfer Web documents across the Internet.

hyperlink See *link*.

hypermedia Loosely used to mean a *hypertext* document that contains, or has links to, other types of media such as pictures, sound, video, and so on.

hypertext A system in which documents contain links that allow readers to move between areas of the document, following subjects of interest in a variety of different paths. With most browsers, you use the mouse to click a link to follow the link. The *World Wide Web* is a hypertext system.

IAB See *Internet Architecture Board*.

IAP Internet Access Provider, another term for *service provider*.

ICANN The Internet Corporation for Assigned Names and Numbers, the organization that is responsible for managing *domain names* and *IP addresses*.

IE A common abbreviation for *Internet Explorer*.

IETF See *Internet Engineering Task Force.*

IMAP Internet Message Access Protocol, a system used to provide access to Internet email. Although this sytem is often used by corporations that link their networks to the Internet, most Internet service providers use a system called *POP.*

IMHO An abbreviation for In My Humble Opinion, which is often used in email and newsgroup messages.

index document A *Web* document that lets you search some kind of database. This term and *index server* are not used much these days; you'll hear the simple term 'search page' instead.

index server A special program, accessed through an *index document*, that lets you search some kind of database.

inline images A picture inside a Web document. These graphics must be .GIF, .JPG, or .XBM format files because those are the formats browsers can display.

Instant Messenger A software program that allows the user to see which of his friends are online and to exchange short conversational messages with any of them in real time. IM software is free, with programs available from AltaVista, Yahoo!, AOL, Microsoft, and others.

Integrated Services Digital Network (ISDN) A digital telecommunications system that everyone's been waiting for but that the telephone companies seem unable to get installed in a decent time. ISDN allows voice and data to be transmitted on the same line in a digital format – instead of the normal analogue format – and at a relatively high speed. ISDN is an Albanian acronym for 'Yesterday's Technology Tomorrow'. Despite the fact that ISDN was invented around the time of the Spanish–American War, the telephone companies just can't seem to figure out how to install this technology – and now ISDN's days are numbered because it will be superceded by *ADSL* (if the phone companies can manage to install *that* system, that is).

interactive service See *dial-in terminal connection.*

internal loop See *loop, internal.*

internet Spelled with a small i, this term refers to networks connected to one another. 'The Internet' is not the only internet.

Internet II The Internet used to be a nice little secret, a special toy for members of academia and the military–industrial complex. But since all you plebs got onto the Internet, it's been pretty crowded and slow. So a new network, called Internet II, is being created just for academia and military research. Don't expect them to make the same mistake twice and invite you to join!

Internet address See *IP address.*

Internet Architecture Board (IAB) The council of elders elected by *ISOC*; they get together and figure out how the different components of the Internet will all connect.

Internet Engineering Task Force (IETF) A group of engineers that makes technical recommendations concerning the Internet to the IAB.

Internet Explorer A Web browser from Microsoft. It's generally accepted as the best browser available, having beaten Netscape Navigator some time ago.

Internet Protocol (IP) The standard protocol used by systems communicating across the Internet. Other protocols are used, but the Internet Protocol is the most important one.

Internet Relay Chat (IRC) A popular *chat* program. Internet users around the world can chat with other users in their choice of IRC channels.

Internet Society The society that, to some degree, governs the Internet; it elects the Internet Architecture Board, which decides on technical issues related to how the Internet works.

InterNIC The Internet *Network Information Centre*. Run by the National Science Foundation, this centre provides various administrative services for the Internet.

IP See *Internet Protocol*.

IP address A 32-bit address that defines the location of a host on the Internet. Such addresses are normally shown as four bytes, each one separated by a period (for example, 192.156.196.1). See *dot address* and *hostname*.

IRC See *Internet Relay Chat*.

ISDN See *Integrated Services Digital Network*.

ISOC See *Internet Society*.

ISP An abbreviation for Internet Service Provider that's much loved in geekdom. See also *service provider*.

Java A programming language from Sun Microsystems. Programmers can create programs that will run in any Java 'interpreter', so a single program can run in multiple operating systems. (That's the theory at least; in practice, the programs often malfunction.) Netscape Navigator and Internet Explorer both have built-in Java interpreters.

JavaScript A sort of subset of Java, JavaScript is a scripting language that's simpler to use than Java. Both Netscape Navigator and Internet Explorer can run JavaScripts at least some of the time.

JPEG A compressed graphic format often found on the World Wide Web. These files use the .JPG or .JPEG extension.

JScript Microsoft's version of *JavaScript*; it contains as much of JavaScript as Microsoft can manage to add (Netscape develops JavaScript, so they're always ahead of Microsoft), plus some JScript-specific commands.

Jughead Jonzy's Universal Gopher Hierarchy Excavation And Display tool. A *Gopher* search tool that's similar to *Veronica*. The main difference between Veronica and Jughead is that Jughead searches a specific Gopher server whereas Veronica searches all of Gopherspace.

Knowbot A program that can search the Internet for requested information. Knowbots are in an experimental stage.

LAN See *local area network*.

leased line See *dedicated line*.

link A connection between two *Web* documents. Links are generally pieces of text or pictures that, when clicked, make the browser request and display another Web document.

linked image An image that is not in a *Web* document (that's an *inline image*), but is connected to a document by a *link*. Clicking the link displays the image. Often known as an external image.

LISTSERV list A *mailing list* that is handled by the popular LISTSERV mailing list program.

local area network (LAN) A computer network that covers only a small area (often a single office or building).

log in The procedure of *logging on* or logging in. Also sometimes used as a noun to mean the ID and password you use to log on.

logging off The opposite of *logging on* or logging in; telling the computer that you've finished work and no longer need to use its services. The procedure usually involves typing a simple command, such as **exit** or **bye**, or, in more recent days, clicking a **Disconnect** button.

logging on Computer jargon for getting permission from a computer to use its services. A logon procedure usually involves typing a username (also known as an account name or user ID) and a password. This procedure makes sure that only authorized people can use the computer. Also known as logging in.

loop, internal See *internal loop*.

lurker Someone involved in *lurking*.

lurking Reading newsgroup or mailing list messages without responding to them. Nobody knows you are there.

mail reflector A mail program that accepts email messages and then sends them on to a predefined list of other email addresses. Such systems provide a convenient way to distribute information to people.

340

mail responder A system that automatically responds to a received email message. For instance, many companies use **info@hostname** addresses to automatically send back an email message containing product and company information.

mail robot An email system that automatically carries out some sort of email-related procedure for you.

mail server 1. A program that distributes computer files or information in response to email requests. 2. A program that handles incoming email for a host.

mailing list 1. A list of email addresses to which a single message can be sent by entering just one name as the To address. 2. Discussion groups based on a mailing list. Each message sent to the group is sent out to everyone on the list. (*LISTSERV lists* are mailing-list groups.)

MB Abbreviation for *megabyte*.

megabyte A measure of the quantity of data. A megabyte is a lot when you are talking about files containing simple text messages, but not much when you are talking about files containing colour photographs.

The Microsoft Network A major online service (at one point the fastest growing service in history) that was launched in 1995 when Windows 95 was released. Also known as MSN.

MILNET A US Department of Defense network connected to the Internet.

MIME (Multipurpose Internet Mail Extensions) A system that lets you send computer files 'attached' to email. Also used to identify file types on the Web.

mirror site A copy of another site. (There are *FTP* mirror sites and *Web* mirror sites.) Every so often the contents of the other site are copied to the mirror site. The mirror site provides an alternative location so that if you can't get into the original site, you can go to one of the mirror sites.

modem A device that converts digital signals from your computer into analogue signals for transmission through a phone line (modulation) and converts the phone line's analogue signals into digital signals your computer can use (demodulation). (So-called ISDN modems and cable modems are not true modems; they don't modulate and demodulate.)

Mosaic The first popular *GUI Web browser*, created by *NCSA*. This was the first graphical browser; some of the original Mosaic programmers helped to found Netscape Communications, the publisher of *Netscape Navigator*.

MP3 Short for *MPEG* Layer-3, an audio format that can hold one minute of CD-quality music in a single megabyte, along with pictures (album art, for instance) and notes (such as lyrics and contact information for the musician or band); good MP3 players can not only play the music but display the text and images.

MPEG A computer video format. With the right software and, in some cases, hardware, you can play MPEG video files on your computer.

MUD A type of game popular on the Internet. MUD means Multiple User Dimensions, Multiple User Dungeons, or Multiple User Dialogue. MUDs are text games. Each player has a character; characters communicate with each other by the users typing messages.

navigate Refers to moving around on the Web using a *browser*. When you jump to a Web document, you are navigating.

navigator A program that helps you find your way around a complicated online service. Several navigator programs are available for CompuServe, for instance. Navigators can save you money by letting you prepare for many operations (such as writing mail) offline and then go online quickly to perform the operations automatically.

NCSA National Centre for Supercomputing Applications, the people who make the *Mosaic* Web *browser*.

netiquette Internet etiquette, the correct form of behaviour to use while working on the Internet and in *Usenet* newsgroups. These guidelines can be summarized as 'Don't waste computer resources, and don't be rude'. Apparently neither dictum is widely observed.

Netnews See *Usenet*.

Netscape Communicator A suite of programs based on *Netscape Navigator*. It contains Navigator (a *Web browser*), Messenger (*email* and *newsgroups* – the newsgroups portion is called Collabra in some versions), AOL Instant Messenger (*talk*), and Composer (a *Web* page editing program).

Netscape Navigator At one time the Web's most popular *browser*, created by some old *NCSA* programmers who started a company called Netscape Communications. Recently dropped down to second position, after *Internet Explorer*.

Network Information Centre (NIC) A system providing support and information for a network. See also *InterNIC*.

Network News Transfer Protocol (NNTP) A system used for the distribution of *Usenet newsgroup* messages.

newbie A new user. The term may be used to refer to a new Internet user or a user who is new to a particular area of the Internet. Because everyone and his dog is getting onto the Internet, these loathsome creatures have brought the general tone of the Internet down a notch or two, upsetting long-term Internet users who thought the Internet was their own personal secret.

news server A computer that collects newsgroup data and makes it available to *newsreaders*.

newsgroup The Internet equivalent of a *BBS* or discussion group (or *forum* in CompuServe-speak) in which people leave messages for others to read. See also *LISTSERV list*.

342

newsreader A program that helps you find your way through a *newsgroup's* messages.

NIC See *Network Information Centre*.

NNTP See *Network News Transfer Protocol*.

NOC Network Operations Centre, a group that administers a network.

node A computer device connected to a computer network. That device might be a computer, a printer, a router, or something else.

NREN The National Research and Education Network.

NSF National Science Foundation; the US government agency that runs the *NSFnet*.

NSFnet The National Science Foundation network, a large network connected to the Internet.

offline The opposite of *online*; not connected.

offline browser A program that automatically collects pages from Web sites and then makes them available for viewing *offline*.

online Connected. You are online if you are working on your computer while it is connected to another computer. Your printer is online if it is connected to your computer and ready to accept data. (Online is often written 'on-line,' though the non-hyphenated version seems to be gaining acceptance these days.)

online service A commercial service (such as *CompuServe*, *The Microsoft Network*, and *America Online*) that provides electronic communication services. Users can join discussion groups, exchange email, download files, and so on. These services now have Internet access, too, so they may also be considered as Internet *service providers*.

P2P A geek term meaning Peer to Peer, a networking configuration in which computers communicate directly with each other, as opposed to communicating via *servers*.

packet A collection of data. See *packet switching*.

Packet InterNet Groper (PING) A program that tests whether a particular host computer is accessible.

packet switching A system that breaks transmitted data into small *packets* and transmits each packet (or package) independently. Each packet is individually addressed and may even travel over a route different from that of other packets. The packets are combined by the receiving computer.

permanent connection A connection to the Internet using a *leased line*. The computer with a permanent connection acts as a host on the Internet. This type of service is often called *direct*, *permanent direct*, or *dedicated service* and is very expensive to set up and run. However, it provides a very fast, high *bandwidth* connection. A company or organization can lease a single line and then allow multiple employees or members to use it to access the Internet at the same time.

343

permanent direct See *permanent connection.*

personal certificate An electronic certificate containing *encryption* data used to encrypt and sign email or computer files or to identify the owner to a *Web site.* See also *public-key encryption.*

PING See *Packet InterNet Groper.*

plug-in A special type of *viewer* for a *Web browser.* A plug-in plays or displays a particular file type within the browser's window. (A viewer is a completely separate program.)

point of presence Jargon meaning a method of connecting to a service locally (without dialing long distance), often abbreviated *POP.* If a service provider has a *POP* in, say, Podunk, Ohio, people in that city can connect to the service provider by making a local call.

Point-to-Point Protocol (PPP) A method for connecting computers to the Internet via telephone lines; similar to *SLIP,* though a preferred, and these days more common, method.

POP See *point of presence* and *Post Office Protocol.*

port Generally, port refers to the hardware through which computer data is transmitted; the plugs on the back of your computer are ports. On the Internet, port often refers to a particular application. For instance, you might *Telnet* to a particular port on a particular host.

Post Office Protocol (POP) A system for letting hosts get email from a server. This system is typically used when a dial-in direct host (which may only have one user and may only be connected to the Internet periodically) gets its email from a service provider. The latest version of POP is POP3. Do not confuse this with another type of POP, *point of presence.*

posting A message (article) sent to a newsgroup or the act of sending such a message.

postmaster The person at a host who is responsible for managing the mail system. If you need information about a user at a particular host, you can send email to **postmaster@hostname**.

PPP See *Point-to-Point Protocol.*

private key The code used in a *public-key encryption* system that must be kept secure (unlike the *public key,* which may be freely distributed).

protocol A set of rules that defines how computers transmit information to each other, allowing different types of computers and software to communicate with each other.

PSP (Payment Service Provider) A company that acts as a go-between in online credit card transactions at a Web site. The PSP's servers are used to verify the transaction details, before passing confirmation of a successful transaction to the seller in return for a percentage of the sale price. UK PSPs include Netbanx, WorldPay and SecurePay.

public domain software Software that does not belong to anyone. You can use it without payment and even modify it if the source code is available. See also *shareware* and *freeware.*

344

public key The code used in a *public-key encryption* system that may be freely distributed (unlike the *private key*, which must be kept secure).

public-key encryption A system that uses two mathematically related keys: a *private key* and a *public key*. Information that has been encrypted using one key can only be decrypted using the associated key. The private key is used to digitally sign an electronic document or decrypt files that were encrypted using the public key.

push A push program periodically retrieves data from the Internet and displays it on the user's computer screen. A push program is a sort of automated *Web browser*. See also *Webcasting*.

RealAudio A well-known streaming audio format.

reflector, mail Messages sent to a mail reflector's address are sent automatically to a list of other addresses.

reload (or refresh) A command that tells your browser to retrieve a Web document even though you have it in the cache. Microsoft uses the term refresh for this command in its Internet Explorer browser. (In Netscape Navigator, the Refresh command simply redisplays the Web page to clear up any display problems.)

remote login A BSD (Berkeley) UNIX command (rlogin) that is similar to *Telnet*.

rendered An *HTML* document has been rendered when it is displayed in a Web browser. The browser renders it into a normal text document by removing all the HTML codes, so you see just the text that the author wants you to see. An unrendered document is the *source HTML* document (with codes and all).

rlogin See *remote login*.

rot13 Rotation 13, a method used to scramble messages in *newsgroups* so that you can't stumble across an offensive message. If you want to read an offensive message, you'll have to decide to do so and go out of your way to decode it.

router A system used to transmit data between two computer systems or networks using the same *protocol*. For instance, a company that has a permanent connection to the Internet will use a router to connect its computer to a leased line. At the other end of the leased line, a router is used to connect it to the service provider's network.

RTFM Abbreviation for 'Read the F***ing Manual', which is often used in reaction to a stupid question (or in response to a question which, in the hierarchy of *newbies* and long-term Internet users, is determined to be a stupid question).

Serial Line Internet Protocol (SLIP) A method for connecting a computer to the Internet using a telephone line and modem. (See *dial-in direct connection*.) Once connected, the user has the same services provided to the user of a permanent connection. See also *Point-to-Point Protocol*.

345

server A program or computer that services another program or computer (the *client*). For instance, a *Gopher* server program sends information from its indexes to a Gopher client program, and *Web servers* send Web pages to Web browsers (which are Web clients).

service provider A company that provides a connection to the Internet. *Online services*, although generally regarded as different from service providers, are in fact also service providers because, in addition to having their own services, they provide access to the Internet.

shareware Software that is freely distributed, but for which the author expects payment from people who decide to keep and use it. See also *freeware* and *public domain software*.

shell account Another name for a simple *dial-in terminal* account.

Shockwave A popular multimedia *plug-in*.

shopping cart A program that enables visitors to a Web site to place orders and purchase products.

signature A short piece of text transmitted with an email or newsgroup message. Some systems can attach text from a file to the end of a message automatically. Signature files typically contain detailed information on how to contact someone: name and address, telephone numbers, Internet address, CompuServe ID, and so on – or some strange little quote or poem.

Simple Mail Transfer Protocol (SMTP) A *protocol* used to transfer email between computers on a network.

SLIP See *Serial Line Internet Protocol*.

smiley A symbol in email and newsgroup messages used to convey emotion or provide amusement. Originally, the term referred to a symbol that seems to smile, but the term now seems to refer to just about any small symbol created with text characters. You create smileys by typing various keyboard characters. For example, :-(means sadness. Smileys are usually sideways: turn your head to view the smiley. The more technical term for a smiley is *emoticon*.

SMTP See *Simple Mail Transfer Protocol*.

snarf To grab something off the Web and copy it to your computer's hard disk for future use. Snarfing is often illegal if done without permission (a copyright contravention).

source document An *HTML* document, the basic ASCII file that is *rendered* by a browser.

spam The term given to unsolicited email sent to large numbers of people without any regard to whether those people want to receive the mail. Originally, the term referred specifically to a single message sent to large numbers of newsgroups. The term comes from the Monty Python Spam song, which contains the refrain, 'Spam, Spam, Spam, Spam, Spam, Spam, Spam, Spam'.

346

stack See *TCP/IP stack*.

start page A term used by Microsoft in some versions of its Internet Explorer browser to refer to the *home page*. Just to confuse users, some versions of Internet Explorer refer to the home page as Home Page.

streaming In the old days, if you transferred an audio or video file, you had to wait for it to be transferred to your computer completely before you could play it. Streaming audio and video formats allow the file to play while it's being transferred.

tags The codes inside an *HTML* file. Web *browsers* read the tags to find out how they should *render* the document.

talk A program that lets two or more Internet users type messages to each other. As a user types a character or paragraph, that text is immediately transmitted to the other user. There are several common talk programs: talk, ntalk, and Ytalk are old UNIX systems, but these days AOL Instant Messenger and ICQ are becoming very popular. Talk is similar to *chat*, although chat systems are intended as meeting places, whereas talk programs are private. See also *chat*.

tar files Files *compressed* using the UNIX tape archive program. Such files usually have filenames ending in .tar.

TCP/IP (Transmission Control Protocol/Internet Protocol) A set of *protocols* (communications rules) that control how data transfers between computers on the Internet.

TCP/IP stack The software you must install before you can run TCP/IP programs across a dial-in direct connection. You might think of the TCP/IP stack as an Internet driver. In the same way you need a printer driver to send something from your word processor to your printer, you need the TCP/IP stack to send information to (and receive information from) your dial-in direct programs.

Telnet A program that lets Internet users log in to computers other than their own host computers, often on the other side of the world. Telnet is also used as a verb, as in 'Telnet to debra.doc.ca'.

Telneting Internet-speak for using Telnet to access a computer on the network.

TLA Three-Letter Acronym. An acronym for an acronym. What would we do without them? See also *EFLA*.

TLD (Top Level Domain) The final part of a *domain name* which indicates the type and/or country of the domain, such as .gov or .mil for US government and military sites, .co.uk for UK sites, and .com and .info for generic international sites.

tn3270 A *Telnet*-like program used for *remote logins* to IBM mainframes.

trojan horse A computer program that appears to carry out a useful function but which is actually designed to do harm to the system on which it runs. See also *virus*.

UNIX A computer operating system. Many – probably most – host computers connected to the Internet run UNIX.

upload The process of transferring information from one computer to another. You upload a file from your computer to another. See also *download*.

URL (Uniform Resource Locator) A Web address.

Usenet The 'User's Network', a large network connected to the Internet. The term also refers to the *newsgroups* distributed by this network.

UUCP UNIX-to-UNIX copy program, a system by which files can be transferred between UNIX computers. The Internet uses UUCP to provide a form of email, in which the mail is placed in files and transferred to other computers.

UUCP network A network of UNIX computers connected to the Internet.

uudecode If you use *uuencode* to convert a file to ASCII and transmit it, you'll use uudecode to convert the ASCII file back to its original format.

uuencode The name given a program used to convert a computer file of any kind (sound, spreadsheet, word processing, or whatever) into an ASCII file so that it can be transmitted as a text message. The term is also used as a verb, as in 'uuencode this file'. There are DOS, Windows, UNIX, and Macintosh uuencode programs. In Windows, a program called Wincode can uuencode and *uudecode* files. Most email programs handle *MIME* transmissions properly these days, so uuencode is falling out of use.

VBScript A scripting language from Microsoft, which is similar in concept to *JavaScript*.

Veronica The Very Easy Rodent-Oriented Net-wide Index to Computerized Archives, a very useful program for finding things in *Gopherspace*.

viewer A program that displays or plays computer files that you find on the Web. For instance, you need a viewer to play video files you find. These programs are sometimes known as *helpers*.

virus A program that uses various techniques for duplicating itself and travelling between computers. Viruses vary from simple nuisances (they might display an unexpected message on your screen) to serious problems that can cause millions of pounds' worth of damage (such as crashing a computer system and erasing important data).

Voice on the Net (VON) A service through which you can talk to other Internet users. You need a sound card, microphone, speakers, and the right software; then you can make Internet phone calls. They're warbly, but very cheap.

VoIP (Voice over IP) Another name for *Voice on the Net*.

VON See *Voice on the Net*.

348

VRML Virtual Reality Modeling Language, a system used to create three-dimensional images. Internet pundits claimed, a year or two ago, that most Web sites would be using VRML by now and lots of it, but the pundits forgot that VRML doesn't run well on most people's computers.

VT100 The product name of a Digital Equipment Corporation computer terminal (DEC). This terminal is a standard that is emulated (simulated) by many other manufacturers' terminals.

W3 See *World Wide Web*.

WAIS See *Wide area information server*.

WAP (Wireless Application Protocol) Special Web-like pages written in a language called *WML* (similar to the Web's own HTML) can be downloaded into the new breed of WAP-enabled mobile phones, pagers and PDAs and read while on the move. These devices have four- or eight-line displays for text and simple graphics.

Web Pertaining to the *World Wide Web*.

Webcasting Distributing information via *push* programs.

Web forum A discussion group running on a Web site.

Web-hosting company A company that sells space on a Web server to people who want to set up Web sites.

Web server A computer system – a computer running special server software – that makes *Web* documents available to Web browsers. The browser asks the server for the document, and the server transmits it to the browser.

Web site A collection of *Web* documents about a particular subject on a *host*.

Webspace The area of cyberspace in which you are travelling when working on the *Web*.

WebTV A system used to display Web sites on a television. A box containing a *modem* is connected to a TV; the signals from the Internet are transmitted on the phone lines (not along the TV cable line) and displayed on the TV screen. WebTV is manufactured by Sony and Philips/Magnavox (and recently bought by Microsoft), although the term is also widely used to describe the technology in generic terms. If you're excited about getting onto the Internet, a good way to dissipate some of that excitement is to buy WebTV.

White Pages Lists of Internet users.

Whois A UNIX program used for searching for information about Internet users.

Wide area information server (WAIS) A system that can search particular databases on the Internet.

Winsock A *TCP/IP stack* for Microsoft Windows.

WML (Wireless Markup Language) A text-based language used to write pages of (mainly textual) information that can be viewed on WAP-enabled devices. WML is based on *XML* and could be thought of as a very cut-down version of the Web's own HTML.

World Wide Web A *hypertext* system that allows users to travel through linked documents, following any chosen route. World Wide Web documents contain topics that, when selected, lead to other documents.

WWW See *World Wide Web*.

XML Extensible Markup Language, *HTML*-like *tags* that extend HTML by allowing designers to create their own tags. Particular industry groups could then create programs that could recognize those tags. For instance, the medical industry could create special programs that recognize tags such as <MD>, <RX>, <WHINER> and <VERYSICK>.

Windows Internet Features

In small steps over the last few years, Microsoft has integrated the Windows operating system more closely with the Internet, and Windows 98, Me and XP have a plethora of Internet-related tools. This appendix is a quick summary of the features included in these Windows versions at the time of writing.

Internet Features in Windows 98 and Windows Me

In Windows 98, 98 Second Edition, and Millennium Edition (Me), you can pick and choose which features are installed. Note that some of the Internet features listed below may not be installed on your computer yet – it all depends on the choices made by the person who installed Windows onto your computer. You can add any missing programs by running Windows Setup (assuming you have the installation disk, that is). If the item has not been installed, select **Start**, **Settings**, **Control Panel** and then open the **Add/Remove Programs** icon and click the **Windows Setup** tab. In the list box you'll see, click the category, then the **Details** button, and then select the item you want to install.

These are the optional programs, sorted by category (the category you'll see in the Add/Remove Programs dialog box).

The optional Internet features in Windows 98 and Me

Category	Feature
Communications	Dial-Up Networking
	Microsoft NetMeeting
	Virtual Private Networking
Internet Tools	MS FrontPage Express
	Microsoft VRML Viewer
	Microsoft Wallet
	Personal Web Server
	Real Audio Player
	Web Publishing Wizard
	Web-Based Enterprise Management
Microsoft Outlook Express	(Email, newsreader, and address book; this is a category by itself)
Multimedia	Macromedia Shockwave Director
	Macromedia Shockwave Flash
	Microsoft NetShow Player
	Windows Media Player
Online Services	AOL
	CompuServe
	The Microsoft Network
WebTV for Windows	(Category by itself)

The exact features will vary a little according to which flavour of Windows you're running. To complicate the issue, Microsoft has online upgrades (choose **Windows Update** from the Start menu). If you upgrade your system, it might not match what's shown here. You should be able to find the latest programs in this Windows Update area, though.

Internet Features in Windows XP

Unlike earlier versions of the Windows operating system, with Windows XP Microsoft doesn't offer much control over which features are installed and which are not. (Unless, that is, you've installed Service Pack 1 – see the box headed 'Choose Your Own XP Setup' below.) For a look at what you can install or remove, go to **Start**, **Control Panel**, **Add or Remove Programs** and click the **Add/Remove Windows Components** button. As far as Internet-related programs are concerned, there are only three:

➤ **Internet Explorer:** Rather than installing and removing Microsoft's Web browser, this option simply hides its desktop and Start menu icons.

➤ **MSN Explorer:** A bright, cheerful reworking of Internet Explorer aimed at MSN subscribers and beginners.

➤ **Internet Information Services** (XP Professional only): Microsoft's powerful Web server, provided for use by expert users, and Web authors and developers.

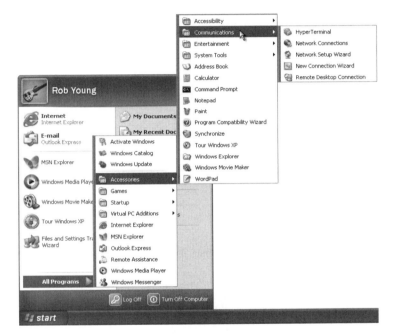

Finding Internet-related programs in Windows XP

Choose Your Own XP Setup

Microsoft has spent a large chunk of the last couple of years in the courts, trying to defend its bundling of ordinary utilities (such as Internet Explorer) with its Windows operating systems. The US Justice Department claimed that these actions harmed other companies who would otherwise be creating and selling similar software. Microsoft has been forced to back-pedal on this, and make it possible for Windows users to remove (well, *hide*) some of these programs. If you have Windows XP Service Pack 1 (SP1) installed, look for a **Set Program Access and Defaults** icon on the Start menu and choose the **Custom** option, and you'll be able to hide a few components, although it won't give you anything new to install.

Finding The Windows Internet Programs

In the remaining pages of this appendix, we'll wander through the Internet programs provided with Windows and see what they're all for. But first, *where* are they? In short, they're all accessible from the Start menu, but exactly where on the Start menu depends (again) on your Windows version:

➤ **Windows 98:** Go to Programs, Accessories, Internet Explorer or Programs, Accessories, Communications. You can also start Internet Explorer and Outlook Express by clicking their icons on the Quick Launch bar beside the Start button, or by double-clicking their icons on the desktop.

➤ **Windows Me:** Go to Programs, Accessories, Communications, or just to Programs for Internet Explorer, Outlook Express and Windows Media Player. You can also start those last three from the Quick Launch bar beside the Start button, or from icons on the desktop.

➤ **Windows XP:** Go to All Programs to find icons for a few of the Internet-related tools, and continue to Accessories, Communications for the rest. Internet Explorer and Outlook Express are also 'pinned' to the top of the Start panel for quick access.

Finding Internet-related programs in Windows Me

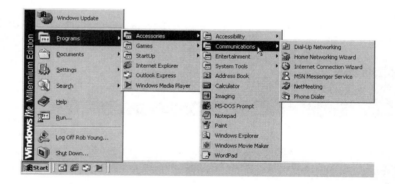

What's It All For?

Some of the programs we'll discuss below are included with some versions of Windows and not with others, so keep an eye on the headings to know whether a particular feature is included in the Windows version you're using.

Internet Explorer Web Browser (Windows 98 Onwards)

Internet Explorer is the Web browser that the US Justice Department – and the folk at Netscape – are so upset about. From a slow start, Explorer has become the most popular browser available, responsible for a good 90% of Web-site visits. It was also included with some later editions of Windows 95.

Outlook Express (Windows 98 Onwards)

Outlook Express combines an email program (see Chapters 2 and 3) and a newsreader (see Chapters 9 and 10). Although Outlook Express is widely used, this is at least partly by virtue of just *being there* – many Windows users will happily use it because it's readily available. In addition, many online services and ISPs provide setup programs which automatically configure OE to work with your new email account, whereas you'd almost certainly have to do this manually if you chose a different program. (In some later editions of Windows 95, the forerunner to OE, the catchily-titled Internet Mail and News, was included.)

Address Book (Windows 98 Onwards)

Many users believe this is Outlook Express's address book (probably because most of us only use it when we're using Outlook Express) but it's actually a separate utility. Yes, you can open it from Outlook Express, select people to email, or add new email addresses, but you can also open it from the Start menu any time you want it. Not only does it store email addresses, but it can store addresses, phone numbers, birthdays, anniversaries, notes, and much more.

Windows Media Player (Windows Me, XP)

An all-in-one media centre capable of playing most of the audio, video and animation formats the Web can throw at it. WMP is also 'skinnable' (you can download free *skins* that radically change the way the program looks), and can be used as a stand-alone player for all your media files. In Windows 98, there's a utility named **Media Player** which can play a few types of media, as well as **ActiveMovie** which handles a few more.

System Setup Tools

Windows has several tools to help you set up your Internet connection.

➤ **Dial-Up Networking (Windows 98, Me).** The Make New Connection wizard in this folder creates connections to Internet service providers (ISPs), so you can get onto the Internet. In theory it provides a simple point-and-click configuration system. In practice, it doesn't – you always have to edit the properties of the connection it creates. Note, however, that in many cases you don't need to use this wizard at all: you can use the friendlier and more capable Internet Connection Wizard (below) instead.

➤ **Internet Connection Wizard (Windows 98, Me).** Simply called the Connection Wizard in Windows 98, this program leads you through the process of setting up Dial-Up Networking. Whenever you want to sign up with a new ISP (one that doesn't provide a CD-ROM, which most now do) just run this wizard and enter the details as prompted.

➤ **New Connection Wizard (Windows XP).** This is XP's somewhat beefed-up equivalent of the Internet Connection Wizard, mentioned above. Use this when you want to create a connection to a new ISP, or connect to a computer on any other accessible network.

➤ **Network Connections (Windows XP).** Windows XP's replacement for the Dial-Up Networking folder included in earlier versions. The Network Connections folder contains icons for all your network connections (not just those to Internet services) – just double-click an icon to connect to that ISP or computer. There's also a handy icon to start the New Connection Wizard, mentioned above, and create a new connection.

Communications Tools

Distinct from email and newsgroups (in which the communication has a built-in delay), these are tools Windows provides for 'real-time' chat, talk and conferencing.

➤ **NetMeeting (Windows 98, Me).** This 'conference' program enables you to communicate with people across the Internet instantly by typing messages, drawing on a white board, or transferring files (see Chapter 13). You may even be able to include voice and video. In Windows Me, this sits alongside MSN Messenger which offers a friendlier way to do many of the same things.

➤ **MSN Messenger (Windows Me)/Windows Messenger (Windows XP).** In Windows Me, Messenger is a friendly instant messaging program (see Chapter 13) with a few added features. What you couldn't do with Messenger you could use NetMeeting to achieve. In Windows XP, both are replaced by the more flexible Windows Messenger, which allows instant messaging, voice or video conversations, file transfer, application sharing, white boards, and text messaging to mobile devices – pretty much all the communications options you can think of.

Web Publishing Tools

Windows 98 provides several Web publishing tools (which were also included with Internet Explorer 4, making them accessible to Windows 95 users too). In later Windows and Internet Explorer versions these have been removed.

➤ **FrontPage Express (Windows 98).** This is a 'light' version of Microsoft's heavyweight Web-page design tool, FrontPage. It's a sort of Web-page word processor; you type all the text and select formats, font types, colours, and so on, and FrontPage Express adds all the HTML codes for you.

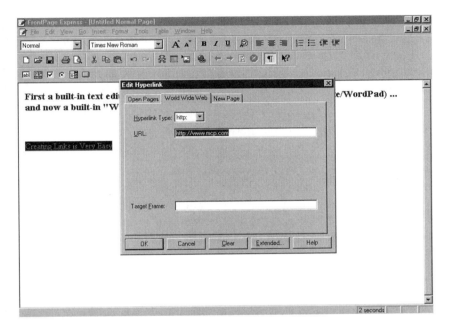

FrontPage Express, the simple HTML editor included with Windows 98.

➤ **Web Publishing Wizard (Windows 98).** This program simplifies the process of transferring Web pages from your computer to the computer that will host your Web site.

➤ **Personal Web Server (Windows 98).** PWS is a very simple Web server that you configure by filling in forms in your Web browser. You can use it to test a Web site on your own computer before publishing it on the Internet for the world to see.

Corporate Tools

Windows has several tools that I think of as 'corporate' – that is, programs that you're unlikely to use at home, but might work with if you are employed by a medium to large corporation.

➤ **Virtual Private Networking (Windows 98 onwards).** This system can be used to build a private network on the World Wide Web. Authorized people can use a 'tunnel' through the Web to access the corporate network. So, wherever you happen to be travelling, as long as you can access the Internet you can get to the network. This system is something that the network administrator must set up.

➤ **Web-Based Enterprise Management (Windows 98 onwards).** This tool is used for managing various corporate and network tasks through a series of Web pages on the network. It's another toy for the network administrator.

➤ **Remote Desktop Connection (Windows XP).** This tool lets you connect directly to another computer and work with it as if you were sitting right in front of it: The desktop of the remote computer is shown in place of your desktop, but you work with it in exactly the same way. For example, you can use RDC to connect to your work computer from home to run applications or work on documents you don't have on your home PC.

Other Internet Features

Each successive Windows version strives to further integrate your computer with the Internet. Here are a few additional Internet-related features you'll find in the latest Windows operating systems:

➤ **Internet Connection Sharing (Windows 98 SE, Me, XP).** If you have more than one computer, you can easily create a home network using Windows Me or XP (Me has a Home Network Wizard for the purpose, and XP offers the Network Setup Wizard). And one big advantage of a home network is that multiple computers can use the same Internet connection, simultaneously.

➤ **Internet Connection Firewall (Windows XP).** A *firewall* is a type of safety-barrier (albeit a software one) that watches what passes into and out of your computer to and from the Internet, and helps to protect it from unauthorized access. ICF is basic as firewalls go, but you certainly have more protection by enabling this for your Internet connections. (If you have a broadband connection, you should consider investing in something more capable than ICF, though.)

➤ **Multiplayer Internet Games (Windows Me, XP).** Five multiplayer games that you can play with online opponents from around the globe. There are no Web sites to access or software to download. Windows will help you locate players from around the world who match your skill level and speak your language – or not. You can even choose from a list of standard chat messages that can be automatically translated if your opponent is from another country or speaks a different language.

Maintainance and Configuration

Look in the Control Panel (**Start**, **Settings**, **Control Panel**, or in Windows XP, **Start**, **Control Panel**) and you'll find an Internet Properties icon (Internet Options in XP). The Internet Properties dialog box provides all sorts of Internet-related settings, from how to automatically dial the Internet to how to keep your kids away from 'bad' Web sites. You can also open this dialog box from inside Internet Explorer; select **View**, **Internet Options**.

You can also update Windows across the Internet. Open the Start menu and you'll see a **Windows Update** option. This option opens your browser, connects to a Microsoft upgrade Web site, and runs the Windows Upgrade Wizard. If there are any bug fixes waiting for you – ahem, I mean 'system enhancements' – the Wizard will automatically transfer and install them.

Windows Update

The Windows Update area of the Microsoft Web site has lots of goodies you can download free. Some of these are 'critical updates' – usually fixes for security-related bugs in the system – and both Windows Me and Windows XP should check for these and prompt you to install them automatically, without waiting for you to use the Windows Update feature manually. (This automatic checking is a feature you can turn off, but it's not advisable; if you can, be content just to tweak the options covering *how* it works.) Some of the software and add-ons you'll find on the Windows Update site are actually useful, though, so it's worth taking a look every so often.

Check This Out...

Bug-Fix Watch!

It can be fun to visit the Windows Update area. See whether you can spot the bug fixes cleverly disguised as product improvements! Here's a tip. If you can't understand exactly what the file is supposed to do, yet Microsoft says it's a critical or recommended update, it's probably a bug fix. Or if you download it and find the new features are so minimal as to be almost worthless, it's probably a bug fix.

All The Software You'll Ever Need

In This Appendix

➤ Finding software at the online services

➤ Finding the browsers

➤ Macintosh, Windows, and UNIX software libraries

➤ Plug-ins and viewers

➤ Demos and drivers

You've read about a lot of software in this book, and there's much more that hasn't been mentioned. Literally thousands of shareware, freeware, and demoware programs for the Macintosh, Windows 3.1, Windows 95/98/Me, Windows NT/2000/XP, and all flavours of UNIX are available for you to download and use. 'Where are they'? you ask. 'How do I find all these programs?' It's easy to find software once you know where to look.

Different Types Of Software

Shareware is software that is given away for free, but which you are supposed to register (for a fee) if you decide to continue using it. *Freeware* is software that is given away with no fee required. *Demoware* is software that is generally free, but is intended to get you interested in buying the 'full' program.

The Search Starts At Home

You can always begin looking at home. If you use one of the online services, you'll find stacks of software within the service itself; no need to go out onto the Internet. All the online services have Internet-related forums (or BBSs, or areas, or whatever they call them). They are good places to begin and you can usually download the software more quickly from there than from the Internet. In addition, many online services have forums set up by software vendors and shareware forums. These are good places to get to know, too.

If you are with a true Internet service provider, you'll often find that your service has a file library somewhere. The library will have a smaller selection than the online services do, but it's a good place to start nonetheless.

The Software Mentioned

I've mentioned two programs in particular – Netscape Navigator and Internet Explorer – that you need to know how to find. You may already have one or the other of these. Many online services and service providers already provide one of them in the software package you get when you sign up. But if you want to try Netscape or Explorer, or if you simply want to get the very latest version, go to one of these sites:

> Netscape Navigator: **http://www.netscape.com/**

> Internet Explorer: **http://www.microsoft.com/ie/**

I've mentioned dozens of other programs throughout this book. Most of those programs can be found at the sites I discuss next.

The Internet's Software Libraries

The Internet is full of wonderful software libraries that are based on either FTP or Web servers. Check out some of the following sites, but remember that there are more, which you can find using the links mentioned in the section 'Finding More', later in this appendix.

ZDNet's Mac Software Library
Go to **http://www.zdnet.com/downloads/mac/download.html** to find one of the largest and most comprehensive libraries of Macintosh software. It's well organized, and you can run keyword searches for the programs you're looking for.

Info-Mac HyperArchive (Macintosh)

This is a large collection of Macintosh software at MIT (**http://hyperarchive.lcs. mit.edu/HyperArchive.html**). It contains lots of files, but it's not very easy to work with.

MacShare

It might sound like a financial stake in a Scottish company, but it's actually a great site for well-sorted Mac software, tips, and reference information, at **http://www.macshare.com**.

TUCOWS (Windows)

TUCOWS, which stands for The Ultimate Collection of Winsock Software, is a large library of software for Windows, Linux, and the Mac. Go to **http://tucows. mirror.ac.uk** for this one, shown in the next screenshot.

The TUCOWS site is an excellent place to find all sorts of useful software.

The Consummate Winsock App Page (Windows)

Another excellent Windows software archive is at the **http://cws.internet.com** Web site.

Winsite (Windows)

You can find another good Windows archive at the **http://www.winsite.com/** Web site or at the **ftp.winsite.com** FTP site.

363

Shareware.com (Everything)

This site (the **http://www.shareware.com/** Web page) contains a huge collection of software for all major operating systems. You can search for a keyword and come up with all sorts of interesting things here.

CNET Downloads

Another excellent site for Windows users (although you'll also find software here for Mac, UNIX, Palm and handheld PCs). Visit **http://download.cnet.com**, shown in the next figure.

Winsite uses Yahoo!-style categories to help you track down the software you need.

ZDNet Software Library (Windows)

This site (**http://www.hotfiles.com**) contains over 10,000 Windows files. It's well organized, with detailed descriptions.

KeyScreen (Windows)

This unusual site at **http://www.keyscreen.com** (shown in the following figure) only has about 470 programs, but it provides pictures of programs so you can see whether you might like them before you bother downloading.

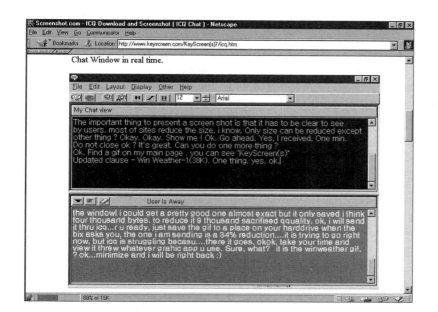

KeyScreen lets you see what the programs look like before you download them.

Nonags (Windows 95, 98, NT)

This site (at **http://www.nonags.com**) is dedicated to software that has 'no nags, no time limits, no disabled features, or any other tricks. Most are really free, a few are shareware ...'

Jumbo (Windows, DOS, Macintosh, UNIX)

Another excellent site, **http://www.jumbo.com** contains thousands of programs (it claims to have over 300,000). It also provides a variety of 'starter kits', collections of programs for decompressing files and checking them for viruses.

Browsers.com

This site at **http://www.browsers.com** has links to all sorts of browser-related software and information.

Finding More

New software archives appear online all the time, many of which are specialized. You can search for more at the search sites discussed in Chapter 16. For example, you can go to Yahoo's **http://dir.yahoo.com/computers_and_internet/software/** page and find links to all sorts of software sites – software for amateur radio, CAD (Computer Aided Design), astronomy, and just about everything else. Also try Pass The Shareware (**http://www.passtheshareware.com**), a site with loads of links to shareware sites.

Don't Forget Demos And Drivers

Thanks to the Internet, the distribution of demo software has increased greatly. Commercial software publishers often create versions of their software that they give away. Some of these programs are full working versions that just stop working after a while; others are 'crippled' in some way from the very beginning (perhaps a few important features don't work). These offer a good way to find out if the company's product is worth buying and, in some cases, they even have enough features to make the demo itself worth having. You'll often see these demos advertised in the computer magazines with the URL of the company's Web page.

Many companies also give away software such as the latest drivers for your hardware arsenal. It's worth checking companies' home pages periodically to make sure that you're always using the latest version, or go to Ziff-Davis' excellent Driver Finder site at **http://updates.zdnet.com/updates/drivers.htm**.

Looking For Something Strange?

If you're looking for a program that you simply can't find at the popular software libraries, remember that you can always search for it using the techniques discussed in Chapter 16. It's amazing what those search sites can turn up sometimes! So if you're looking for something really obscure that the average library doesn't hold, don't give up too soon. You can even try Archie (see Chapter 11) to search for a file at an FTP site if you have a good idea of the filename.

> **Check This Out...**
>
> **Looks Can Be Deceiving**
>
> I've seen some demos that were obviously created by companies that seemed to think the way to make sales was to create a totally worthless demo that didn't even show what the full product could do.

Finding A Service Provider

If you are reading this, either you don't have a service provider, or you are considering changing the one you have. Let's deal with the first major question: which is the best Internet service provider?

I Want the Best! Where Do I Get It?

Ah, so you want the best Internet account you can get. Well, if that's the case, be prepared to empty your bank account. You're going to need a special high-speed line from the phone company, a fast computer with special hardware to connect it to that line, a system administrator to set it up and maintain it ... and on and on.

But for the rest of us, the ordinary Joe or Jane who wants to get hooked up to the Internet, what's the best way to do it? There's no easy answer to that, unfortunately. It's rather like asking 'who makes the best spouse'? Needless to say, everyone has a different answer. A service that you think is good might prove to be a lousy choice for someone else.

Basically, what you need to do is pick a service provider that is cheap, helpful, and has a reliable and fast connection to the Internet and easy-to-install software. Of course, that's very difficult to find. I've had Internet accounts with a couple of dozen providers and I haven't found one yet that I would rave about. They've ranged from pretty good to absolutely awful.

How Do You Choose?

Internet accounts vary quite a bit in just about every respect: what they cost, what you get for your money, and how reliable they are. That means that there's a fair amount of choice to be had, so a good place to start is in deciding what you want and how much you're willing to pay. You'll always have to pay *something*, whether it's a regular fee to your chosen ISP or online service, or call charges to your phone company, so unless you're determined to stick to a fixed budget, it's best to start by deciding what you want. Here's a quick look at the options available:

➤ **Free Internet service provider account.** With a free ISP account, you only pay per-minute phone charges to your phone company when you actually go online. If you spend an hour a day online, for example, your total outlay is the cost of 30 hours of local phone calls. At the moment, this is one of the UK's favourite access methods. If there's a catch with this option, it's that you may find the service unreliable at times – tough to connect, slow, unexpected disconnections, and so on – since most free-access subscribers are home users who all want to go online at the same time.

➤ **Pay-for Internet service provider account.** Some ISPs have resisted the temptation to provide free access, and continue to charge around £10 to £15 per month (sometimes in conjunction with a SurfTime option mentioned below). In theory this should give you a more reliable service, although the jury's still out on that one, and you'll probably get one or two features and services not included in a free account.

➤ **BT SurfTime (or similar) ISP account.** The SurfTime package gives you free Internet calls during evenings and weekends for about £6 per month (or, for about £20 per month, unlimited Internet calls at any time). Many of the free ISPs offer SurfTime as an alternative, so if you pick a free ISP and the cheaper of the SurfTime options, you'll pay a fixed monthly charge of £6 plus the cost of any Internet connection calls made during weekdays.

➤ **Unmetered ISP account.** Unmetered access is similar to the SurfTime option, letting you connect to the Internet at any time, for as long as you like, without incurring any call charges. Instead you pay a fixed fee of between £13 and £15 per month. In the last edition of this book I said I'd bet my boots that most ISPs would be offering unmetered access in 6 months' time. My boots survived: from the major providers (Freeserve, Virgin Net, BTOpenWorld, Tiscali, AOL, and others) to the smaller companies, an unmetered option is almost always available. If you want to use the Internet whenever you like without worrying about the cost, this is a very worthwhile option.

➤ **Broadband account.** As mentioned in Chapter 1, broadband connections are finally within reach of a large percentage of the UK population, and the prices are beginning to fall to levels at which we'd consider using them. Many of the larger companies that offer unmetered connections (above) now offer a broadband option at around £25–£30 a month. If you decide to go for one of these (and you currently have an ordinary phone line rather than a Home Highway or ISDN line), look out for self-installation packages which can reduce the setup costs by more than half.

Auto-Disconnection Alert!

Some unmetered access providers (and a few ISPs who offer free calls at particular times) don't really expect you to stay online indefinitely. Read the small print to find out what steps they take to deter you from using your connection too much. Some disconnect you automatically after a certain period, such as every two hours, forcing you to dial in again. Others disconnect you if your connection is idle for a period (no data passes through it). Some access providers take a draconian approach, disconnecting you after only a few minutes of inactivity. You may be able to get around the 'inactivity' problem by installing a small program that regularly sends a little packet of data (called a 'ping') over the connection to keep it alive.

➤ **Online services.** Online services have always been the expensive option, although they're catching up fast now. You may have to compromise in your choice of software (not being able to choose a decent email program, for instance, or putting up with the plethora of windows thrown at you by AOL), but online services give you an easy way to get the whole family online, a fair degree of security, and high-quality content including friendly, moderated chat rooms. Most online services now offer a choice of packages to rival ISPs. As an example, AOL offers unmetered access for £16 per month, or for £10 per month they'll subsidize your phone charges to leave you paying a fixed 1p per minute any time you use the service.

The free service providers are as keen to sign you up as those that charge, so the 'extras' that come with a fee-paying account – such as Web space to host your site or multiple email addresses – are also included with most free accounts. The main difference between the two types is that free-account providers usually charge a premium rate for phone calls to their help-lines when you get stuck.

Tips For Picking A Provider

Consider the following guidelines when you're trying to find an Internet service provider:

➤ The major online services (MSN, AOL, CompuServe) make it very easy to connect to the Internet: you just run the setup program and you should be surfing merrily within 15 minutes. Many service providers now supply easy-setup programs, too (particularly the free providers), but it's not yet universal.

➤ Try to choose a service provider that provides telephone support at times when you're likely to need it (evenings and weekends, for example).

➤ *Always* make sure you'll be dialling a local phone number to go online (or a local-rate 0845 or equivalent number). Many Internet service providers have dial-in nodes all over the UK. Others might be smaller outfits with, perhaps, a single computer in Blackpool. That could be ideal if you live in the Blackpool area, but if you're in Torquay, forget it.

➤ Make sure your service provider (or your local dial-in phone number) supports a fast modem speed. If you have a 56Kbps modem, you don't want to dial in to a slower line. If you have ISDN or BT Home Highway, make sure your provider supports it and doesn't make an extra charge. It's also worth finding out whether you can link the two 64Kbps lines to create a single high-speed 128Kbps connection, although very few ISPs support this.

Finding A Service Provider

The two most reliable ways to find a good service provider (especially now that there are so many hundreds to choose between) are to ask friends and colleagues with Internet access whether they're happy with the service they use, or to check some of the popular Internet magazines for reviews. If you already have Internet access and you're thinking of changing to a different provider, here's a short list of contact details for some of the most popular free service providers with full UK coverage. In some cases, you may even be able to sign up for a new account online.

Online Services

Name	Telephone	Email	Web
America Online (AOL)	0800 279 1234	queryuk@aol.com	www.aol.co.uk
CompuServe	0870 6000 800	UKCSSVC@cs.com	www.compuserve.co.uk
MSN	0870 60 10 100		www.msn.co.uk/internetaccess

Internet Service Providers

The following is a list of UK Internet service providers, between them offering a choice of connection options. Remember that although these details were correct at the time of writing, there may have been some changes by the time you read this – the ISP business scoots along pretty quickly!

blueyonder
www.blueyonder.co.uk
0800 953 9000
Unmetered anytime, cable broadband

BTOpenWorld
www.btopenworld.com
sales@btinternet.com
Unmetered anytime, ADSL broadband

clara.net
www.uk.clara.net
info@clara.net
0207 903 3310
Unmetered offpeak, unmetered anytime, ADSL broadband

Demon Internet
www.demon.net
enquiries@demon.net
0800 027 9200
Standard dial-up (monthly fee), unmetered options via BT SurfTime, ADSL broadband

Freeserve
www.freeserve.com
info@freeserve.com or freeserve.broadband@freeserve.com
0800 970 8890
Unmetered anytime, ADSL broadband

ic24
www.ic24.net
support@ic24.net
0906 302 0176
Free access (pay for calls only)

ntl
www.ntl.co.uk
01256 752000
Cable broadband

SurfLink
www.surflink.co.uk
support@zoo.co.uk
0870 7474 746
Unmetered access

Tiscali
www.tiscali.co.uk
enquiries@tiscali.co.uk
0845 660 1001
Free access (pay for calls only), unmetered offpeak, unmetered daytime, unmetered anytime, ADSL broadband

UK Online
www.ukonline.co.uk
sales@ukonline.net
0800 053 4500
Free access (pay for calls only)

Virgin Net
www.virgin.net
advice@virgin.net
0500 558800
Free access (pay for calls only), unmetered offpeak, unmetered daytime, unmetered anytime, ADSL broadband

Index

O

off-line working 29
online services 18, 22, 24,
       369, 370
   grocery shopping 304–5
   radio/TV listings 282
   shopping 300–7
   user profile 256
Opera 51
opera information 283–4
.org 268–9
Outlook Express 23, 41,
       141–2, 355
   newsgroups 143
   sending a message 152

P

padlock icon 79–81
pagers 229
pages, multiple 80
paragraphs, Web page 116
parking meters 231
partner, finding 307–8
partnerships 277–8
password 21, 40, 253
penfriends 325
people, finding 245
Personal Digital Assistants
       (PDAs) 228
PGP (Pretty Good
       Privacy) 38–9
phone
   calls 200
   cards 10–11
   number, local 370
phones
   cell p. 227
   on Internet 5–6
pictures *see* graphics
plug-ins 92–3, 97, 100–1

installing 100–1
politics 297
POP (Post Office
       Protocol) 18–19
premium rate services 11
printers 230
private
   chat 179
   sites 166
products, selling 212–3
Protect Document
       Command 40
public-key encryption 40–2
Public News Servers 133
publishing on the Web 118

Q

quotations online 312
quoting 26–7

R

RAM (random access
       memory) 66
Recreational Software
       Advisory Council *see* RSAC
refresh 262
reload 70, 82
remailers 266
research online 309–20
Reply-to Address 21
right click 71–2
ROT13 150–1
RSAC 253–4

S

satellite listings 282
saving 72–5
schools online 317–18

scripting language 85
search engines 236–50, 276
searching 366
   instant 244
security 79–81
self-extracting archives 220
server 49
   push 87
service provider *see* ISP
setting up 15, 20
setup, Windows 355–6
sex, accessibility 252
Shockwave 96
shopping 300–7
shortcuts 71
shorthand in messages 32–3
signatures 41–3
slow connection *see* speed
smileys 31–2
sound 93–6, 151
   linking to 126
soundcard 7, 201
source document 53
SMTP (Simple Mail
       Transfer Protocol) 21
Smart Download 175
software 351–6
space and the universe 315–17
speed 8, 14, 15, 66, 91–2, 99
sport 326
SSL (Secure Sockets
       Layer) 68
start page 52
starting 1
subdirectories 212
subscribe to newsgroups
       142–4
superhighway *see* Web
support groups 323–4
SurfTime 11
survey 4
system
   setup tools 355–6
   which one? 18

376